Reflections on Multiliterate Lives

BILINGUAL EDUCATION AND BILINGUALISM

Series Editors: Professor Colin Baker, *University of Wales, Bangor, Wales, Great Britain* and Professor Nancy H. Hornberger, *University of Pennsylvania, Philadelphia, USA*

Other Books in the Series
At War With Diversity: US Language Policy in an Age of Anxiety
James Crawford
Bilingual Education and Social Change
Rebecca Freeman
English in Europe: The Acquisition of a Third Language
Jasone Cenoz and Ulrike Jessner (eds)
Foundations of Bilingual Education and Bilingualism
Colin Baker
Japanese Children Abroad: Cultural, Educational and Language Issues
Asako Yamada-Yamamoto and Brian Richards (eds)
Languages in America: A Pluralist View
Susan J. Dicker
Learning English at School: Identity, Social Relations and Classroom Practice
Kelleen Toohey
Language, Power and Pedagogy: Bilingual Children in the Crossfire
Jim Cummins
Language Revitalization Processes and Prospects
Kendall A. King
The Languages of Israel: Policy, Ideology and Practice
Bernard Spolsky and Elana Shohamy
The Sociopolitics of English Language Teaching
Joan Kelly Hall and William G. Eggington (eds)
Studies in Japanese Bilingualism
Mary Goebel Noguchi and Sandra Fotos (eds)
Teaching and Learning in Multicultural Schools
Elizabeth Coelho
Teaching Science to Language Minority Students
Judith W. Rosenthal

Other Books of Interest
Beyond Bilingualism: Multilingualism and Multilingual Education
Jasone Cenoz and Fred Genesee (eds)
Encyclopedia of Bilingualism and Bilingual Education
Colin Baker and Sylvia Prys Jones
Guía para padres y maestros de niños bilingües
Alma Flor Ada and Colin Baker
A Parents' and Teachers' Guide to Bilingualism
Colin Baker

Please contact us for the latest book information:
Multilingual Matters, Frankfurt Lodge, Clevedon Hall,
Victoria Road, Clevedon, BS21 7HH, England
http://www.multilingual-matters.com

BILINGUAL EDUCATION AND BILINGUALISM 26
Series Editors: Colin Baker and Nancy Hornberger

Reflections on Multiliterate Lives

Edited by

Diane Belcher and Ulla Connor

MULTILINGUAL MATTERS LTD
Clevedon • Buffalo • Toronto • Sydney

Library of Congress Cataloging in Publication Data

Reflections on Multiliterate Lives/Edited by Diane Belcher and Ulla Connor.
Bilingual Education and Bilingualism: 26.
Includes bibliographical references.
1. Multilingualism. 2. Literacy. 3. Autobiographies. I. Belcher, Diane Dewhurst.
II. Connor, Ulla. III. Series.
P115.R44 2001
404′.2–dc21   00-050058

British Library Cataloguing in Publication Data

A CIP catalogue record for this book is available from the British Library.

ISBN 1-85359-522-5 (hbk)
ISBN 1-85359-521-7 (pbk)

Multilingual Matters Ltd

UK: Frankfurt Lodge, Clevedon Hall, Victoria Road, Clevedon BS21 7HH.
USA: UTP, 2250 Military Road, Tonawanda, NY 14150, USA.
Canada: UTP, 5201 Dufferin Street, North York, Ontario M3H 5T8, Canada.
Australia: P.O. Box 586, Artarmon, NSW, Australia.

Typeset by Wordworks Ltd, Gairloch.
Printed and bound in Great Britain by the Cromwell Press Ltd.

Contents

Acknowledgements

We are indebted to a number of people: first and foremost, all of our contributors, without whose accomplished multiliteracy and eloquent self-reflections this book would not exist; Steve Fox, for his inspiring work with student literacy autobiographies; Mike Grover and many others at Multilingual Matters, for their enthusiastic support of our project; Alan Hirvela and Andrea Lunsford, for their feedback and encouragement; Iveta Asons, Vera Belcher, and Darlene Oglesby, who helped immensely with the time-consuming task of transcribing; Peter Brandt and Stephen LeBeau for their amiable technical assistance; and last but never least, John Connor and Jim Belcher, whose emotional and intellectual support we have come to count on.

Editors' Introduction

A second generation American, **Diane Belcher** began her career in TESOL as a teacher of English literature and composition in the People's Republic of China. She received her BA in English from George Washington University and her MA and Ph.D., also in English, from The Ohio State University, where she is currently director of the ESL Composition Program. She serves as co-editor of the journal *English for Specific Purposes* as well as co-editor of the Michigan Series on Teaching Multilingual Writers (University of Michigan Press). She has also co-edited several books: *Academic Writing in a Second Language: Essays on Research and Pedagogy* (1995) and *Linking Literacies: Perspectives on L2 Reading–Writing Connections* (2001). A former chair of the TOEFL Test of Written English Committee, she is now a member of the TOEFL Committee of Examiners.

Born and raised in Finland, **Ulla Connor** received her BA and MA in English language and literature from the University of Helsinki and her second MA, in comparative literature, from the University of Wisconsin, where she also received her Ph.D. in education and English linguistics. She has taught ESL/EFL and applied linguistics for the past thirty years in the US, Finland, Sweden, Japan, Venezuela and Slovakia, and has lectured at universities around the world. Her research has been on L2 reading and writing, with special emphasis on cross-cultural aspects and contrastive rhetoric. Her current interests are EAP (English for academic purposes) and ESP, especially the language of business and nonprofit organizations. She has edited and authored a number of books, including *Contrastive Rhetoric: Crosscultural Aspects of Second Language Writing* (1996). She is also the author of close to 100 articles and book chapters.

In planning this book, eighteen highly successful second-language users were asked to outline in their own words their struggles and successes along the path to language learning. The result is a volume in which the contributors, using interview as well as narrative formats, compellingly recount their formative literacy experiences, with the aim of helping others to understand better how advanced second-language literacy can be achieved.

In many respects, all the contributors to this volume are 'fortunate travelers', to borrow the term that Suresh Canagarajah himself borrows from Derek Walcott for the title of his narrative. Both physically and mentally, the contributors have traveled great distances to arrive at their wished-for destinations. Robert Agunga, for example, now a professor of agriculture, still keenly recollects his early childhood marches of a dozen miles daily through Ghanaian forest to attend a village elementary school. Jun Liu, now a professor of English, remembers surreptitiously reading, when he was growing up in China, the English-language books hidden under his family's beds for fear of a sudden 'revolutionary inspection' by Red Guards. María Juliá, currently a professor of social work, still finds it painful to recall her early days of graduate study in the US as a new arrival from Puerto Rico – days marred by the anxiety of constant translation, sleep deprivation, and lost opportunities to interact with others. All of our contributors, in fact, eloquently articulate similarly vivid recollections of earlier selves that they obviously value, memories that may well continue to help shape their present-day achievements (see Ross & Buehler, 1994).

Though well aware of how far they have come, none of the contributors, according to their own self reports, feels able or willing to now comfortably sit back and contentedly survey all that s/he has achieved. Ming-Daw Tsai, for instance, whose extensive scientific writing in English has garnered numerous grants, special honors and appointments on editorial boards, remarks that he still feels the need to put every paper he writes 'through at least ten rounds of revision before submission'. Miyuki Sasaki observes of herself that, despite the accomplishment of annually publishing in highly respected English-language journals for a number of years, she is still not comfortable composing in English: 'I think in Japanese, take notes in Japanese, and write the first rough drafts in Japanese because I can't think thoroughly about any complicated matters in English'. Some of the contributors who now live in English-speaking environs also regret and worry over first language loss resulting from greatly diminished contact and use. María Juliá is appalled by the Spanish-usage errors her mother finds in her letters home because, as Juliá explains, 'I was always very proud of how well I could write in my first language'. Anahid Kulwicki finds that the hectic pace of her life as an academic in the US leaves no time for the Armenian and Arabic literature that she loved as a girl in Lebanon. Nevertheless, the contributors to this volume, all extraordinarily productive scholars and teachers with well-established reputations in their fields, are clearly not significantly hampered by feelings of inadequacy, frustration, or loss. They are, rather, notably aware and indeed appreciative of where they have been and where they are going, conscious of how the world, especially an English-dominated academic world, has impinged on them but also of how they have responded to it and, through their linguistic expertise and finely honed literate practices, put their own imprint on it.

Our contributors are precisely the types of 'multicompetent' language users, successful users of more than one language, that Vivian Cook (1999) has argued researchers and teachers of language need to know far more about, and students of language need to have more exposure to. Research, after all, has tended to focus on what language learners lack rather than on what they have achieved. And our classrooms, Cook reminds us, have too seldom provided second language (L2) students with access to examples of skilled L2 use. The collection of personal accounts of the formative literacy experiences of highly successful – both linguistically and professionally – L2 users assembled in this volume should help address the needs expressed by Cook and certainly felt by many others. The contributors to this volume, who are well known L2 specialists in applied linguistics and the teaching of English as well as L2 academic writers from the physical and social sciences, represent a broad spectrum of linguistic and academic accomplishments. The language educators who have contributed provide both a personal and, at the same time, linguistically informed view of language learning by reflecting on their own language and literacy experiences. The contributors from other disciplines share their insider awareness of what it takes to attain and sustain literacy in fields that those of us who specialize in teaching academic literacy can usually view only from the outside. Since all of the contributions have been authored, or co-authored in the case of interviews, by L2 users themselves, the array of accomplished multiliterates' language-learning reflections presented here appears in their own words. Thus, the contributors have constructed their own representations of themselves.

The value of the type of autobiographical narrative, or auto-ethnography, provided by our contributors has received increasing recognition over the past few decades from both researchers and teachers. From the point of view of second language acquisition (SLA) researchers, autobiographies (or another variant called 'diary studies') are seen as providing windows on learners' metalinguistic awareness, capable of telling us much about their conscious use of language-learning strategies (Bailey & Nunan, 1996; Bailey & Ochsner, 1983). From the teachers' point of view, narratives can be a powerful teaching tool, in that they are highly accessible, easy to relate to and, when either read or written, can increase learners' awareness of their own learning processes (Bailey & Ochsner, 1983; Bell, 1997).

Further evidence of the growing recognition of the value of narrative can be found in the wealth of recently published collections of narratives in L1 and L2 studies recounting the experiences of language educators and writing teachers, e.g. Casanave & Schecter (1997) *On Becoming a Language Educator*; Meyer (1996) *Stories from the Heart*; Roen et al. (1999) *Living Rhetoric and Composition*, and Trimmer (1997) *Narration as Knowledge*. All of these collections are rich sources of data on the language teaching experience. The second-language learning experience has been the focus of a number of essays that present first-person accounts of language learners who are also language specialists, e.g. Bell (1995), Campbell (1996), Connor (1999), and Shen (1989). There are also compelling book-length first-person accounts of second-language learners, some of which have been authored by language specialists who are language learners, such as Ogulnick (1998) *Onna Rashiku [Like a Woman]* and Lvovich (1997) *The Multilingual Self*, and others of which have come from outside the education field, such as Hoffman (1989) *Lost in Translation* and Liu (1984) *Two Years in the Melting Pot*. All of these narratives offer thick description of the emotional peaks and valleys of language learning and teaching that no one knows more intimately than the language learner or teacher her/himself.

One of our primary aims in this book has been to widen the range of voices available in published language-learning narratives by including contributions from representatives of a wide range of academic disciplines as well as linguistic and educational backgrounds. The multicompetent language users in language education and other academic fields that we have invited to contribute to this volume have lived and worked in core English-speaking countries, e.g. Australia and the US, in the 'periphery,' e.g. Hong Kong, and in EFL (English as a foreign language) environments, such as Japan and Finland. We have also included one L1 English speaker who has functioned professionally as an academic in another language, Hebrew, in a country, Israel, where English is not the dominant language. When we chose potential contributors, we also kept gender representation in addition to distribution of L1/L2s and geographic locations in mind in an effort to select a group of women and men representative of the global academic community. The world represented by our contributors, in terms of their countries of origin, includes the following: Austria, China (PRC and

ROC), Finland, France, Ghana, Germany, India, Iran, Japan, Lebanon, Lithuania, Mexico, Sri Lanka, and the US (with Puerto Rico included).

Our hope is that students, teachers and others who read the highly personalized, often poignant accounts of our diverse group of contributors will have little difficulty in appreciating their past and present struggles and successes, and in recognizing our contributors' obvious strengths (which include admissions of weakness) as remarkably self-aware learners of language and of much else. That so many of the multicompetent language users represented here have attained so many of their goals in life, already having achieved what relatively few monoliterates accomplish in their entire lifetimes, suggests not just that these particular multiliterate individuals are unusually high achievers but also argues compellingly, we feel, for the inherent values of multiliteracy.

Overview

Our book is divided into two sections: Part I, consisting of narratives by professional language educators, and Part II, narratives (some in interview format) from professional academics representing disciplines across the curriculum. These two sections have somewhat different organizing principles owing to the varied nature of their components.

Since all the contributors in Part I, as language educators, share essentially the same discipline (a domain that includes specialists with backgrounds in linguistics, literature, and teacher training), we have organized this section along nation- (or region-) of-origin lines. In other words, language educators from the same part of the world appear side by side, allowing for differing, often complementary perspectives on the same or similar cultures of origin (or C1). Thus, we begin with an American-educated Sri Lankan, followed by a British-educated Indian; then two Finns of different generations; followed by an Austrian and a Lithuanian, both of whom immigrated, the former to Australia, the latter to Israel, and an American of Russian heritage who also immigrated to Israel; finally two Japanese and one Chinese, with the former currently residing in different nations, one in the US and the other in Japan, and the latter, the Chinese academic, currently living in the US.

Part II, which is organized along disciplinary lines, moves from the physical and mathematical sciences to the social sciences, and finally concludes with academics who have crossed over into administration and reached the pinnacle of professional university life, as presidents of their institutions. More specifically, the progression in Part II is as follows (with contributors here identified by their C1 and discipline): a Chinese biochemist, a French mathematician, an Iranian electrical engineer, a Lebanese nursing educator, a Ghanaian agricultural communication specialist, a Puerto Rican social work researcher, and two university presidents, Mexican and German. While all of the above now reside in the continental US, they still, as will be seen in their personal accounts, proudly identify themselves as products of their C1, e.g. as Chinese or Ghanaian or Mexican.

The diverse range of contributors should, it seems to us, make it abundantly clear to all who read this collection of life stories that (1) no C1, no matter how apparently distant from the target culture, should be perceived as an obstacle to success in that culture (in fact, quite the reverse, as some argue in this volume, since awareness of difference can be a source of strength that those without the lived experience of difference lack), and (2) no discipline should be seen as out of reach for L2 users, for highly successful L2 academics can be found across the curriculum.

Part I

Having worked as a professional academic both in his home country and in the United States, **Suresh Canagarajah**, whose narrative 'The Fortunate Traveler: Shuttling Between Communities and Literacies by Economy Class' opens this section, is able to present a dual perspective on L2 academic literacy training and experiences that may challenge some readers' notions of literacy objectives. After struggling to master the discourse expectations of his American professors and succeeding as a graduate student as few L1 speakers of English do, with articles accepted by several prestigious journals, Canagarajah returned home to discover he had become an outsider. When his efforts to produce academic prose in Tamil were met by disappointment in his 'pompous' and 'over-confident' style', Canagarajah consciously readjusted his style yet again so as not to 'put off' his readers. Upon returning to the US to teach, Canagarajah faced new complaints about what some perceived as an overly passionate style, a reaction possibly to his 'flirtations with vernacular [Tamil] academic writing' or perhaps evidence that 'issues of tone and style could have ideological implications'. Well aware of the advantages of academic life in the US, Canagarajah now feels that the conveniences of affluent, high-tech US life have made him 'intellectually and rhetorically lazy', while the competitiveness of 'publish or perish' American academia has taken much of the pleasure out of the writing process. Canagarajah's reflections thus give us much to reflect on. Should, Canagarajah leads us to wonder, academic literacy mean far more for citizens of the world than merely mastering the survival strategies required in one's degree- or tenure-granting institution?

Canagarajah makes us mindful that, despite the onslaught of English in disciplines around the world, there are other academic worlds beyond the English-dominated one – with their own sets of norms and priorities. To be truly academically literate, Canagarajah suggests, means being able to reach the audiences one chooses to reach, utilizing 'available conventions and discourses from the standpoint of one's [own] ideological and rhetorical preferences'.

Although **Vijay Bhatia** is from the same part of the world as Suresh Canagarajah, namely, the postcolonial Asian subcontinent, Bhatia traveled a very different route to L2 academic literacy. In 'Initiating into Academic Community: Some Autobiographical Reflections' Bhatia recounts his intellectual and psychosocial journey from India to Great Britain, from the perspective of his current professional academic life in Hong Kong. Unlike Canagarajah, Bhatia focuses much more on academic socialization than on academic literacy *per se*. In his account of admittedly fortuitous life events, Bhatia underscores the importance of situated learning, or serving a sociocognitive apprenticeship. To Bhatia, finding one's niche, by which he means both the right academic field for one's talents and interests and the right community of scholars to apprentice oneself to, is more important than any cross-linguistic or cross-cultural issues. Bhatia feels that, ideally, learning is not confined by the walls of an institution of higher learning but is 'an ongoing process, which could take place anywhere, on a cricket field, or in front of the TV in a video room while watching Wimbledon finals'. Bhatia observes that friendly and relaxed contact with academic professionals, who gave him the opportunity to disagree and think for himself, enabled him to develop the habits of mind essential to success on his own terms. Such mental habits no doubt served Bhatia well as a junior professional academic in his determination to resist an editor's attempts to change his phrasing – a battle that Bhatia won and which further empowered him. Bhatia does not argue that language use is never an issue for NNSEs (non-native speakers of English), but that academic gatekeepers can make it more of one than it should be. He urges fellow NNSEs not to allow concerns about their L2 competence to discourage or distract them from the exercise of their academic expertise that will truly qualify them for professional academe.

With **Nils Erik Enkvist**'s 'Reminiscences of a Multilingual Life', we enter into the realm of those who lead bi- and multilingual private and professional lives in their home countries. Finland's best-known applied linguist and truly an international scholar, having lectured and published around the world in English and other languages, Enkvist presents an account of literacy development that began in pre-World War II Finland, when French and German, not English, were the dominant European languages. A maverick in his youth, Enkvist was one of the few students of English linguistics in Finland to seek language experience in the US and the UK. But what will perhaps appear most noteworthy about Enkvist to many mono- and bilingual readers is how normal it seems to Enkvist to have grown up and lived his adult life as a multilingual. With a Swedish-speaking father and Finnish-speaking mother, as well as numerous other language-learning experiences, including German, French, English, Estonian, Russian, Italian, Spanish, Portuguese, Norwegian and Danish, Enkvist's usual response to queries about how many languages he speaks is '... unless you define what you mean by "knowing" a language, choose any number between three and something like a dozen...'. For Enkvist, being multilingual is so natural that there is no reason to fear loss of one's 'native' identity. His description of 'personality switching' reveals not a static, unitary identity but rather a dynamic sense of self that seems quite postmodernist:

> People often ask if I change personality when switching from one language to another. Yes, I do. In Finnish I am an honest straightfor-wardly homely down-to-earth person, occasionally digging into the politer layers of a wartime military substratum of language. In Swedish I am pedantic and, also, sound precisely like the academic administrator I used to be. And in English, a language I originally learned through formal education, I am stuck with an RP variant, which strikes today's Britons as a relic from high society in the days of Edward VII.

A lifelong student of stylistics, which Enkvist believes can be universally defined, his own elegant and witty English prose is testimony both to his understanding of style and his achievements as a multiliterate.

If Nils Enkvist's narrative projects the development of personal multiliteracy as an enjoyable journey, **Håkan Ringbom's** reflections in 'Developing Literacy Can and Should be Fun – But Only Sometimes Is' makes the pain and hard work of the development process conspicuous. A student of Enkvist and an internationally known scholar in his own right, Ringbom, who came of age in post-World War II Finland, is more inter-ested in linguistic difference (or relativity) than in stylistic universals but, like his teacher Enkvist, he is also an astute observer of his own experiences with language. Ringbom has observed that, despite the relatively privi-leged status of the Swedish minority in Finland, his fellow Swedish Finns are very much aware of their language minority status and choose carefully when and where to use Swedish. Ringbom is conscious of the impact his

Swedish has had on his use of Finnish, noting that it was many years before the 'flexibility and beauty' of Finnish 'dawned' on him. Although a native-like speaker of Finnish, Ringbom feels less confident as a writer of Finnish. But writing, Ringbom observes, has never been easy for him, and learning to write academic English was an especially arduous process:

> When writing my first postgraduate thesis [in English] ... I reckoned that the result of half a working day was only two or three sentences most days during two years.... And at least one of the sentences I had produced I deleted or altered considerably the following day. Yet, the result of my labors, qualitative and quantitative, bore very little witness to the time and energy spent.

Students and teachers of writing may find it heartening that, despite his struggles as a writer, Ringbom's written English has served him well as a professional academic. Ringbom himself now sees his having been forced to function in more than one language as a definite advantage: 'Language takes on a wider dimension and you ... become aware of the possibilities and restrictions each language [whether L1, L2, or L3] possesses'.

In 'Straddling Three Worlds', **Anna Söter** provides another European language speaker's perspective; however, as an immigrant to an English-speaking country, Australia, Söter's language learning and literacy experiences differed quite markedly from Enkvist's and Ringbom's. Söter's immersion into Australian English at age six led to immense success as an adult L2 user – an early career as a high school English literature teacher and eventually, a school administrator. It was not until she traveled to the US for graduate studies that she felt somewhat disadvantaged as a writer – perhaps because of her Australian variety of English, having been steeped in British literature, and some residual L1 (German) influence. Her writing style, 'a vehicle for success in Australian educational contexts', was a 'problem' in the US. Even though not perceived as a 'non-English speaker', Söter was forced to 'clean up' her academic writing in English. A more daunting challenge has been the effort to retain and develop her command of her L1. Like many first-generation immigrants, as a child Söter had wanted to blend in with the majority as quickly as possible, although parent-enforced correspondence with Austrian relatives enabled her to sustain a feeling of 'Austrian-ness' until she was able to return to her native country in her twenties. Developing her German literacy was, and continues to be, a struggle. Today Söter still finds that, while she can effortlessly converse in German, her dominant literacy experiences in English make it difficult 'without a great deal of work ... [to] maintain a line of unbroken thought [in written German] ... and appropriately express it in that language'.

Interestingly, the emotional power of her L1 has remained constant, for she still finds herself reaching for German words when engaged in creative writing in English. As a mature, accomplished adult, a tenured professor of English education living in the US, Söter values all her prior language experiences, especially that of her L1: 'If I have any advice to pass on to others, it is to accept the influence of one's mother tongue, embrace it and understand it, for in denying it, one denies a part of oneself'.

It is easy to see clear parallels between both Enkvist's and Ringbom's as well as Söter's language learning-experiences and those of **Adina Levine** as recounted in 'How a Speaker of Two Second Languages Becomes a Writer in a Foreign Language'. Growing up in Russian-dominated Lithuania, Levine found, as did Enkvist and Ringbom in Finland, the ability to speak and be literate in more than one language to be essential. Despite the imposition of Russian on her homeland, Levine's literacy in Russian led to an infatuation with Russian culture, especially Russian literature, that continues to have positive effects on her today. These happy early literacy experiences established a love of reading that, Levine is convinced, has buttressed all her subsequent literacy learning, no matter what the language. When she immigrated to Israel as an adult and was faced with the need to learn 'from scratch' a new 'second' language, Hebrew, as well as master a foreign language, English, because of 'the need "to compete" with native English speakers as my colleagues at work', Levine found that her lifelong interest in reading, especially her ability to read attentively and engage in more than simple decoding, helped her master the new academic English genres she needed to produce in order to survive professionally. Though the academic text types were new to her, textual analysis, thanks to her years of reading literature, was not. While Levine still feels not fully able to anticipate NSE (native speaker of English) reader response to her writing and 'a strong element of suspense when a manuscript is sent off for review', that feeling of uncertainty has never stopped her from writing and being published in English.

Although like Adina Levine's, **Andrew Cohen**'s narrative, 'From L1 to L12: The Confessions of a Sometimes Frustrated Multiliterate' describes an adult language learner's immigration to Israel, Cohen, an American whose production of academic publications in English has continued unabated since early adulthood, focuses on acquisition of Hebrew for academic purposes. It should be noted that Cohen, the only L1 English speaker contributing to this collection of multiliteracy autobiographies, is a member of what is no doubt a quite small minority given the *Tyrannosaurus rex* nature of academic English worldwide (Swales, 1997) – NSEs who function as academics in a language other than English. Cohen is very straightforward about his struggle to acquire academic Hebrew, which proved quite a formidable task despite his obvious talent and enthusiasm for languages and success in learning such non-Indo-European tongues as Quechua and Aymara. Cohen recounts a number of the strategies he developed in his efforts to cope with academic Hebrew, such as, reliance on Hebrew word processing and spell checking programs, compilation of a glossary of professional terminology for lectures in his field, reformulation of his Hebrew academic writing by Israeli colleagues to heighten his discoursal consciousness, and pleasure reading in Hebrew to increase his reading speed. Cohen confesses, however, that even after sixteen years as an academic in Israel, reading an advisee's doctoral dissertation was still a challenge, and his academic speaking was perceived as 'an excellent example of a mixing of registers'. Upon finally returning to live in the US, Cohen himself was surprised by how appealing it was to be working again in an English-language environment, where he could comfortably and confidently function without excessive concern over sending or receiving the wrong message. It is difficult to read Cohen's narrative without being impressed, not only by his own academic career in Hebrew, but by the achievements of all who succeed as professional academics in a language other than their L1.

Ryuko Kubota is one of a number of East Asians living and working as professional academics in English-speaking countries, in her case the US. In 'My Experience of Learning to Read and Write in Japanese as L1 and English as L2', Kubota readily admits that reading and writing are for her still far more time-consuming and painstaking processes in English than in her native Japanese. Yet, that she has succeeded in accomplishing what she already has as a professional academic in English education – publishing in English and teaching in a tenure-track position at a prestigious American university – is largely owing, Kubota feels, to her early literacy experiences in Japanese. Having retained all of her childhood books and writings in Japanese, Kubota is able to vividly recount her L1 literacy training and development. What may strike readers as especially noteworthy are the great quantity and varied types of writing Kubota did as a child. As her private diaries and group anthologies at school suggest, personal expressive writing played a substantial and significant role in her youthful literacy. Kubota notes that one of the genres she practiced as a child, *seikatsu-bun*, or lived-experience writing, with its emphasis on observing human society and seeking ways to transform it, bears a striking similarity to Freirean pedagogy. Such literacy experiences may have predisposed Kubota toward the apparently Freire-inspired emancipatory interests that her academic work in English exhibits today. Kubota herself, however, is not entirely satisfied with what she has accomplished so far as an L2 writer. She wishes that she could reveal in English more of her 'authentic voice,' yet is aware too, as a teacher of Japanese in the US, that the error density of 'authentic' writing can have a definite effect on readability – an awareness that makes her appreciative of feedback on her own L2 writing. Kubota concludes her narrative by pointedly warning us that her personal experiences and observations are not generalizable, situated as they are 'at a certain time and location'. She encourages 'continuous investigation' of the ever-changing literacy environment of her country of origin, Japan.

Whereas Ryuko Kubota has forged a professional academic life for herself in the US, **Miyuki Sasaki** returned to Japan to pursue an academic career after her graduate education in applied linguistics in the US. Being a professional academic in Japan, however, has not meant that she no longer works in English, as Sasaki feels compelled to continue to write academically in English in order to reach an international audience. One of the parallels between Sasaki's and Kubota's narratives that readers are likely to find of interest is the significance that both attribute to their early L1 literacy experiences. Like Kubota, Sasaki sees her childhood L1 literacy experiences as having an enormous influence on the scholar she is today. Sasaki credits her parents with providing a rich literacy-learning environment in their home, full of books and magazines, but also the example of parents who write. Some of the important formative experiences for the future biliterate academic also took place outside Japan – e.g. her year as an undergraduate exchange student at the University of Michigan, where she studied English composition and realized for the first time that writing is a learnable, improvable skill. Now as a gatekeeper of academic writing in English herself, i.e. a manuscript reviewer, Sasaki has discovered that 'even the most established researchers' drafts are not perfect when they are first submitted' and often undergo extensive revision before publication. Sasaki reveals much about her own L2 composing strategies in her narrative, e.g. that she finds L1 pleasure reading and writing a great restorative from the rigors of L2, and that, as mentioned earlier, her most productive conceptualizing still occurs in L1. After almost three decades of studying English, Sasaki still views academic work in L2 as a struggle, but one well worth the effort given the 'world of research' it has opened up to her.

Jun Liu's account in 'Writing from Chinese to English: My Cultural Transformation' of his early literacy experiences in his native People's Republic of China is so strikingly different from those of Miyuki Sasaki and Ryuko Kubota that the difficulty of attempting to draw conclusions about East Asian learners in general will likely be readily apparent. Liu's youth in

China took place during tumultuous times, the Cultural Revolution, when his English-teacher father was seen as 'one of the suspicious targets ... poisoned by Western thoughts and ... in possession of Western books'. Despite the danger involved, Liu and his sister, under their father's tutelage, engaged in the traditional Chinese practice of memorizing and reciting literary texts – including L2 texts well beyond what Krashen would call 'comprehensible input'. Liu is convinced of the lasting benefits, to both his L1 and L2, of his early literacy experiences, i.e. his early exposure and performance approach, not only to English literary works but to classical Chinese poetry and Beijing Opera as well. Although sidetracked for a time by a forced sojourn as a hospital lab technician, Liu eventually obtained a college education, but another decade passed before he was permitted to leave for graduate study in the US. Not until his graduate education did Liu feel that he had truly learned to write in English, thanks to the process approach of an ESL composition class, and not until he became an ESL composition instructor himself at a US university did he feel deservedly confident: 'for the first time in my life I felt that I was accepted as a member of the target community.' Liu sees himself as having benefited as a writer from his L2 social identity which, in turn, has benefited from his efforts to 'understand the fundamental thinking processes of the target culture and the way that my L1 culture can be accepted'.

Part II

The multi-disciplinary half of this volume opens with **Ming-Daw Tsai**'s 'Learning as a Life-Long Process.' Although a Chinese speaker like Jun Liu, Tsai, who is from Taiwan, or the Republic of China, focuses far less than Liu on the early political and cultural influences on his literacy development. Tsai's story is that of steady, if not always smooth, progress towards success in the international scientific community. The point that Tsai stresses most emphatically in his narrative is that literate practices figure far more prominently in the life of a scientist than is likely realized by those outside the academic scientific professions. Having published over one hundred papers in chemistry and biochemistry, 'not a single one [of which] was written in Chinese', Tsai has found himself spending increasingly less time in the lab and more time in front of his computer, composing. That arriving at this high level of literate productivity was not an easy journey for Tsai is clear in his account of several unsettling discoveries made after arriving in the US for graduate study: that despite ten years of English study and a high TOEFL score, he lacked communicative competence, spoken and written, in English; and that, even after greatly improving his communicative skills, he still lacked the ability, or at least the confidence, to lecture to large audiences and write research proposals independently. After years of practice as a speaker and writer of scientific English, Tsai is now confident in his abilities in these areas. He is pleased in particular with the results of, as described earlier, his multi-draft writing process but, outside the scientific milieu, Tsai feels less accomplished, noting that his children, raised in the US, read faster, write better (in English), and 'their speaking ability ... is something I will never reach in my life'. Yet Tsai is not sorry that he continues to feel the need to learn English, for it helps him avoid the trap of *ping-yong*, or passive contentment with mediocrity. As Tsai sees it, to continually learn English means to continually be in growth mode – both in terms of constant improvement of self-expression and of world knowledge.

As does Ming-Daw Tsai, **Louis de Branges** argues in his narrative 'Linguistic Expression of a Mathematical Career' that language is far more important in his field than is often realized. A French speaker till age nine, when he and his family took refuge from World War II France in the US, de Branges found that his struggle to master written English as an adolescent in an American school taught him to 'respect good writing in any language as a major achievement'. He notes too that his experiences as a bilingual reader while growing up actually led him to mathematics for, having learned 'through reading French [on his own] to read independently of instruction', he eagerly sought reading matter that captured his imagination. The realization of the importance of language to mathematics came to de Branges when he began his teaching career and found that all 'teaching is a challenge in the use of language', including the teaching of mathematics, which requires 'decoding a technical language of symbols and translating it into a verbal pattern'. As a mathematics textbook writer, de Branges has stayed true to his belief that 'words and ideas [should] dominate over symbols and formulas'. Now an internationally recognized professor of mathematics, de Branges remains intensely interested in undergraduate mathematics as a means of teaching 'logical thought [dependent] on words'. While de Branges sees himself as fortunate to be a speaker of 'the international language of mathematics, which is English', he also strongly believes that, without the experience of learning more than one language, he would have 'underestimated the value of language as opposed to symbols and formulas for the expression of mathematical ideas'.

For **Hooshang Hemami**, not just language but also the humanities in general are seen as crucial to success in his field. In 'Taking the Best From a Number of Worlds: An Interview with Hooshang Hemami', Hemami describes the foundations on which his career as a professor of electrical engineering with over 200 publications in English has been built. Basically, Hemami feels that he has had to come to terms with what Liu (this volume) would call his 'cultural transformation' in his adopted homeland, to develop a sustaining philosophy of life, and to stay in touch with the non-scientific sides of himself in order to function effectively as a scientist. Hemami's cultural adjustment to life in the US has not meant relinquishing his C1 for his new C2 but focusing instead on the best that both the Iranian and American, or Western, cultures have to offer. Although Hemami did make a conscious decision to stop speaking Farsi, his L1, because of its apparent interference with his English and also the flood of memories it gives rise to, he now finds himself spontaneously writing poetry in Farsi: '... suddenly this stuff flows out and ... it is beautiful...'. Hemami's personal philosophy of life, which guides his 'normal' and his 'scientific life', has helped him develop an open-minded, undogmatic attitude toward all cultural beliefs. As for the non-scientific sides of himself that he feels he must stay in touch with –'investments' in music, sports, creative writing, painting, and reading in psychology and literature, mainly in English and German – Hemami contends that all of these are needed not just as respites from his professional life but as essential complements to it that help sustain his productivity as a researcher and academic writer. Hemami's advice to L2 students is not to lose sight of the world outside their formal academic work, but to 'try to understand this culture [i.e. C2] and take advantage of it'.

In 'Growing Up Trilingual: Memories of an Armenian/Arabic/English speaker', **Anahid Kulwicki** focuses to a large extent on her earliest language and literacy experiences in multilingual Lebanon. For Kulwicki, as with many of the European contributors to this volume, being multilingual seemed entirely natural to her as a child. While the language of her family was Armenian, a minority language in Lebanon, at school she was required to study Armenian, Arabic, and English. Television shows were broadcast in Arabic, French, and English. Interestingly, Kulwicki does not remember being at all impressed by English in her youth. Far more appealing were Armenian and Arabic: the former as a means of maintaining her Armenian identity; the latter as more 'romantic' and 'less restrictive' than English. Now, however, as a professional academic, a nursing educator in the US, she finds that English has supplanted her two first loves as the language of both her academic and personal life. Virtually all of her literate activities are in English, a language she is still not entirely comfortable with as a writer. Not helpful, Kulwicki observes, is the unspoken bias of many NSE colleagues – revealed in reactions to her texts, or texts believed to be hers – that she must contend with despite her advanced level of L2 proficiency and publication record. While Kulwicki's observations are disturbing, they also remind us that L1 reactions to texts perceived to be L2 may indicate as much or more about the L1 readers themselves than about L2 texts.

As the son of a Ghanaian chief and the first in his family to receive a formal education, **Robert Agunga**'s multiliteracy experiences, recounted in 'How Can I Help Make a Difference?: An Interview with Robert Agunga', have been in many respects unlike those of most of the other contributors to this volume. Few of the other contributors had to overcome the types of obstacles Agunga did: e.g. traveling increasingly greater distances from his family, even as a small child, as he advanced up the educational ladder and, as a young adult with a new doctorate in agricultural communication, forced to face the reality that to go home to help his fellow villagers, which was always his goal, meant returning to a place with no electricity and no books, where he could be 'lost forever'. Yet Agunga views his personal past as remarkably fortunate. He is especially grateful for having had people in his life willing to push him to achieve: e.g. a father who insisted that education was 'not a choice' for his son but a must, and a graduate advisor/mentor from Malawi who insisted he rewrite and rewrite until he achieved 'flow' in his dissertation. Agunga's decision to stay in the US as a professional academic is also not one that he regrets, for it is here that, through his academic writing on topics such as sustainable agriculture and his communication with the World Bank and United Nations, he can have the greatest impact on international development. Not surprisingly, Agunga's advice to graduate student writers is to find a research area that inspires them: '...you have to look at what is happening in society and ask, "How can I help make a difference?"'

Like Robert Agunga, **María Juliá**, as she observes in 'A Professional Academic Life in Two Languages: An Interview with María Juliá', was pushed to achieve, especially linguistically, during her youth, but her family's and teachers' impatience with her progress left her with a lingering lack of confidence in her abilities as both an English speaker and a writer. For Juliá, in spite of years of early exposure to English at home and school in Puerto Rico, coming to graduate school on the US. mainland was, as pointed out earlier, a traumatic experience that she still vividly remembers: e.g. '... there were times when I was sleeping four or five hours a night because I felt I had to read things over and over to be able to be at the same pace that the rest of the students were'. That Juliá succeeded in her efforts is abundantly evident, as she is now a tenured professor at the same research institution where she obtained her doctorate – a university that only rarely hires its own graduates. Though Juliá now struggles with what she perceives as the deterioration of her Spanish, she is committed to making her contributions to social work research available to both English- and Spanish-speaking audiences and insists that her NSE colleagues acknowledge both her L2 and L1 academic accomplishments. Yet Juliá, like Kulwicki, still senses 'implicit messages of inadequacy' from NSE faculty. The best course of action, Juliá has found, is to attempt to ignore the unjust and often tacit criticism that can otherwise 'paralyze' you intellectually and emotionally, and focus instead on the well-deserved validation that others who do appreciate your contributions will provide.

Luis Proenza, who, like María Juliá, is a native speaker of Spanish, has strong feelings about the advantages his Mexican background has given him. In 'On Being a Citizen of the World: An Interview with Luis Proenza', Proenza reflects on his journey from early childhood in Mexico to his leadership roles in university administration in the US, as dean of graduate students at Purdue University and now President of the University of Akron. Far from feeling disadvantaged when he first arrived in the US at age eleven, Proenza found himself a full two years ahead of his US classmates. It was not until he immersed himself in scientific writing at graduate school, however, that Proenza felt that he had become a truly literate person. As an administrator, Proenza's academic communication is now mainly in the form of speeches, which he often submits to from three to ten 'edits' before delivery. Although English dominates his life now, Proenza, who considers himself 'more of a citizen of the world rather than ... a particular country' is grateful to be able to use Spanish in his professional work and believes that knowledge of it has enriched his English writing by sensitizing him to the 'power' and 'rhythm' a language can have.

As editors of this volume, we are very pleased to be able to conclude this collection of literacy autobiographies of highly accomplished L2 academics with not one but two university presidents. **Steven Beering**, like Luis Proenza, a university president (in fact, the administrator to whom Proenza reported when still in his deanship at Purdue), also believes that he has greatly benefited from his NNSE past. In 'The Advantages of Starting Out Multilingual: An Interview with Steven Beering', Beering describes the impact that growing up comfortable with German, his L1, as well as French, English, and even Latin has had on his professional and personal life. Although he arrived in the US at age thirteen, Beering maintained his German and French well enough to be able to work his way through college by teaching both languages at the University of Pittsburgh. However, an American accent which, as a young adult, Beering greatly desired, was not easily or naturally acquired, but rather very consciously learned with the aid of elocution drills from his college's drama department.

As President of Purdue University, Beering has found, as has Proenza, that most of his public communicating is in the form of speeches, with an average of 250–300 speeches delivered per year. Beering's current speaking skills in his L1, German, however, are much more limited, he readily admits, than they once were, constrained by limited vocabulary and a lack of familiarity with contemporary German. Nevertheless, Beering, again like Proenza, still views his L1 as useful professionally, and he is convinced that his well-developed metalinguistic sensitivity is the result of 'early education in several languages'. For Beering, as with so many other contributors to this volume, life may well not have been, as D. J. Clandinin and F. M. Connelly (1991:265) put it, 'a matter of growth toward' so many of his 'imagined futures' were it not for the benefits of being multilingual.

Notes

1. Kathleen Bailey and David Nunan (1996) have pointed out that language learning narratives have been criticized as either lacking accuracy, as the products of naive language users without the formal linguistic training needed to adequately describe their language learning, or as lacking authenticity, when produced by those with linguistic training who view their own (or others') language learning processes through the lens of that training. These criticisms encouraged us to include both those with and without formal linguistic backgrounds among the contributors.
2. Ruth Spack (1997) has noted the too-often-heavy authorial hand of the researcher in the representation of cultural 'others'. However, another problem arises when anyone constructs his/her own self-representation for an audience. Space/time constraints, the limitations of introspection and perspective, and interest in preserving or establishing a particular self image make the presentation of the 'facts' of one's life an inevitably highly selective process. Linda Brodkey (1987:47) has observed, though, that pursuit of the social construct known as objective truth is not what drives, or should drive, our interest in narratives:

    > One studies stories not because they are true ... but for the same reason that people tell them, in order to learn about the terms on which others make sense of their lives: what they take into account and what they do not; what they consider worth contemplating and what they do not; what they are and are not willing to raise and discuss as problematic and unresolved in life.

References

Bailey, K. M. and Nunan, D. (1996) *Voices from the Language Classroom: Qualitative Research in Second Language Acquisition.* New York: Cambridge University Press.

Bailey, K. M. and Ochsner, R. (1983) A methodological review of the diary studies: Windmill tilting or social science? In K. M. Bailey, M. Long and S. Peck (eds.) *Second Language Acquisition Studies* (pp. 188–198). Rowley, MA: Newbury House.

Bell, J. (1995) The relationship between L1 and L2 literacy: Some complicating factors. *TESOL Quarterly* 29, 687–704.

Bell, J. (1997) *Literacy, Culture, and Identity*. New York: P. Lang.

Brodkey, L. (1987) Writing ethnographic narratives. *Written Communication* 4, 25–50.

Campbell, C. (1996) Socializing with the teachers and prior language learning experience: A diary study. In K. M. Bailey and D. Nunan (eds.) *Voices from the Language Classroom: Qualitative Research in Second Language Acquisition* (pp. 201–223). New York: Cambridge University Press.

Casanave, C. and Schechter, S. (1997) *On Becoming a Language Educator: Personal Essays on Professional Development*. Mahwah, NJ: Lawrence Erlbaum.

Clandinin, D. J. and Connelly, F. M. (1991) Narrative and story in practice and research. In D. Schon (ed.) *The Reflective Turn: Case Studies in and on Educational Practice* (pp. 258–281). New York: Teachers College Press.

Connor, U. (1999) Learning to write academic prose in a second language: A literacy autobiography. In G. Braine (ed.) *Non-Native Educators in English Language Teaching* (pp. 29–42). Mahwah, NJ: Lawrence Erlbaum.

Cook, V. (1999) Going beyond the native speaker in language teaching. *TESOL Quarterly* 33, 185–209.

Hoffman, E. (1989) *Lost in Translation: A Life in a New Language*. New York: E. P. Dutton.

Liu, Z. (1984) *Two Years in the Melting Pot*. San Francisco: China Books & Periodicals.

Lvovich, N. (1997) *The Multilingual Self: An Inquiry into Language Learning*. Mahwah, NJ: Lawrence Erlbaum.

Meyer, R. (1996) *Stories From the Heart: Teachers and Students Researching Their Literacy Lives*. Mahwah, NJ: Lawrence Erlbaum.

Ogulnick, K. (1998) *Onna rashiku (Like a Woman): The Diary of a Language Learner in Japan*. Albany, NY: State University of New York Press.

Roen, D., Brown, S. and Enos, T. (1999) *Living Rhetoric and Composition: Stories of the Discipline*. Mahwah, NJ: Lawrence Erlbaum.

Ross, M. and Buehler, R. (1994) On authenticating and using personal recollections. In N. Schwarz and S. Sudman (eds.) *Autobiographical Memory and the Validity of Retrospective Reports* (pp. 55–69). New York: Springer-Verlag.

Shen, F. (1989) The classroom and the wider culture: Identity as a key to learning English composition. *College Composition and Communication* 40, 459–466.

Spack, R. (1997) The rhetorical construction of multilingual students. *TESOL Quarterly* 31, 765–774.

Swales, J. (1997) English as 'Tyrannosaurus Rex'. *World Englishes* 16, 373–382.

Trimmer, J. (1997) *Narration as Knowledge: Tales of the Teaching Life*. Portsmouth, NH: Boynton/Cook.

Part I: Language Specialists as Language Learners

The Fortunate Traveler: Shuttling between Communities and Literacies by Economy Class

Suresh Canagarajah is an associate professor in English at Baruch College of the City University of New York. He teaches postcolonial literature, Masterpieces of World Literature, ESL, and composition. His research interests span bilingualism, discourse analysis, academic writing, and critical pedagogy. He hails from the Tamil-speaking northern region of Sri Lanka, and taught in the University of Jaffna from 1984 to 1994. Among his publications are *Resisting Linguistic Imperialism in English Teaching* (1999), and research articles in the professional journals *TESOL Quarterly, College Composition and Communication, Language in Society, Written Communication, World Englishes, Journal of Multilingual and Multicultural Development*, and *Multilingua*. His book *Geopolitics of Academic Literacy and Knowledge Construction* is to be published by the University of Pittsburgh Press in 2001. He has worked with inner-city community service organizations in the South Bronx, Los Angeles, and Washington DC. He contributes to the literary and cultural activities of Tamil refugee groups in North America and Europe.

> 'You are so fortunate, you get to see the world – '
> Indeed, indeed, sirs, I have seen the world.
> Spray splashes the portholes and vision blurs.
> Derek Walcott, *The Fortunate Traveller* (1986)

While we are seated under the mango trees outside our house on a warm breezy afternoon in Jaffna chatting in Tamil, my Dad suddenly whispers something in English to my mother and they both sneak into the room inside, letting me play with the maid. They would emerge a couple of hours later seeming tired and exhausted, leaving me curious as to what they had uttered in English earlier. There are other occasions when we'll be talking about some wayward relatives, when my parents would switch to English to discuss some unpleasant episodes that shouldn't be understood by a four year-old like me. Or, while planning my upcoming birthday party, they would quickly switch to English to talk about a gift or invitee they'd like to keep hidden from me. These early experiences would leave a lasting impression on me of English as a language of secrecy, power, and mystery; a language owned by others, not belonging to me; a language that could put into disadvantage those who aren't proficient in it.

Many weeks and months later I would continue to put one and one together, understand with the help of context, guess the meaning, till I gradually began to break the code. Thus, even before I started attending school, I grew into some rudimentary levels of proficiency in English. My parents later learnt – much to their dismay – that they couldn't use English as a secret code any more between themselves. More dramatically, I joined the in-group now, sharing with them jokes, secrets, and gossip that we kept away from the monolinguals around us (like our maid). It was exhilarating to join the exclusive club of bilinguals (at least the two adults in my house) as we teamed up to put others into disadvantage. It would be much later in life that I would become politically sensitive enough to question the unfair power enjoyed by this language. It is after developing this sensitivity that I would understand the need to teach English critically and share its resources widely in my community to democratize its possibilities. But the strategies that helped me acquire proficiency in the language in my pre-school days would remain with me as I strove to become literate in English. These are the strategies: a curiosity towards the language, the ability to intuit linguistic rules from observation of actual usage, a metalinguistic awareness of the system behind languages, and the ability to creatively negotiate meaning in context. The characteristics of humility, wonder, and excitement over the power and complexity of language have also encouraged my coming into voice in English literacy. In an educational context where there was little explicit teaching of writing, and a social context that was predominantly oral in communicative tradition, such were the inner resources required to develop bilingual literacy. Perhaps these are the secrets of everyday learning – characterized by reflective understanding, strategic thinking, and contextual reasoning – that are at the heart of any educational experience. They sustain me as I negotiate the communicative traditions in Tamil and English – not to mention the hybrid discourses of diverse institutions and contexts – as I continue to develop a literate voice as a bilingual.

Childhood Literacy

I was born into a family that was already bilingual. In fact, both my parents were teachers of English, having done teacher training locally. Our relationship with the dual languages was complicated. We used Tamil for everyday oral communication. But the language of choice for literate activities for my parents was English. Literacy in our family involved more reading than writing. Moreover, we rarely indulged in academic or 'serious' reading and writing. Being literate meant the reading of the bible, newspapers, and some light fictional texts. As children, we were given simple books of nursery rhymes and stories that depicted the life of amiable pigs, ducks and sheep. I remember that these books had a gloss and color that was lacking in locally produced nursery readers in Tamil. Writing meant sending letters to acquaintances or business institutions. This was quite frequent in a community that lacks widespread use of telephones. (My family never had a telephone in Sri Lanka.) The relative status of the type of oral/literate and reading/writing activities we did in either language (which has remained largely the same throughout my life) would influence my written discourse. The Tamil of my oral interactions influences the English of my writing. I have used rhetorical skills of Tamil oral discourse in my English academic texts. This is partly because my family hadn't developed a discourse for English oral interactions or that of Tamil written traditions. The awkward tensions it creates and the creative ways in which it has been negotiated constitute the story of my development as a bilingual writer.

Another important reason why my oral discourse in the vernacular influenced my writing is because there was no explicit teaching of writing during my education in Sri Lanka. The language classes in my secondary school in Jaffna did have a component called essay writing (in addition to grammar, speech, and reading). But the writing instruction consisted of teachers assigning topics for our essays, taking them home for correction, and students reading out aloud their exemplary essays in the next class. The correction usually focused on grammatical, syntactic, and spelling errors. A grade was assigned using a vague/undefined notion of expressive effectiveness. With hindsight, I may call this a product-oriented practice towards writing – although there was no explicit rhetorical theory or teaching practice that motivated teachers to adopt this approach.

I emerged as a writer of no mean standing in this background. I still remember an essay in the Tamil class that was praised by my teacher in grade 6. I was asked to read this to the class as a model of good writing. It was one of those ubiquitous topics in secondary school, i.e. the most memorable experience in my life. I adopted some reflexive moves and dramatic twists that impressed the readers. I narrated an incident during an educational tour organized by my school. I first evoke the excitement and fun among the students as we begin the tour in a chartered bus at daybreak. Then I move to the tragic climax around the middle of the tour: as our bus approaches a railroad crossing on one of those bridges common in Sri Lanka which the trains and cars use alternately, the guard rails on both sides close with the bus trapped in the middle. With the train approaching us, I pause before the inevitable conclusion. I employ a stream of consciousness to dramatize the various feelings and thoughts that rush through my mind in a mixture of flashbacks composed of reality and illusion. As the train nears us, I awake from sleep to realize that all that I had narrated was in fact a dream. Thus I cheat the reader. The expressive effects, the emotional climaxes, suspense, excitement, and personal involvement were very much appreciated. This constituted 'good writing' for my vernacular teacher, my classmates, and me during those days.

My English essays were also usually commended. But before I left school I had an experience that taught me that not everything was okay with a style that heightened feelings and sensation. This occurred in the annual essay-writing competition held by the school for the senior classes. There were many subjects given for us to choose from. Knowing my strength, I chose the subject 'A Day in the Life of a Beggar'. In a chronologically structured essay that begins with daybreak and accompanies the beggar as he goes through the streets to beg for food, I end with his monologue under the awnings of a shop where he spends the night. He reflects on his sad plight and is in tears. I bring out the contrast between the plight of the beggar and the indifference of the rest of the society, much of this through the self-pitying musings of the beggar himself. I was certain that the examiner would be moved to tears by this expressive writing and offer me the prize.

But the decision surprised me. The prize went to a classmate, Seelan, who was in the science stream. He wrote on the subject 'Airplanes'. This was a technical essay on the recent developments in aerospace technology. The differences in both our essays were glaring. Seelan had adopted a restrained prose packed with information. (For the record, my friend was from a considerably more anglicized bilingual family that used English as the home language, and was also an avid reader in English.) It is possible that he was more influenced by the literate discourse in English while my writing showed the trace of oral discourse from the vernacular. We must also note here the background of the examiner. Though other English teachers had appreciated my expressive writing in English, this teacher (who was very senior in the school) had done some education in England, held a Master's degree, and was deeply inducted into English literacy. It is possible that this teacher's background made him appreciate a different discourse. But, interestingly, no explanation was given as to why the prize was awarded to the essay on airplanes. Our teachers didn't have the language to theorize decisions and assessments on writing. (There was only a single examiner for this contest, implying the belief that conclusive judgments could be made by anyone according to presumably universally accepted standards.) Since we weren't given any explanations, I was left to learn by trial and error. But one incident of negative feedback was not sufficient to teach me that expressive/emotional writing was not the only or best mode of writing in the world.

College Literacy

There was not much difference in my writing strategy when I proceeded to the more cosmopolitan capital city to obtain my first degree. I was majoring in English. The course work consisted mainly of lectures on literature – from Chaucer to Eliot and after. There was just one course on 'language' – which featured a structuralist approach to the description of grammar. What were called 'tutorial classes' – an hour a week – were reserved for writing assignments deriving from the lectures. A tutor was assigned to small groups of four or five students. The essays we wrote weekly were graded largely according to content. The rhetorically oriented comments were scribbles in the margins, like 'original insight', 'interesting idea', or 'meaning not clear' and the flagging of awkward syntax. The discussions in the class featured our reactions to the content of the essays. In a sense, these tutorial classes were somewhat personalized versions of our other lecture classes. In fact, in some tutorial classes there was very little writing. The hour was spent discussing the assigned texts in a collaborative, discussion-oriented manner. While the English department recognized the need for effective writing skills by assigning an hour for this purpose, there was no understanding about how this was to be inculcated.

I was left to learn by trial and error once again. When one of my essays in the first year was praised by my tutorial instructor for original insights and fresh use of language and was awarded an A, I thought this approach was what was appreciated in the university. I took my style a step further in my next essay. This was on the short story by Faulkner, *Dry September*. In this story a black man is lynched after being falsely accused of rape by an aging white woman. My essay was an interpretation of the evils of racism. In passionate prose, replete with rhetorical questions and exclamations, I moralized on the implications of the story: 'O why, why should people be judged on the basis of their skin? When will prejudice ever end? When will we begin to look at people as human beings and not as black, brown, or yellow?!...'. This paper was rewarded with an A and praised for its 'powerful language', its very 'personal response,' and relating the text to life.

There was some evidence that this style was not widely appreciated even in Sri Lanka. I recollect that the lecturers who gave me good grades (two of them in particular) had earned their first degrees locally and were doing their postgraduate degrees in Sri Lanka. They were also more deeply grounded in the vernacular literary and language traditions. But our examination scripts were marked by senior instructors who had obtained their doctorates in British universities. Here I didn't fare that well. I didn't see any As for my essays in the final tests. In fact, I remember one of my senior lecturers asking whether I really needed all the exclamations in my essays! (There goes another of my exclamations.) But that was the closest they came to posing a meta-textual (or even textual) comment on my writing. I began to intuit that the exaggerated, passionate, personalized style of writing wasn't universally appreciated in the academic community. But since there was little overt theorization or meta-discursive commentary on styles of writing, it was difficult for me to understand the rationale behind these different responses.

I must remark here, with the benefit of hindsight, that some of the different discursive influences – that of my local communicative tradition and the Western tradition – were coming into conflict in this formative experience of my literacy development. The predominantly oral influence in the vernacular tradition values the feelings, personalization, exaggeration, and hyperbole of communication. The restraint typical of serious Western writing is considered bland and mechanical. It is not surprising that my instructors who were rooted in the vernacular tradition (even though they were teachers of English) appreciated the discursive strengths I brought from this tradition. Of course, teachers who came from the traditional bilingual elite (with postgraduate education in the West) had an instinctive discomfort with this style – although they didn't have the language or tools to explain their preference. On the whole, both kinds of my teachers show the hybrid discursive traditions and styles of textuality that exist in postcolonial bilingual communities.

Joining The Academic Community

When I moved to the USA for my graduate studies, many of my sources of cultural shock pertained to text construction. In the very first essay I

wrote in my first semester at Bowling Green State University – an appreciation of a poem by Randall Jarrel – I found the instructor's red pen used a bit
too much for my liking. He wanted to know why I didn't have two spaces
after my periods, a single space after my commas, and five spaces at the
beginning of my paragraphs. He wanted to know why the first sentences of
my paragraph announced one thing while the rest of the paragraph went on
to talk about different matters. He underlined my occasional typographical
mistakes and called them spelling errors (I was new to typing: all my essays
in Sri Lankan schools and universities had been handwritten, as typewriters and computers are hard to come by). He also referred to my
occasional Sri Lankan idiom as grammatical or syntactical errors. His B
minus was by now not surprising to me. I knew that he had gone totally out
of his mind. With much exasperation I asked him, 'Don't you have
anything to say about the original ideas I was developing in this essay? Did
you only look at these insignificant mechanics of my paper to give me that
grade?' I was, of course, expressing the bias of my community that content
is more important than form. He blurted out something like, 'But these
things _are_ important'. What struck me as peculiar about his approach was
the heightened sensitivity to the materiality of my text – the physical representation of what I was trying to communicate. It was shocking to learn that
there were such numerous detailed rules and conventions relating to the
encoding of ideas on the page.

It was fortunate that my graduate advisor had enrolled me for a course
titled 'Bibliographical and Research Methods' in my very first semester. I
soon learnt the documentation methods and citation conventions of
various style manuals – like the MLA, APA, and Chicago. Although my
real induction into academic discourse was to come later, this introduction
to the textual conventions of writing was important to me. I also learnt to
consider books as 'products' and understand such matters as copyright,
reprints, and other conventions of the publishing process. Another component of the course was the introduction to word-processing. As I went
through the routines of opening, saving, closing, and reopening files in the
Macintoshes in the university computer lab, I realized what a fortuitous
move this was. Not only did word-processing erase all the traces of my bad
typing, the ease of producing successive drafts enabled me to give the kind
of attention to the text demanded by my American professors. I enjoyed
re-reading and revising my texts, as I didn't have to hand-write or manu-
ally type each draft all over again.

As for mastering the discoursal aspects of academic literacy, this took a
more difficult route. My reflective learning and critical thinking on the
feedback of my professors enabled me to make some crucial insights into

differences in style, structure, and tone. When a young assistant professor teaching American Transcendental literature used his red pencil liberally – and pointed out that my introduction didn't lay down the outline of my argument or announce my thesis, and that my essay started at one point and ended at another point – I was disturbed. Soon I couldn't take it any more. After carefully choosing my words, I met him in his office to tell him that my strategy of developing an argument had a different logic all its own. I chose the terms inductive and deductive to articulate the difference. While he was demanding a deductive approach, which already anticipated the concluding point of the argument, mine was an inductive approach that proceeded gradually towards the thesis in the last paragraph after providing the relevant evidence first. When this failed to break his resistance, I brought my trump card. I said that, since I was from a British colony, I was inducted into a more leisurely writing style (that sustained a certain amount of suspense, discovery, and involvement in communication typical in British scholarly writing) while the American academic style was too rigid, calculated, circular, and self-confirming. This explanation seemed to make better sense to the professor and he began to comprehend my essays. But I must say that the professor's careful attention to the construction of my paragraphs and development of my essay sensitized me to a more self-conscious use of language and discourse.

The real watershed in my transition to the literacy expected in the American academy would come through a more ironic route. I *learnt* a lot about academic writing by *teaching* composition to undergraduate students. Around this time, I was also registered for a course on Rhetoric and Composition – a requirement for teaching assistants in the English department. As I perused the textbooks of my students and also studied the recommended reading from my course (featuring the cognitive process approach of Flower, Hayes, Emig, and others of this period), I could understand better the thinking of my American teachers. The textbooks defined for me such textual structures as topic sentences, thesis statements, body paragraphs, supporting details, and transitions. The course work introduced me to the processes of brainstorming, outlining, and idea development. Used to valuing the poignancy of spontaneous communication, these cognitive routines and structural features forced me to detach myself from my writing and thus develop a more restrained, objective prose. Having mastered the magic formula of academic writing, it was not difficult to cruise through graduate school with effortless ease. I thought I had reached the culmination of my progression into academic literacy. This feeling was confirmed when my early submissions to leading professional journals like *TESOL Quarterly, World Englishes,* and *Language in Society* got accepted without much fuss.

An Outsider at Home

That this formula of academic text construction was not universally appreciated I was to discover when I returned to Sri Lanka to teach in my hometown after my doctorate. The reactions of my colleagues to my publications were not that enthusiastic. While some of them had praised my style in the articles I had written to local newspapers and magazines before my departure to the West, now they were enigmatically silent. Though they did not express openly their dissatisfaction at the new discourse I was adopting, their feelings were conveyed in other subtle ways. The only essay that one of my colleagues (who frequently edits my essays) approved was the article I published in *World Englishes.* This was different from my other articles. While the others reported empirically-based ethnographic or sociolinguistic research, this essay was on literature. I did a close reading of some Sri Lankan poets in English to bring out the ways they negotiated the competing discourses (i.e. of the vernacular and English). The essay was thus more impressionistic and less detached than my other essays, which fell into the typical IMRD (i.e. introduction-methodology-results-discussion) structure of research reporting. The fact that my colleagues appreciated my imaginative evocation of poetry in *World Englishes* did suggest their tastes and preferences in academic writing.

Another instructive experience was my first attempt at writing an academic paper in the vernacular. Since the main contribution to the academic life in the local context was in Tamil, I had to write in the vernacular in order to show the relevance of my scholarship at home. In an essay on contemporary Tamil poetry, I adopted my newly learnt writing skills from my American graduate school. For example, my introduction followed a move typical of the well-established CARS model (standing for 'Creating A Research Space' as formulated by John Swales). I outlined my purpose in that essay, defined how my contribution differed from existing scholarship, indicated the structure of my argument, and spelt out my thesis statement. My colleagues, who rarely indulged in meta-talk on writing styles, were suddenly quite vocal in expressing their disappointment. Even some of my students came up to me and said that the introductory paragraph had sounded a bit too pompous and over-confident. They explained that in the vernacular tradition (in lectures if not in writing) one opens with an *avai aTakkam* (i.e. humbling oneself in the court). The speaker starts with a brief confession of his/her limitations, praises the knowledge of the audience, and attributes whatever knowledge he might develop in his/her talk to others (i.e. elders, teachers, God). As the term *avai* (court) reveals, this rhetorical practice must have developed in the feudal social formation of the past. But the ethos of the scholar/rhetor is still influenced considerably by such an attitude. My cocksure way of beginning the essay – announcing my thesis, delineating the steps of my argument, promising to prove my points conclusively – left another bad taste in the local reader-ship. They said that this excessively planned and calculated move gave the impression of a 'style-less,' mechanical writing. Although I had attempted this mode of writing half-mischievously, I understood that a better strategy was to find ways of encoding the planned/disciplined/organized ways of writing without putting off my readers by sounding self-conscious, self-controlled, or self-confident.

In terms of material resources and institutional support for literate activity, there were striking differences between the academic cultures of USA and Sri Lanka. Initially, the lack of many of the facilities I had enjoyed in the United States was a source of discomfort. I couldn't word-process my drafts anymore. I had to first write them by hand, before typing the final draft for submission. Also because stationery was not easily available in war-torn Jaffna, I had to write fewer drafts. The lack of electricity and power reduced my writing time to the daylight hours. The badly equipped libraries didn't always help me in my citations and documentation of refer-ences. My colleagues couldn't help me much in the writing process. They would read my essays and enjoy discovering the new information, but rarely comment on them. At most, they would comment on some editing and typographical problems. It was difficult to expect too much from my colleagues as they lacked the induction into the Western publishing culture to comment authoritatively on matters of convention, style, or content. I had to develop the practice of re-reading my papers many times from different angles to aid revision. This contrast from the writing process in the West made me experience keenly the ways in which material/social contexts influence writing. I developed a cynicism towards cognitive process theories and pedagogues that reduce writing to an idealized mental activity.

But after a period of despondency, I adjusted my literate life style to suit my new context of work. I gradually opened my eyes to some of the features in the local academic culture that would help my writing activity. Most significant of these advantages is the lack of a publish-or-perish axiom in my institution. This removed the pressure from writing, and provided more time for reflection/revision. Gradually I adopted the prac-tice of composing sections of my paper in the daytime (when the sun was still up), while the night-time was spent on mulling over my points and working out my arguments mentally. Since there was no electricity, I couldn't read or write during the nights anyway. Furthermore, I had to plan the whole paper well in advance as it was difficult to write multiple drafts of revision (especially because I had to write them by hand with little spare paper). In retrospect, these were some of the best organized papers I wrote in my academic life. I ended up having a greater sense of control over what I was writing. The papers appear to be more coherent and smooth flowing. The relaxed nature of the writing enabled me to enjoy the writing process. Despite the disadvantages here, the papers I published in *Multilingua, Language and Education*, and *Language Culture and Curriculum* – in addition to *TESOL Quarterly, World Englishes*, and *Language in Society* – were all written in Jaffna.

An Outsider in the Western Academy

I moved again to the United States in Fall 1994 after four years of teaching in Sri Lanka. It was partly my frustration with the conditions of academic work there that drove me to relocate. For instance, the postal system and all form of communication between my hometown and the rest of the world had literally broken down. I couldn't get the latest research information in time. I faced tremendous practical problems in keeping up with academic developments elsewhere. However, I have mixed feelings about my literacy life here in the West. The facilities for writing are all in place (i.e. computer, laser printer, stationery, mailing services, libraries, internet). But I feel that my writing process has suffered in some important ways. The availability of all these facilities has made me intellectually and rhetorically lazy. I plan less extensively now, as I know that the word processor will let me revise things as much as I want to. I cut and paste from other drafts more often. (Though I eventually revise for coherence and erase all traces of pastiche, I find these drafts less powerful than the drafts I hand wrote.) In fact, I don't enjoy the writing process as I used to in Sri Lanka. Sometimes the very thought that all this writing contributes to earning my tenure deadens my enthusiasm. Even the recent papers I have managed to publish in coveted journals like the *College Composition and Communication* and *Written Communication* seem overworked, littered with references, and convoluted in argument in an effort to satisfy scrupulous reviewers.

Traces of my vernacular discourse are increasingly visible in my writing nowadays. Perhaps it is the fact that I am less in control of my writing process, perhaps it is the influence of my brief interlude in the culture of my native academic community, or perhaps it is my flirtations with vernacular academic writing that is to blame for this. But some of the criticism of my reviewers has in fact made me aware of the ways in which issues of style and tone could have ideological implications. A case in point is the paper titled, 'American textbooks and Tamil students: A clash of discourses in the ESL classroom.' It presently appears in the journal *Language Culture and Curriculum* (1993:6/2: 143–156). It was first sent to an 'international' ESOL journal published in America. The American reviewers (whose identity is betrayed by the spelling conventions, as you will see in the quote below) rejected publication based on the view that the display of feelings in the paper shows me as too ideologically biased against the West. This is how one reviewer opens his/her comments:

> Certainly, impassioned writing is to be admired, especially if it is grounded in theoretical writings, as much of this article is. Despite these valid aspects of the article, the unnecessarily hostile tone of the writer towards the specific materials used and towards Western society and values in general undermines the logic of this argument.... While I will always support provocative articles which enable readers to re-examine long-held beliefs, articles whose logic is obscured by hostility are counterproductive. Rather than open dialog, they preclude it. For this reason, I am not recommending publication.

It is interesting how this reviewer (in such an important gate-keeping context) still adheres to the classic Western stereotype that feelings are against logic. More importantly, the display of feelings becomes an excuse to proscribe writing that is ideologically critical. Hostility (which is defined as 'unnecessary') can be a reason to bar a paper from publication.

Although I always remind myself of the need to restrain my display of feelings in my writing, feelings get encoded in my texts quite unknown to me! There is a limit to how much I can suppress my subjectivity in my writing. In papers such as the above, where I had done considerable rounds of revision to subdue my feelings before sending it to the publisher, feelings do get displayed nevertheless. In fact, in most cases it appears to me that the level of feelings I find acceptable in an academic paper differs for center and periphery scholars. Coming from an oral rhetorical tradition where feelings are an index of one's conviction in one's position and of truth, I have come to think of feelings as never totally eradicable in my writing. It is therefore no more surprising to me to hear reviewers saying that they detect feelings in my paper.

That such differences in attitudes towards affect can have ideological implications is conveyed by what followed in the case of the paper mentioned above. Since I was working on another project at the time the reviewers sent back that paper, I couldn't start revising it immediately. I therefore decided to send it to another journal for consideration before I reworked it. So I sent the paper without any revision to *Language Culture and Curriculum*. To my surprise, the paper was accepted with absolutely no requests for changes. In fact, the manuscript was not sent back to me for any further work. The editor's letter simply stated that the reviewers had found the paper eminently publishable and that they would go ahead with scheduling the paper for printing. (I must point out that the editor of this journal is from Ireland, where much of the production seems to be taking place, although the publisher, Multilingual Matters, is based in Clevedon, England.) The issue here is not only that the British/Irish reviewers had a greater tolerance level for affect. It is possible also that their own feelings were not ruffled by the critical comments I was making of American textbooks and pedagogical dominance. They probably sympathized with my argument against American dominance, as they themselves are victimized by it!

The reactions of my colleagues in Sri Lanka to my publishing activity in the United States has further impressed upon me the way in which style can be ideological. Consider their ironic reactions to the paper I published in *Written Communication* (1996), where I articulated the problems periphery scholars face in getting their papers published in mainstream journals. My colleagues felt that my political insights didn't go far enough or were diluted or compromised by the type of writing I was indulging in. Some felt that there was a tone of condescension in my attitude to periphery scholars since I was addressing center academics as an insider in the latter's circles. In making accommodations to the writing conventions of center publishing institutions, I had also ended up representing my colleagues in ways that were not appreciated by them. To my surprise, my attempts to represent my colleagues was judged by them as a misrepresentation of their interests and values. Thanks to my colleagues from Sri Lanka, I have become alert to the contradictions of representing periphery concerns and subjects in a discourse that is so alien to their interests and traditions.

Such experiences have taught me many things: that the conventions governing academic discourse are partisan; that the judgements on the acceptability of feelings/affect and other matters of tone or style are considerably subjective, differing according to the culture of the various scholarly communities; that matters of style can be ideological with different prospects for highlighting or suppressing a critical perspective. I have been emboldened by these experiences to now reconsider my literacy development. Perhaps I shouldn't have gone to such lengths to suppress my feelings and ethos in my early journal articles. My writing strategy has been to write myself out of my texts. Thus my entry into the respectable center journals may have been earned at the cost of my subjectivity. On the other hand, I realize that I have always encoded feelings and personal modes of argumentation quite unwittingly, even when I focused on satisfying primarily the dominant modes of academic communication. I now consider ways in which I should infuse my vernacular rhetorical strengths into the academic discourse more consciously and confidently. I also feel more comfortable about attempting new forms of coherence in my writing that incorporate different voices and discourses. The current critique of texts and discourses defined in univocal and homogeneous terms has also given me confidence to construct multivocal, heteroglossic texts that show an active negotiation of the academic conventions from the basis of my vernacular oral rhetorical strengths. I am now constantly trying out ways of reconciling the competing discourses in a manner that is more satisfying to both my politics and poetics. This approach enables me to be at peace with myself in my writing activity.

Conclusion

Can I provide any hints for other non-native writers that will help them engage in academic discourse confidently in their professional life? Is there a secret for my success? I have mixed feelings about these questions. On the one hand, I don't feel I am 'successful' – I am still a student of academic discourse, restlessly experimenting in order to find a suitable voice in this discourse. (It is possible that it is this creative tension that has given life to my writing so far.) I also feel that I have not been provided with pedagogical or technical recipes that have helped me achieve mastery in writing. This is because I had my formative education in a community which doesn't indulge in much meta-talk about writing, and the theories handed to me during my graduate studies in the West have not always understood the unique challenges confronting a periphery scholar like me. But from another point of view, there *are* some lessons I have learnt during my literacy development that can help others. These are largely intuitive realizations and reflective insights that derive from the diverse contexts and cultures of writing I have been situated in.

To begin with, I find that being caught between conflicting and competing writing traditions, discourses, or languages is not always a 'problem.' These tensions can be resourceful in enabling a rich repertoire of communicative strategies. The conflicts I have faced as I shuttled between my native community and Western academic community generated many useful insights into the ideological and rhetorical challenges in academic communication. I developed a keener appreciation of the strengths and limitations of either discursive tradition. It was probably a blessing that I was an outsider in *both* the center and periphery academic communities! The restlessness that was created by these rhetorical contexts generated a sense of experimentation towards finding ways of cultivating my voice in the academy. Perhaps all writing involves ways of appropriating the available conventions and discourses from the standpoint of one's ideological and rhetorical preferences. Coming from a non-native language group, this truth was conveyed to me all the more glaringly. I learnt about appropriating the dominant conventions or developing multivocal texts, not from postmodernist academic scholarship, but from the painful personal experience of shuttling between discourse communities. Perhaps the qualities that helped me treat my conflicts positively and educationally were the traits I identified at the beginning of the essay – i.e. humility in the face of knowledge, a reflective learning attitude, critical questioning of dominant practices, and contextually grounded theorization. It is somewhat anticlimactic to point to these very fundamental learning strategies as those that helped me in my progress towards a confident play with academic conventions. But these are, after all, the skills and strategies that lead to a constructive, self-directed, everyday learning experience. This is how I became a bilingual when I was a child. This is how I have grown to manipulate competing literacy conventions as an adult.

References

Walcott, D. (1986) The Fortunate Traveller. In *Collected Poems 1948–1984* (p. 460). New York: Farrar, Straus and Giroux.

Canagarajah, S. (1996) Non-discursive requirements in academic publishing, material resources of periphery scholars, and the politics of knowledge production. *Written Communication* 13 (4), 435–472.

Initiating into Academic Community: Some Autobiographical Reflections

Vijay Bhatia was born and raised in India, where he received his first degree in science and mathematics and an MA in English and American literature. His Ph.D., in discourse analysis, is from the University of Aston in England. He has taught English and applied linguistics in India, Singapore and Hong Kong. Currently a professor of English at the City University of Hong Kong, he teaches courses in discourse and genre analysis and ESP (English for specific purposes) and also directs the MA program in the teaching of ESP. His research has focused on legal language and genre analysis, and his 1993 book *Analyzing Genre-Language Use in Professional Settings*  (1993) is widely used as a graduate textbook around the world. His publications have appeared in journals such as *English for Specific Purposes, World Englishes* and others.

It is often said that either you are born with creative abilities or you don't have them. I am not sure to what extent it applies to writing. What seems more likely is that some are born in a literate environment, while others acquire literacy through hard work. I belong to neither of these two categories. I adventitiously walked myself into an environment where I had little choice. I was born in the India of the British Raj immediately after World War II in a family of businessmen with almost no tradition of academic literacy or use of English. Since the colonial rulers of my country did not believe in making higher education widely accessible to the ordinary masses, I was sent to an ordinary government school, where I had absolutely no chance of having any contact with the language of the colonial masters till I was old enough (aged eleven) to appreciate the niceties and intricacies of elegant expression in the master's voice. At the time, I was unaware of my good fortune at having escaped the painful struggle that in my later life I saw my second language learning students go through in mastering the master's tongue. My mother tongue was far more convenient and accessible than my master's tongue, so I thought. Even now I think I was lucky to have had the opportunity to postpone my eventual confrontations with a foreign tongue, i.e. in English-medium subject-area classes, till I got to my high school. Considering the family background, English education seemed unlikely to contribute to my professional development in any significant way, I had thought. Therefore, I was told that I should not harbour any pretension to excel in the academy.

Initial Influences

Although I can't say we had a family tradition of academic literacy, I did have a distant uncle, a professor of philosophy, who lived next door after his retirement. In his early sixties, to me he often seemed very impressive, representing all that I would have liked to be. After thirty years even today I distinctly remember talking to him most evenings on almost every topic under the sun, philosophising politics, economics, sciences and of course language. He had many books to his credit, mostly on educational psychology, though his highest degree was in philosophy. To me, he was extremely versatile in his literacy practices. He was a perfect bilingual, using literally two fingers on his very old manual typewriters (one in English and the other in Hindi) completing manuscripts in both the languages to produce some thirty odd books of respectable size and standard. To me, as an undergraduate student in science, he was a perfect epitome of the ultimate in academic literacy. Deep down in my mind and, perhaps in my soul too, I had all the desire to be like him. However, there were several other problems. I was a good student of science, and the discipline carried with it the maximum prestige in the early sixties in India, if not everywhere else too. It was unthinkable for me to expect any significant shift in my career goals to take me away from this prestigious discipline, which personally I didn't fancy very much. On the other hand, I was a very good cricket player, and somewhere deep in my heart I was nurturing an obsession to become a professional cricket player, which I knew wouldn't take me very far in life. There were hardly any promising opportunities for professional cricketers those days. Today, close to the end of the century, things have become rather more promising in this respect, but I was born a little too early perhaps. My career, then, was balanced on two rather divergent objectives, one of which I was not particularly keen to pursue, and the other promised no long-term return of any significance.

When I graduated, I was admitted for a postgraduate degree in physics, about which I was not very enthusiastic. Too demanding a discipline, I thought. It would not leave any time for cricket. I could have applied for chemistry too. My heart was not there either. I thought I had no other choice. For the next few days, it seemed to be the end of the road for me, till I quite accidentally met a professor of English literature in the university, a well-known Irish scholar on W. B. Yeats, although I had no knowledge of this at the time. When she discovered my predicament, she suggested that I could do my master's degree in English literature. It took me only a few seconds to get a glimpse of my Promised Land. I would have enough time to play cricket and yet complete my degree in a respectable discipline, even though the Indian society was up in arms against any continuation of English on the national scene. It was a period in India's political history when nationalistic fervour had started sweeping far and wide, and English was being increasingly seen as the last remnant of colonial hangover. When the nation was going red in favour of abolition of English language from all educational institutions across the country, I was keenly looking for a career that crucially depended on the survival of the threatened language. But deep in my subconscious mind, there was a more serious consideration to resolve the tension created by my first propitious opportunity and my so-called first love, which did not seem to go together. So, as soon as I was offered a second choice, which seemed more compatible with my first love, it didn't take me long to decide what I wanted. The next morning I was formally admitted for a postgraduate degree in English and American Literature, though, at that time, I didn't have even the faintest idea of what I was getting into.

Search for Relevance

The two years of study of English literature were rather uneventful in terms of literary exploits, partly because I had very little acquaintance with Shakespeare, Hemingway or any of the other literary giants, not to mention some of the minor figures. Initially, they seemed to pale in comparison with this philosopher uncle of mine, as I had known him for a long time, inter-acted with him for years, whereas these literary giants, though big names, were unfamiliar and largely inaccessible to me. My literary sensitivities remained largely unsaturated and unresponsive even after two years of my laboured attempts to come to terms with the mystifying realities of fictional characters from the distant and not-so-distant past from the worlds I had little understanding and knowledge of. The cricket field was pure pleasure, whereas literature was simply a painful and tortuous experience. I may have been a bad literary scholar, but thanks to my scientific background, I proved to be a good examinee. Or, was there something wrong with the examination system that some of my seemingly learned classmates ultimately failed to impress the examiners as well as I did in the final analysis? Whatever the case, the die was cast. My fate was sealed. My examination results were so good that I was able to attract a lectureship in English as soon as my success in the examination was confirmed. With all my lack of interest in and under-standing of English literature, I was condemned to educate unwilling learners in their appreciation of the literature of the language they had developed a natural aversion and hostility to. That probably was the time I realised the truth of the saying that one has to pay for everything, but this was not an easy price to pay for a few years of fun in the cricket field.

The real turning point for me on my road to a career came when linguistics as an independent discipline was introduced in some of the Indian univer-sities, especially in the Central Institute of English and Foreign Languages. At that time, I was registered for my doctorate in English literature and I had started working, though not very enthusiastically, on anti-Utopian fiction. I went through my first teacher-training course in linguistics for English-language teaching, where for the first time, I listened to some of the formal linguists claiming linguistics as the scientific study of language. My background in science gave my search for a relevant academic niche for myself a new meaning. I said to myself, if my uncle, after his degree in philosophy, was able to establish himself as a psychologist and author so many books in psychology, why couldn't I turn to linguistics after literature? It seemed a reasonable argument to me. At last, I thought to myself, I had found something I could cope with reasonably well. From then onwards, it was goodbye to literature and welcome to linguistics. I thought this was the end of my problems, but I soon discovered how immature I was. The quest for a niche to establish oneself in academic literacy is a never-ending process. It starts with your first serious academic thought and continues to haunt you till you have written your last. What I was happy about was that the quest had at least begun with some hope of fulfilment. This was the beginning of my career as a teacher, researcher and writer. It took me about ten years of early career to discover and establish a field of research interest where I had some hope of fulfilment.

Period of Apprenticeship

The next stage in the development of my academic literacy practices began, once again accidentally, when I was asked to teach English to law students, which led me to do my first research in legal English. I had abso-lutely no idea that this initial accidental and rather reluctant fascination with the use of English for law was soon to become a life-long obsession.

One thing led to another and, without being conscious of it, I started sinking deeper and deeper into the chaotic complexities of legislative English. There was no other linguist or language teacher that I knew of who had a similar interest in this area.

I soon discovered, once again accidentally, that there was at least one more person who had a somewhat similar interest in the study of the language of the law. I had written a letter to Angela Tadros in the Sudan requesting her to send me a copy of her publication on the language of economics. Unfortunately, she had already left for Birmingham when the letter reached Khartoum. The letter was intercepted by John Swales, who was the Director of the Language Studies Unit, and also had an interest in legal English. As I subsequently learnt from him, he was equally delighted to find another human being on this Earth, other than himself, who was interested in legal English. Such was the size of the discourse community in legal English at that time. He immediately wrote back, sending me, not only the paper I had asked for, but also a few of his own, which were more centrally relevant to my interest. More important than the papers was the opportunity to come in contact with a person who after a few years was to become the most invaluable and lasting influence on my career as an academic and researcher. It was just a coincidence that he intercepted my letter, which was meant for someone else. Moreover, this was not to be the end of the story. It continued when I applied for a research fellowship at the University of Aston in Birmingham. By then, John had returned to Britain and had taken over as the Director of the Language Studies Unit at the same university where I had applied for a fellowship (although I must confess that I had no knowledge of it at that time). That was how I became his first research student. It also ended my search for a research niche, and launched what was to become almost an obsession for me for a long time to come, although I had absolutely no inkling of it at that time.

As I look back at my university days, I realise more now than ever before how valuable and yet enjoyable a time I had. Research, especially leading to a degree, is often stressful, depressing and boring. In contrast, for me, this period of research was perhaps the opposite of what people normally expect it to be. For me, it was a kind of apprenticeship period, which was relaxed, enjoyable and interesting. The institutional environment was almost like what in good old Indian tradition was known as *guru-kul*, where students were sent as apprentices for a period of time in the company of the guru, which was anything but instruction in formalised settings. Research and learning, I remember, was not simply confined to the few rooms of the University. Research supervision was not simply a matter of helping the researcher to develop a proper focus, interpret previous research, identify and collect data, develop a suitable framework and analyse data to arrive at conclusions worthy of reporting. It was also a process of developing the right kind of attitude to knowledge acquisition, creation and dissemination. It was a kind of initiation into the discursive practices of the academic community, for which it was equally important to develop a long-term academic relationship with other members of the academic community. It was very much a question of developing a long-term relationship with the adviser based on mutual confidence, understanding and respect, all of which was made so effortlessly accessible because of the diverse activities, not all of which were directly related to academic supervision. Participation in a range of activities of the unit – research, general academic, pedagogic as well as administrative – was extremely useful in developing a relationship with the adviser and the unit. We regularly played cricket during lunchtimes and weekends, tennis in the evenings, and had frequent social get-togethers. This was all part of the institutional environment. Research supervision involved a lot of discussion of topics and procedures for research, but it became as much a part of our daily life as a number of other extra-academic activities, contributing to a mutual understanding that in no time created a relaxed, enjoyable and interesting environment for an approach to discourse and genre analysis that was to dominate the remaining years of our professional life. A necessary consequence of this approach was that learning was rarely seen as an activity confined only to supervision meetings. It was an ongoing process, which could take place anywhere: on a cricket field, in front of the TV in a video room while watching Wimbledon finals, or during frequent discussion sessions with the adviser and several other colleagues, some regular, others informally arranged. The most important aspect of this informal, relaxed and friendly approach to research supervision is that it encourages individual growth rather than dependence on the adviser, although it is true that for a conventional teacher there could be nothing more difficult than abdication of authority in student–teacher consultation. My own impression is that such a *laissez faire* attitude on the part of the adviser is easier to adopt in traditional British university settings than in more typically American universities. To me, this is the most attractive side of the professional life of researchers because it encourages self-confidence and development in the researcher, which is the most important step in getting accepted as a member of a particular discourse community.

Another important contributor to the development of my personal profile was the research environment during my doctoral days at Aston, where I had excellent opportunities to grow naturally, as it were. I distinctly remember that my adviser and more established members of the discourse community, especially senior colleagues and researchers, never took advantage of their position, status, expertise or professional relationship, particularly in situations where they saw any academic disagreement, to win a point. This allowed me, especially in my early years of academic apprenticeship, to live with disagreements for years before I felt convinced, one way or the other. This often kept me mentally active and thinking about issues I thought were important for my personal academic profile. This, to me, seemed the most important aspect of academic advising: to allow one to take time to resolve a contentious argument or to accept a position against one's own. Thinking about it now, I feel that we were somewhat stubborn in not readily accepting a change in our position unless we felt convinced, even if it took a long time. This kind of continued search for resolution, however, kept me professionally alive. I always felt that I had something to look forward to, something more crucial to resolve, some outstanding issue that needed further investigation and thinking. This was part of the training that I feel was important, especially during my initial attempts at discourse analysis. Unlike many other areas of linguistics, including formal linguistics, discourse analysis is complex and potentially unpredictable and developing. There is always room for negotiation and accommodation. Right or wrong solutions, which are preferred in the sciences, are generally less than adequate in discourse studies. I think this kind of liberal research environment gave me initiative and confidence to grow independently.

The other very significant aspect of academic apprenticeship is active participation in the process of research, where one is invariably unsure of almost everything, including the focus, data, investigative procedures and, of course, the outcomes, even if one has obtained the findings. One needs encouragement, participation and direction. I distinctly remember that, whenever my adviser took home some of the texts I was struggling with and the following day brought back his own analyses and interpretations, however tentative, I used to gain new understanding of the discipline. It was comforting to know that my adviser was also an active participant, collaborator and a fellow sufferer in the investigative process. This kind of involvement in the research process is not only insightful for the struggling researcher but also an important source of confidence building for a long-term academic relationship. It needs tremendous courage for a teacher to risk his credibility by participating in such research initiatives through preliminary, tentative and inadequate or, at times, half-baked analyses, which one is under no obligation to offer. I think it is always helpful to lead by example, to prove a point by demonstration, or to win an argument by convincing others and by consensus. Ideally, academic research is more of a collaborative and co-operative endeavour than an arduous, painstaking and agonisingly lonely chore. This is the essence of what, in the beginning, I called research apprenticeship, which is extremely helpful to the researcher but can be risky for the adviser. Many of us would not like, or have the courage, to take such a risk.

Professional Development

Now when I look back and try to visualise what was valuable for me in that early research exercise, I think the most important aspect of my academic life at that time was my attempt to find for myself a narrow focus in research but with a broad vision. The focus for me was on the analysis of legislative writing, but the main issue I had in mind was the way legal writers attempt to make their writing clear, precise, unambiguous and yet all-inclusive. This kind of broadening of vision, I gradually discovered, opened up a number of other areas of professional discourse for me. To my great advantage, I soon discovered that, although it is crucial to have a narrow focus in your research and publication, it is even more crucial to have a broad vision, as this allows you to raise issues and talk about them in a context that gives more mileage to your efforts. Soon I discovered that I was no longer simply analysing a corpus of legislative writing and asking myself the question, 'Why do legal writers write legislation the way they do?' I soon discovered that it is necessary to ask more general questions of the following type:

- What disciplinary goals do writers set for themselves and how do they fulfil them?
- How do they achieve their disciplinary goals through the discourses they construct?
- Why do most professional writers write their discourses the way they do?
- What makes their discourses typical of the settings in which they are embedded?
- What aspects of their professional demands make these discourses possible?
- To what extent are these discourses recognisable and hence standardised?
- To what extent are these discourses driven by conventions?
- Are there any constraints operating on their construction, interpretation and use?
- What freedom do they have in breaking away from the established conventions?

As you can see, there were two distinct advantages in such an approach, one a short-term and the other a long-term. The short-term view allowed me to have a clear focus for research leading to a degree to be completed within a reasonable time and to claim a reasonable degree of experience and expertise in a highly-focused area of professional discourse. The long-term view was to create a sufficiently broad and sustainable niche for myself in an area that was to last me at least a lifetime, if not more. In order to establish one's academic credentials as a writer in today's highly competitive academic world, one needs both: a proven expertise in a highly focused area of study, where one can claim some authority, however limited it may be, with some degree of confidence, and also published evidence over a sustained period of time, which is possible only if one can broaden the focus by identifying questions and issues of the type I have identified from my own experience. Going back to my last ten years of research and publication, I feel that one can never emphasise enough the importance of high mileage research with a focus on specifically local but broadly significant problems. Research publication is, in a way, a long-term investment, in that it can assure potentially higher returns if one has the capacity to survive over a longer period of time. The broader the vision, the longer one is likely to survive, and the higher the returns. However, in order to start effectively, one must have a focus, without which a broad vision will be no better than a mere aberration.

Writing Professionally

A very important aspect of individual development as an academic writer is the confidence with which one can make a safe claim about one's research insights. Hedging in academic discourse has been given top priority, especially in the context where writers tend to publish in languages other than their own, but it is very rare to find even a suggestion to the effect that, if one is confident about one's claims, one must stick to them. It may be difficult in the beginning, but it pays off enormous dividends in the long run. It has something to do with the mastery of the field you claim to be part of, and is often not difficult to acquire once you have identified a focus for your work.

Let me give you an instance. Very early in my academic career, I had sent one of my initial articles for publication to one of the most prestigious journals in the field. I was fairly confident about the work that had gone into the article, but I had no academic standing, and I was taking a big risk by arguing against a well-established claim made by one of the editors of the journal. I was pleasantly surprised by the reactions from the editor. His comments were very positive and appreciative of the way the arguments were structured. However, one of the major contributions I thought I was making in the paper was seen by the native-speaking editor of the journal to be inappropriate. As a concept, it was perfectly acceptable. It was the use of an expression not available in any of the available dictionaries of the English language that was not acceptable. I was offered a few alternatives to replace what I thought was a significant contribution to the understanding of discourse. None of these suggestions I thought would do justice to the claims I was trying to make. The choice was either to accept the change suggested by the editor, or risk losing the opportunity of almost-certain publication in a very prestigious journal for a new author like myself. I was advised by several of my colleagues and superiors to accept the changes, which, I thought, would damage the argument I was putting forward and the claim I was making in the paper. I realised that taking the path of least resistance, complying with the editor's request, could mean losing confidence in my own work and my own judgement. Thus, I decided to take the risk rather than undermine my conviction in my own claim. I wrote a very lengthy and detailed explanation in support of my decision not to accept the change suggested by the editor. The letter, which I wrote with great apprehension and care, took quite a bit of effort on my part. I don't think I have written a more important letter in my entire life. To my pleasant surprise, the editor very graciously accepted the argument, withdrawing the objection originally raised. Let me acknowledge that it was not easy to get away with an innovation in the use of the language of which I was not a native speaker, especially when it ' jarred' on the ears of a well-established native speaker of the language. Even today after many years I can hardly underestimate the value of that one single outcome, and the support and encouragement it gave me at such an early stage of my academic career.

Myths About Literacy Practices

I have often found uninitiated academic writers, quite rightly I think, complaining about what has been referred to in academic discourse as gate-keeping practices within and across discourse communities. My own experience with this has been rather pleasant, for reasons I find difficult to identify straightaway. I don't deny that there are gate-keeping practices associated with most of the discourse communities in general, but these are relatively less obstructive in academia than in other non-academic discourse communities. There is competition and, although it is often more intensely felt in the early years of apprenticeship than in more advanced years of academic life when one is more comfortably established in the community of practice, it certainly is moderate as compared with what one might expect in other professional communities, especially those associated with business, finance or legal contexts. Disciplinary cultures, quite legitimately, require their members to work toward a certain degree of conformity based on conventions which, it is hoped, will eventually create solidarity within the community, and often language is one of the most important tools to achieve that purpose. In academic and research publications, therefore, it is often found that uninitiated and relatively less experienced researchers, especially in sciences and engineering, publish collaboratively with their more senior and better established colleagues. Although one may justify such a tradition on the basis of somewhat unavoidable collaboration in research laboratories, it is not entirely due to these constraints. I distinctly remember the time when I prepared the draft of my first research paper as a doctoral student in a university dominated by scientists and technologists. Having known several of my fellow researchers in the sciences invariably publishing jointly with their supervisors, I followed their practice and submitted my first paper to my supervisor for comments. It had both names, mine as well as that of my supervisor, as authors. To my great surprise, my supervisor told me that he would not like to claim any credit for the paper, as he felt that he had not contributed to the paper, except by way of normal supervision and guidance. To me, it was exactly the opposite of the established practice in science and technology. Was it a matter of different disciplinary cultures? Or was it a case of different individuals? Whatever the reasons, I felt a little bit nervous at that time. Maybe the paper was not good enough for my supervisor to put his name on it, I thought. I had to take all the blame for the paper. With somewhat nervous apprehensions of several kinds, I submitted it for publication. To my great surprise, it attracted excellent reviews and was accepted for publication in a very prestigious academic journal in the field. Thinking about it now, I feel as if this was a deliberate attempt on the part of my supervisor, who I respect very much, to make me go through the process of initiation all by myself. Obviously the experience turned out to be extremely pleasant and useful. Ever since, I am more than convinced that risk-taking is a great confidence builder in academic publishing.

I have often been reminded of a number of rather disturbing myths prevalent in academic communities of different make-up, but the one that seems to have been more established is the one that cautions non-native speakers of English about the role of grammatical and rhetorical accuracy in research reporting. I have seen researchers claiming linguistic accuracy as the key to success in research publishing. Although it would be preposterous on my part to ignore the role of linguistic competence in academic activity of this nature, one cannot deny the fact that this is only one of the important contributors to academic research. Moreover, linguistic competence is not simply a matter of fixing prepositions or manipulating subject–verb agreement. It is more important to be able to understand, manipulate and even exploit the conventions of research genres, where the obvious advantage of native-speaker competence in the use of the language has a very nominal role to play. Other factors, perhaps more important to my mind, include an ability to locate a suitable and attractive niche for one's research contribution and to position oneself appropriately in the context of existing knowledge, to use effective and acceptable research tools to carry out the intended research, to be able to make a good judgement about the journal where the intended research can make a valid and acceptable contribution, and to be able to conform to the requirements of the different house styles of the journals. One could go on adding to this list. I remember having a discussion with the editor of a well known science journal about this point. I was told that one of the main reasons for not accepting research reports from developing countries in Asia, including India, was the lack of efficient and effective means of communication with the potential authors. It often took editors months to get revisions and corrections done, although in several cases there was nothing wrong with either the quality of research or in the use of language to report such research. Nevertheless, the most common impression is that such a lapse is always due to the lack of what language teachers regard as native or near-native competence in the use of English. To me, it is nothing more than a myth created by language teachers, which is often used for gate-keeping purposes by interested parties. It is also not very uncommon to claim that, since many non-natives have very little confidence in their use of language, they often find it extremely daunting to write their first paper. As far as I know, it is less of a problem that non-native writers lack confidence in their linguistic ability. The far more serious problem is that native-speaker journal editors have no confidence in non-natives and their use of the language. I know of at least three of my colleagues, one native speaker of English born in England and the other two from America, all three now well established writers, who in their early years were made to suffer linguistic indignities at the hands of journal reviewers and editors because their names gave a misleading impression that they were non-native users of English. Their expressions were challenged for linguistic accuracy by other native speakers of the language, but in one case I distinctly remember, the challenge was made by a non-native speaking journal editor. Such is the nature of academic gate-keeping.

In the final analysis, as they say, nothing succeeds like success, but in academic publishing this happens only when one has become established in the community. During the early years of initiation, it is simply a bumpy ride, full of distressing disappointments from editors and publishers, insulting indignities from reviewers, confusing crossroads fabricated by established disciplinary gurus, puzzling predicaments made unbearable by colleagues and fellow researchers from other cultures. By the time you get established, you are so exhausted that you tend to lose your urge and determination to exploit your new-found freedom from all the constraints that bothered you for such a long time. However, the rewards for such a struggle are by no means unexciting. You begin to discover that the recognition from colleagues and members of the wider discourse community have renewed your enthusiasm and determination to continue this struggle in a more positive and meaningful way, and that is when you realise that your only limit is your own capacity to work and to continue to work endlessly.

Reminiscences of a Multilingual Life: A Personal Case History

Nils Erik Enkvist, one of the twelve Finnish Fellows of the Academy of Finland, was born and raised in Finland. He studied at the Universities of Helsinki (MA, Ph.D.), University of Michigan (MA), and University College London. He taught English and linguistics at the University of Helsinki and at Åbo Akademi University, where he served as chair, dean, rector, chancellor, and Distinguished H.W. Donner Professor of Stylistics and Text Research. He has lectured widely, not only in most European countries, but also in the US, Canada, Israel, Singapore, Australia and South Africa. His honours include honorary doctorates from Stockholm, Poznan in Poland, Purdue, and

Indiana University. A member of many learned academies, his presidencies include those of the European Linguistic Society and the International Federation for Modern Languages and Literatures. He has always believed in the necessity of combining research and teaching and has published widely on such topics as the reception of American literature in nineteenth-century England, motifs in Old and Middle English poetry and, since the 1960s, on linguistic stylistics as well as the linguistics of text and discourse, in which fields he has been a pioneer.

It is not altogether without embarrassment that I find myself shanghaied into a text type novel to me, namely the venerable genre of egocentric confessions. On the other hand, I have been persuaded that what I have to tell might be partly exotic to some readers, and partly typical enough of my generation to have some slight general interest. Hence my agreement to contribute.

I have been most forcibly reminded of the role of writing in my family since my parents died and I inherited their archives. For generations, my ancestors were attached to their chattels, and apparently I too have inherited the genes which make throwing things away impossible. Such attitudes are possible as long as people don't move around much. My forebears didn't. So, I find myself blessed with crates and cartons of manuscripts and other impedimenta, including masses of letters and postcards.

Before the advent of the telephone, the normal way of keeping contact within the family was the postcard. There are various historical strata of materials in my collection, but the bulk comes from my paternal grandmother and her circle. She was born in 1870 as one of the eight children of a headmaster of a girls' school. All of those of the original eight who survived, especially the women, conversed incessantly by card, transmitting greetings, gossip and information about health and sickness ('little Ole has the measles'), news about better and cheaper milliners and seamstresses with closer contacts to the fashionable world of Nevsky Prospect in St Petersburg, which was the nearest metropolis. More sombre are the wartime messages about hunger and Ersatz diets and black markets and brutalities and death. A day spent with such correspondence is a lesson in grassroots history and family relationships, though reading a copperplate hand on a card written, not in boustrophedon but at least once across, is a chore for aging eyes. One of my livelier cousins went through similar archives of another family. She has a store of conversational treasures about her discovery of a hushed-down mid-nineteenth-century black sheep, apparently a heart-crusher but dreaded by his bourgeois siblings because of his torrents of requests for money from distant continents. Nothing so dramatic in my archives, unless our black sheep were illiterate or their messages were destroyed.

This voluminous correspondence was intensified during the war years, including the period from 1939 to 1945. In the combat zone, the Finnish Army had never heard of private phone calls. My father was in the medical corps outside Leningrad, my mother nursed the wounded in a base hospital, and I served as a gunner in the ack-ack. We kept in touch by exchanging carefully censored versions of our experiences. When I studied at the University of Michigan, I still wrote regularly to my parents as well as to friends and acquaintances. The telephone, fax and e-mail have made such behaviour obsolete, for better or for worse. The files of letters now make me wonder. I cannot remember when I last had a letter from one of my own children. These days our affections transmit by mobile phone, much favoured by traffic jams when telephone calls have a function in defusing one's fury.

I grew up as one of the bilinguals in officially bilingual Finland (today some 4.7 million speakers of Finnish and 300,000 speakers of Swedish). I had a Swedish-speaking father and a Finnish-speaking mother. I went to school first in Swedish and then in Finnish, and I pass as a native speaker among both groups. But during my school years I also had many years of intensive German and English and did a fair amount of reading in both. I was, of course, a bookworm. The *Galgenlieder* and *Winnie the Pooh* were particular favourites, but most of my diet was adventure, an occasional detective story, history and biography. I had picked up some Estonian in Tallinn and Pärnu during the last months of peace in 1939 and have since tried to keep it up with an occasional book. During visits south of the Gulf of Finland, my sudden bouts of Estonian still strike colleagues and friends with awe. As a schoolboy, I also tried to satisfy my thirst for languages by worrying my way through the odd text in Russian with dictionary and grammar. What remains of my Russian is a somewhat shaky ability to read linguistics and history, with the occasional support of a dictionary. Fiction is beyond my powers. French and Italian came later, though I got to know the Musketeers and the Count of Monte Cristo through Finnish. As an exotic exercise, I browse through occasional texts in Spanish and Portu guese, and during a recent visit to Barcelona, some texts in Catalan. Like all native speakers of Swedish, I can also read traditional Norwegian as well as Danish, after an hour or two of adaptation. Spoken Danish is, however, beyond me. At school, I had plenty of maths and physics, but no Latin or Greek, and I chose to prepare myself for the obligatory Latin test at the university by reading lots of texts instead of memorizing the prescribed dose of grammar. Part of the reading could be squeezed into peaceful moments during the tail end of my military service. My chief pedagogical aid was the Loeb Library. I read the Latin, looked at the English when I got stuck, and hugely enjoyed the process. From time to time, I still take out my well-thumbed Loeb Suetonius to contemplate the iniquities of those in power, being reminded of modern parallels surfacing in present-day newscasts and newspapers.

Like I suppose most bilinguals and multilinguals, I think reading and speaking several languages has had a crucial effect on what literacy I may have in all the tongues I work with. The famous Slavicist Valentin Kiparsky (Kiparsky *père* to today's American linguists) had advised my parents to keep strictly to one language per person, and my father did not react unless addressed in Swedish and my mother unless spoken to in Finnish. Thus I was my own translator and interpreter from the start, and I did not feel I had done my filial duty until I had stated my business in two languages, or three or four if we had foreign visitors. To the despair of my wife and astonishment of many houseguests, this intensive translating went on until my father's death in 1972, though I, of course, well knew that my parents were bilingual too. However interesting linguistically, our slow-motion communication could not help having a somewhat inhibiting effect on small talk, and, worse, intellectual discussion and debate. After the first half hour it did occasionally provoke some tactful but not entirely positive feedback from exhausted visitors bright enough to understand an utterance at first go, especially if their upbringing obliged them to watch the sauce congealing over the steak rather than disturb our linguistic exercises. Still, by the age of two or three or four, I was steeped in most of the problems solemnly discussed today as Translation Science or *Uebersetzungswissenschaft*. My loving parents also liked to entertain all and sundry with hilarious examples of their brilliant son's more wayward childhood translations, to my embarrassment, of course. But I got my own back. Now I cite my childhood achievements to provide relief for those doomed to hear my otherwise boring lectures on translation and intercultural rhetoric.

People keep asking how many languages I know. My answer is, unless you define what you mean by 'knowing' a language, choose any number between three and something like a dozen (for instance, I once studied Portuguese because I wanted to work in Brazil, and still have a basic reading knowledge tested in Lisbon and the Algarve and Madeira, but I would never dare claim that I 'know' Portuguese.) Of my three strong languages (Finnish, Swedish, English), I read each language daily, write in each language almost daily, and lecture gladly in any of the three. To give a concrete example: this morning I am writing this little essay in English. Yesterday I wrote a report for an organization I belong to in Finnish, and some weeks ago I finished a chapter in Finnish on the history of nineteenth-century linguistics in Finland for a history of Finnish science to appear in the year 2000. And this afternoon I shall write two letters to Sweden about a reserve officers' excursion to the Swedish equivalent of West Point. I have written books and articles in all three languages, and have frequently lectured in all three during one working day. Another question I hear occasionally is, what language do I dream in? My wife, who lovingly listens to me talking in my sleep, confirms that the language varies, and I know it adapts to the setting of the dream. The language of the multiplication table and of doing sums used to be another classic test for linguistic dominance, until it was made obsolete by the pocket calculator. I used to do mine in Swedish, the language of my primary school.

People also often ask whether I change personality when switching from one language to another. Yes, I do. In Finnish, I am an honest, straightforward, homely, down-to-earth person, occasionally digging into the politer layers of a wartime military substratum of language. In Swedish, I am pedantic and, alas, sound precisely like the academic administrator I used to be. And in English, a language I originally learned through formal education, I am stuck with an RP variant that strikes today's Britons as a relic from high society in the days of Edward VII. The phoneticians at

Edinburgh once set up a fascinating fake biography for me on the basis of my accent ('What school did Nils go to? What was his regiment? How much money did his father make?'), and Lord Quirk, one of the world's greatest experts on English, once said over a pint of bitter in the bar of the House of Lords, 'Nils, compared to you even the Queen sounds slightly demotic.' After much contemplation, I have decided that this was not altogether a compliment. Some of my American friends have dressed the same opinion into much blunter idioms. My years of study and research in the US actually gave me a temporary mid-Atlantic accent, which stimulated puzzled queries in many parts of the anglophone world. But some years in London and Cambridge took me back to my phonetic roots. I actually majored in phonetics in Helsinki, practising glottal stops and clicks and Welsh fricolaterals in the tram on my way to the phonetics seminars. One of the profits of such exercises was increased elbow-space as my frightened fellow-passengers quickly moved out of range. A troublesome relic of these phonetic drills is that my pronunciation of tourist phrases in divers languages is misleadingly convincing. This in turn leads to the embarrassment of my understanding nothing of the cascades of noises in machinegun staccato with which trusting natives requite my simplest queries. George Bernard Shaw missed many opportunities when he failed to take Professor Higgins on a tour around the globe.

My generation of people in the Nordic countries has experienced a revolutionary shift in the status of foreign languages. When I went to school, Swedish was necessary for inter-Nordic communication, German was the dominant language of learning and science, and French had to be learned by diplomats and fashionable people in polite society. English was still a language mastered mainly by businessmen and a minority of diplomats, scholars and scientists, and the Finns simply refused to learn Russian. Today English has taken over most international linguistic functions. There are indeed people who react against the global dominance of English, fearing that other languages, including their native ones, will suffer under the onslaught of TV, entertainment, international sports and travel, where English is without rival as a lingua franca. You may share my interest in noting that the same people who deplore the decline of Latin and French as international languages now regret the rise of English into a position comparable with first, that of Latin, and then, that of French in past centuries – an inconsistency I point out with a happy smile, as one should as a Professor of English. I trust the vernaculars will survive, as they have so far.

Now back to the autobiography. There is a decided difference in my familiarity with registers in my three strong languages. I have, for instance, done all my military service in Finnish only (that is, not in the Swedish-language units of the Finnish Army), and have no idea what the parts of a machine gun are called in Swedish. The other way round, I began my academic administration in Swedish. But I got elected to various inter-university committees and boards in the Ministry of Education and else-where, and had to learn to write the proper jargon of administrative Finnish more or less overnight (a painful operation but a quick one, I am glad to say). And in linguistics, I suppose English is my strongest language. When preparing a lecture in Finnish or Swedish I insure myself by a sweep through the relevant terminology, and even then I find myself asking for occasional help from audiences familiar with linguistics in English and in other major languages.

As some of my readers may recall, I have written and lectured widely on the linguistics of style, text and discourse. My original interest in style was not academic, but painfully personal. My teachers and tutors in Michigan and London used to worry about my essays. 'What you are trying to put across,' they said, 'may well be all right, but your style is absolutely awful.' 'Excuse me, Sir,' said I, because at that time I was a well-brought-up young man, 'but what actually is style?' The answers I got were all platitudes of the kind, 'make your essay easy to read' and 'try to make the expression fit the subject.' 'But isn't this precisely what I've done?' I asked. I now thor-oughly admire the patient politeness with which my professors showed me the door. Clearly I was a case beyond hope.

I then started teaching in Finland and grading undergraduate essays written in English. In no time I found myself saying to students, 'What you are trying to put across may well be all right and your syntax is by-and-large correct, but your style is absolutely awful.' 'Excuse me,' said the boldest of my students, 'but what is style?' This gave me a strong feeling of *déja-vu*. At the same time, various universities in Sweden and the Swedish School Board started inviting me to speak about teaching litera-ture in a foreign language, or, if you prefer, teaching a foreign language through literature. And one of the recurring questions at these summer courses and seminars was, 'What can we do to give our students a sense of style in a foreign language?' To appreciate the urgency of the question you must remember that the traditional Nordic gymnasium of fifty years ago was a strict, academic institution catering for an intellectual elite. Today reading whole plays by Shakespeare and Schiller in the original is no longer part of the normal school syllabus. Indeed some experts claim that Shake-speare's mantle has been stolen by Donald Duck or, worse, Batman.

But that was an aside. What I wanted to say is that I sat down to read and think about style. I wrote a long essay 'On Defining Style' (OUP 1964) where I recapitulated various approaches people had had to stylistics, and a couple of books – *Linguistic Stylistics, Stilforskning och stilteori* (both 1973) – as well as a large number of papers explaining what I thought about style-consciousness. I followed up these English- and Swedish-language books with another, smaller one in Finnish entitled *Tekstilingvistiikan peruskäsitteitä* (1974). My basic idea was, and is, that what we call 'style' is one of the responses we have to texts. The impressions of style are provoked by style markers, that is, by linguistic features (words, sentence structures and the like) which activate an association with a certain type of text in its situational context, e.g. a sermon, a statute, a sergeant drilling recruits, religious ritual, love letter, sonnet, etc.; sergeant to private, lover to mistress, boss to worker or, at the literary level, text produced by, say, Milton, Pope, or Vonnegut. When we hear or read a new emerging text, we match it with past memories of texts in specific situations: 'This clergyman sounds like all clergymen' or, shockingly, 'This clergyman sounds like a drill-sergeant,' or 'This clergyman sounds as if he were talking to his girl-friend rather than to the Almighty,' or 'This blank verse has a majestic roll like Milton's.' Sometimes, as in laws and statutes and ritual texts, we prefer de-individualized modes of expression that conform to our stylistic expectations by resembling texts we have met before in comparable contexts and situations. Sometimes, as in certain kinds of modern or surrealistic literature, we appreciate surprises and thwarted expectations and fresh effects arising through shock rather than through slavish obedience to conventions.

This leads to corollaries relevant to learning and to teaching. I believe in them because I have been through them myself and have also tested them on students in several countries for almost half a century. It is, for instance, useless to gripe about a student's inability to appreciate and describe styles until that student has experienced a large body of different texts brought from a wide range of contexts. To know what a sermon sounds like you must hear and perhaps read sermons. And to really know what a sergeant sounds like when drilling recruits you should have been a recruit yourself. What you need to identify styles and to respond to them, in your L1 as well as in other languages, is a wide spectrum of experience not only of language but also of different uses of language and indeed of life. Some of it can be had through reading, but a great deal requires the kind of familiarity with spoken idiom that you can only acquire by living with, or in, that language. To a certain extent, you can extrapolate from one language to another, particularly if you are studying styles of major international cultural movements. (There are, to take a trivially familiar example, certain recognizably similar style markers in Renaissance sonnets in Italian, French and English.) But many styles and style markers are culture-sensitive in such a detailed way that they become language-specific. The more we learn about language, the more we notice that texts – even scientific papers – are organized differently in different languages. How students can best gain the necessary experience of discourse across a wide spectrum of situations is a crucial question for all syllabus-builders. At this point I am tempted to produce a diatribe on a favourite topic, and must desist before my essay explodes.

Again, back to the summary of my own linguistic development. With time, I exposed myself to increasing bodies of texts, written and spoken, of various kinds and from various contexts and in various languages. Through exposure and osmosis, I acquired a network of linguistic experiences that I could draw upon when trying to judge whether an emerging text was stylistically successful or not, whether it conformed to pattern or struck an original, perhaps interesting or even epoch-making path. This was the point when I began feeling competent to criticize the language of my students.

Styles, I said to start with, are characterized by features I called style markers. But as many style markers reside, not within individual sentences, but in the ways in which sentences link up into discourse and text, I was soon tempted to venture beyond syntax and beyond the single sentence, to look at style in terms of larger textual patterns. Style, of course, is not a matter of individual sentences torn out of context, but of long sequences of connected discourse. This view was wholly in line with current developments: since the late sixties, when I began working on such problems, in fields variously labelled as text linguistics, discourse analysis, conversation analysis, etc., the study of text has branched off into many directions. In the area of text, we have indeed had an information explosion through which the study of discourse has become arguably the most powerful recent extension of linguistics into new directions. And the study of text and discourse leads us back to venerable traditions in rhetoric and composition.

As I had begun applying concepts of modern linguistics to the study of connected discourse as early as the 1960s, I got a large number of invitations to lecture about these then-new developments. They took me all the way from California in the West via Europe and the Soviet Union to Singapore, Australia and New Zealand in the East. I am grateful, happy and proud to have been a witness to the expansion of linguistics that has brought theory closer to practical concerns in rhetoric and composition. By now, the elements of text and discourse linguistics, as well as their applications to composition, have spread triumphantly around the world and are routinely taught even to undergraduates. The only piece of bad luck I have had was the unhappy coincidence of the beginning of my inevitable period of university administration in the tumultuous late 1960s and early 1970s with the advent of text and discourse linguistics. When I came out of my administrative tunnel, I found a number of my own nascent ideas developed in books and papers by others, in most instances no doubt much better than I could have done. I console myself with the thought that others too have seen the light. And, as there are no lucrative patents in the linguistics of discourse, there is no way of measuring what I may have lost.

As I said at the beginning, this has been a highly egocentric apologia and confession of a kind I associate with modes other than scholarly writing. But I was invited to produce an autobiographical essay, and this is what I have shamelessly tried to do. Also, every bilingual and multilingual person will have a highly personal and idiosyncratic linguistic past. This means that a subjective case history such as mine may not be completely out of order.

References

Enkvist, N. E. (1964) On defining style. An essay in applied linguistics. In N.E. Enkvist, J. Spencer and M. Gregory (eds) _Linguistics and Style_. London: Oxford University Press.

Enkvist, N. E. [in Portuguese] (1970) _Definindo o Estilo. Um Ensaio de Lingüística Aplicada_. In N.E. Enkvist, J. Spencer and M. Gregory (eds) _Lingüística e Estilo_. Sâo Paulo: Editora Cultrix.

Enkvist, N. E. [in German] (1972) _Versuche zu einer Bestimmung des Sprachstils. Ein Essay in angewandter Sprachwissenschaft_. In N.E. Enkvist, J. Spencer and M. Gregory (eds) _Linguistik und Stil_. Heidelberg: Quelle und Meyer.

Enkvist, N. E. [in Spanish] (1974) _Para definir el estilo. Ensayo de lingüística aplicada_. In N.E. Enkvist, J. Spencer and M. Gregory (eds) _Lingüística y Estilo_. Nadri: Ediciones Cátedra.

Enkvist, N. E. (1973) _Linguistic Stylistics. Janua Linguarum, Series Critica_ 5. The Hague: Mouton & Co.

Enkvist, N. E. (1973) _Stilforskning och stilteori_. Lund: CWK Gleerup Bokförlag.

Enkvist, N. E. (1974) _Tekstilingvistiikan peruskäsitteitä_. Helsinki: Oy Gaideamus Ab.

Developing Literacy Can and Should Be Fun: But Only Sometimes Is

Håkan Ringbom was born and raised in Finland, where he received his master's and doctoral degrees in English language and literature at Åbo Akademi University. Most of his teaching has been at Åbo Akademi University, where he is currently a professor of English and the head of the Department of English. He has lectured widely in Europe and the US in the area of second language acquisition and teaching. His publications include countless articles and the following books: *Studies in the Narrative Technique of Beowulf and Lawman's Brut* (1968), *George Orwell as Essayist: a Stylistic Study* (1973), and *The Role of the First Language in Foreign Language Learning* (1987). As a hobby for 45 years, he has played competitive tennis, and his current research interest is the study of third language acquisition.

I grew up in the city of Turku (Swedish Åbo) in an academic, Swedish-speaking family. With only brief interludes, I have spent my whole life in Turku, a bilingual city where, as in Finland as a whole, fewer than 10% have Swedish as their L1 (first language). I learnt basic communication in Finnish quite early, but since practically all my friends were Swedish speakers, my Finnish certainly was – and still is – not really native-like. But growing up in a bilingual environment means a wider perspective on language than a monolingual has: if you are used to hearing two or more languages, you learn that there is more than one way of expressing your ideas. Language takes on a wider dimension, and you also become aware of the possibilities and restrictions each language possesses.

Language minorities are usually well aware that they have to learn the majority language, whereas many or most people belonging to a clear language majority feel they need not learn the minority language. This is the situation Swedish speakers in Finland learn to live with.

Belonging to a small language minority may sometimes involve identity problems of sorts. This may also be the case with some Swedish-speaking Finns, even though we are a very privileged minority, perhaps the most privileged in the world. Our rights are well protected by law, and our relations with the majority normally have little or no friction. I am not conscious of ever having anything resembling identity problems relating to language, and I have hardly ever had personal experiences of negative reactions to my being a Swedish speaker. I belong to a group privileged and important enough to have education in Swedish all through, and I have always had a wide circle of Swedish-speaking friends. All this has shaped my language identity into a fairly uncomplicated one. The history of our country makes us not Swedes, but Finns who merely happen to speak another language than that of the majority.

I speak Finnish well enough to cope with any everyday situation almost as well as a native (writing in Finnish or expressing myself in Finnish at formal meetings is a different matter). I am certainly not ashamed of being a Swedish speaker, but it is true that in most service encounters in town, I don't speak a word of Swedish. Like nearly all Swedish speakers in Finland, I have thus occasionally found myself speaking Finnish to another Swedish speaker behind the counter, but in most such situations, speakers do not expressly reveal their Ll at all. The reason for not keeping to my Ll, even in contexts where the law requires civil servants to know Swedish, is that a service encounter started in Swedish in Turku or in Helsinki too often leads to a blank face or even irritation behind the counter. Swedish speakers in these cities learn their territory: when and where communication in Swedish works, and when and where it doesn't. Young Swedish speakers moving around in town on Friday or Saturday nights may prefer to communicate with each other in Finnish, since particularly Swedish, but occasionally even English or any other language than Finnish, is not popular with the 'tough guys' in town. The tough-guy attitude here actually has little to do with language: it is simply a question of gangs trying to establish who is 'one of us' and who isn't on whatever basis available. Some members of tough-guy gangs may actually be bilingual Swedish speakers.

Finnish has to me been primarily a means of communications in ordinary situations (the flexibility and beauty of the language dawned on me at a very late stage). As my L1, Swedish makes for emotional attachment.

In my home, reading was much encouraged and there were lots of books around. At an early age, at or possibly even before the age of 4, I learnt to read. I don't remember being read to very much as a child, but since there was a war going on in Finland during my childhood, from age 3 to age 8, conditions were rather exceptional. At any rate, I became a fast and avid reader and had certainly ploughed through plenty of books before I started intermediate school at the age of 10. One of these early books I remember most vividly was my grandmother's old torn copy of the *Iliad*, written in very old-fashioned Swedish hexameters. Otherwise I read what was available in boys' literature: Richmal Crompton's William books, Biggles books, James Fennimore Cooper's and Karl May's Indian books and any other books that came my way as Christmas or birthday presents. The town library did not figure prominently in my early life, partly because I felt the age limit when one was allowed into the ordinary adult section was disgustingly high – ageism in those days.

My father's family, most of whom lived in or near Turku, were keen on family gatherings for New Year and other occasions, and both young and old took part in games, including language games, of various kinds. The game that appealed particularly to me as a nine year old was one where one member wrote a little story, leaving gaps for the adjectives to be filled in, one by one, by the other group members who knew nothing about the story. The results were, I thought, hilarious, since some cousins, aunts and uncles obviously had a fair amount of such verbal imagination and wit as appeals to a nine year old. I tried to play this game with some of my friends but somehow the result was disappointing: the collocations were trite even when I as story-writer cheated a little by trying to select a good place for the proposed adjective.

Any activity involving linguistic creativity of some sort is obviously good for children, and most children would find such pastimes enjoyable, at least for a time. And it is clear that my early reading experiences helped me a lot in my later development. However, in intermediate and partly even in high school, sports seemed more important to me than intellectual pursuits. I did very little homework, but managed well at school simply by being a fairly attentive listener during lessons. I was lucky not to have the kind of parents who are constantly checking that their children do their homework properly. But if I needed help, as occasionally happened in high school maths, I could always rely on getting pedagogically good guidance from my father.

The school I went to between 10 and 18 was a boys' school where few of the teachers could be said to be pedagogically brilliant. Also, the going was pretty rough in these post-war years and the focus of the educational system in Finland those days was largely on memorizing facts, understanding basic principles of mathematics and being able to translate from and into foreign languages. Certainly the general atmosphere among the boys at school up to their middle teens was not very conducive to individual linguistic or literary activities. L1 teaching might have provided some such stimuli – as it did for some of my contemporaries in other schools – but the main feeling my L1 teacher inspired was a fear of his bad temper. He was a competent marker of written compositions, though, and used to do his marking in class whenever we wrote a composition in class. We noticed that the average time he spent on marking one essay was about 38 seconds. He did not feel inclined to do more marking than was absolutely necessary, and that meant that I don't remember having to write any essays at home after the age of 12. Everything was done in class. About once a semester we had to give a talk in front of the class, often on a Swedish author writing in the seventeenth, eighteenth or nineteenth centuries whose work nobody had read. This meant that most papers were copied from an encyclopedia and then read out aloud in class. Unlike most of my classmates, I always tried to produce a version that was my own, not copied. When I was about 15, one of my classmates read a paper on an author that he illustrated with a picture from a book that was circulated in class. As it happened, this book contained not only the picture, but also the whole text my friend had read out in his talk. I was sufficiently lacking in solidarity to point this out in the 'discussion' afterwards. Our teacher happened to be in a good mood that day and his reaction was a hearty guffaw and a comment to me, 'you're a tough one.' He obviously knew very well how most of his students composed their papers, but didn't really mind.

On another occasion, when I was 13, my teacher selected me to take part in the annual public recitation contest between the four Swedish schools in town. I did not like the idea at all, and was quite horrified, but my teacher was not one to take no for an answer. I therefore selected the shortest piece I could possibly find and on the dreaded day, according to my friends, ran up to the podium in the awe-inspiring university hall, rattled off my piece as fast as I could and ran down again. The local paper reporting on this event was charitable enough to write that 'the piece Håkan Ringbom read was so short that it was not possible to form any idea of his ability.'

Immediately after World War II, English began to replace German as the first foreign language in Finnish schools, and I started reading English at school when I was 11. In these early days, there was naturally a shortage of qualified teachers, but whatever could be said about the efficiency of the English teacher during my first year, he certainly made me interested, or at least managed to maintain my interest, in the English language. My father, a professor of science, had read six languages at school (Swedish, Finnish, German, French, Russian and Latin), but no English, and he started taking a correspondence course and conversation lessons in English a year or two before I started my English at school. I got a new English teacher at the age of 13 and for five years I then had competent teaching of English, mainly along traditional lines (grammar and translation) but also with some conversation practice, which was not very usual at that time.

I had read a long course in Latin at school – a very useful basis for learning other languages – and started reading Latin, Swedish and English at Åbo Akademi University. My interest in English was always the strongest, particularly since I was fortunate enough to have Nils Erik Enkvist as my professor of English. In those days, the Department of English had no more than two faculty members, a professor and a lecturer. The change from school to university was certainly abrupt, but my family background helped to make the shock milder for me than for most of my friends. I enjoyed my student life and occasionally also exercised a certain amount of linguistic creativity by producing some light entertainment items, often in rhymed verse or mock hexameters, for student occasions. In fact, I still enjoy writing some light verse, like Christmas rhymes on parcels, but I would not normally try to attempt doing that in English. And, like bad verse in general, my verses are largely based on rhymes. One year I was also the editor of our student rag and for three other years a member of the editorial committee. The meetings meant lots of fun, but the funniest jokes we came up with were of a kind that could not possibly be published after all.

As for L2 writing, I produced some undergraduate essays in English, but my MA thesis had to follow the regulations of those days and be written in Swedish. This lack of practice certainly contributed to the laboriousness I always in earlier days associated particularly with L2 writing, though L1 writing never came easy to me, either. When writing my first postgraduate thesis for the licentiate degree, I reckoned that for two years the result of half a working day was only two or three sentences most days – almost every single day of the year, though. And at least one of the sentences I had produced I deleted or altered considerably the following day. Yet the result of my labours, qualitative as well as quantitative, bore very little witness to the time and energy spent.

Devoting my active life to research and teaching in English language and literature has naturally improved the pace of writing, at least some-what. And since I write more English than Swedish, at least some types of texts are now easier to produce in English than in Swedish. But I still write very slowly in both L1 and L2.

The computer has improved matters for me: while I previously always had to write by hand a first draft of even the most conventional letter, I am now moving over to writing at least ordinary texts directly on to the computer.

If linguistic creativity can be encouraged by whatever means during childhood and school years, this will undoubtedly be good for one's future development, not only of language skills. At school at least a little time should sometimes be devoted to more relaxed activities of a linguistic nature. I certainly wish that the attitudes to language could have been loosened up during my school days so that we could occasionally have had some fun with language games or other potentially enjoyable linguistic activities in both L1 and L2. Such play can, of course, easily be exaggerated, and not all students at school can be motivated to enjoy it, but the development of literacy is something that needs to be stimulated by many different means.

I am certainly very much aware of my non-nativeness in English. In speech as well as writing I have to choose from a more limited lexical repertoire than native speakers at a comparable educational level and may not always have the linguistic competence to realize the connotations of certain phrases. The label 'near-native speaker of English' may be appropriate for me. This means that I make few direct 'errors' in my writing, which, however, will always include a few slightly odd or awkward phrases. Native speakers may, of course, also produce awkward phrasing at times, but when experienced writers do so, they would probably produce similarly awkward rather than identically awkward phrases.

Some research that a student of mine and I have carried out has shown that even competent native speakers find it difficult to distinguish between native and near-native texts. There is surprising variation when educated speakers are asked to say whether a particular text is written by a native speaker or not. One British and one American group of postgraduate students of language or literature were given eight near-native texts (one of them written by me) and two American undergraduate essays. They were asked to provide a label NS or NNS for each text and to state their reasons for each choice. They certainly had problems: none of the 23 referees had more than eight correct assessments, one had only four and the rest had five, six or seven. It is also interesting to note that the accompanying reasons given were often contradictory: some referees praised a near-native writer's rhetorical ability and complete mastery of the language, while others detected an overall rhetorical ineptness and lack of clarity in the same text. When the referees gave examples of non-nativeness, they generally focused on one or two concrete examples, but each example was hardly ever mentioned by more than one referee.

Almost every time I have written something in English for publication, I have had a native speaker check it before sending it in. I have been fortunate enough to have Anthony Johnson as my colleague for the last dozen years, and this means that I have always been able to count on excellent language-use feedback, which has not been restricted to isolated phrasing. He has made constructive suggestions on textual coherence and contents as well. This is a point I would like to emphasize most strongly: the importance for non- natives to use *competent* native language consultants who also know something about your topic. Merely being a native speaker is not sufficient for a language consultant: I have seen some amazingly bad English texts that have been checked by a native speaker.

The advice I have for anyone writing in his or her L2 is, 'Find your own Anthony Johnson!' There are heavy demands on the perceptiveness of a language consultant. If native speakers sometimes do a bad job there, non-natives certainly are at an even greater risk. Even if a near-native language consultant seems perfectly competent in L2, there are likely to be more oddities that will pass unnoticed by him/her than by a native speaker. Recent research in Finland by Eija Ventola and Anna Mauranen (1990) has shown that, for the best result, discourse linguistic competence may be needed together with native speaker proficiency.

Finally, I would like to say that even though my school experiences were uninspiring, without really being unhappy (most of my contemporaries in Finland would probably have had similar ones), I have been lucky in having so many favourable background variables contributing to the development of my literacy.

Note

1. I remember how shocked our (male) native speakers at the English Department were when one of our brightest girl students returned from a year in Britain, speaking very genuine English of a singularly unacademic type with frequent use of expletives like 'fucking'. At our department we certainly encourage our travelling students to integrate with the natives, but there may be limits to that! As a non-native speaker I wasn't as shocked as my colleagues were, primarily since English swear words do not convey the same emotional force to me as they do to native speakers of my generation. In both Finnish and Swedish, though, I am well aware of the emotional force of the swear words, having grown up hearing them all around me at school or on the streets.

References

Ventola, E. and Mauranen, A. (1990) *Tutkijat ja englanniksi kirjoittaminen* (Researchers and Writing in English). Helsinki: Yliopistopaino.

Straddling Three Worlds

Born in Austria, **Anna Söter** was educated in Australia and the United States. Currently an associate professor of English education at The Ohio State University, she received a BA in English and history from the University of Western Australia, an MA in English literature and language from the University of Sydney, and a doctorate in education from the University of Illinois, Champaign-Urbana. In addition to numerous book chapters and journal articles, she has authored *The New Literary Theories and Young Adult Literature* (in press) and co-edited *Essays in Literacy: Implications for English Teaching* (1990) and *Reading across Cultures:*

Teaching Literature in a Diverse Society (1997). She is also co-author of the popular textbook *How Porcupines Make Love: Readers, Writers, Texts in a Response-based Literature Curriculum* (1996). Her hobbies and pursuits include skiing, hiking/bushwalking, creative writing and alternative health and spirituality.

> To me, my mother's English is perfectly clear, perfectly natural. It's my mother's tongue. Her language, as I hear it, is vivid, direct, full of observation and imagery. That was the language that helped shape the way I saw things, expressed things, made sense of the world.
> (Tan, 1996: 40)

Introduction

As I read Amy Tan's autobiographical essay, *Mother Tongue*, I found myself recalling some of the marvellous phrases of my own mother's letters, sent to me from Australia but still rich with the flavour of her Austrian dialect, and realized what I had always known: that it was *her* language, a language that evolved over 45 years of living in the far north of Australia following her transplantation as a European refugee shortly after World War II. She arrived in Fremantle, Western Australia, as a young adult, three children and a Hungarian husband in tow, and was immediately sent to a tiny mining town, 1400 miles from the nearest large city, Perth, with no English lessons, no migrant support system, no other family, to make her new life in a place as removed from the Austrian Alps as the moon is from the Earth. With no local library to aid her, she managed to instill in us a love of reading and writing and education in general, for which I am, still, immensely grateful. She taught herself to write in English, although she continues to write to her family in Austria in the German that she had learned in school. It is an English that, with its idiosyncratic turns of phrase, still has the power to surprise me, but it is also the English that influenced me as I found myself needing to abandon German in favour of the new language as a sign of my 'belonging'. Mine, however, does not have the richness of hers:

> I just let the pictures talk. I do hope you are enjoying your summer vacations. I am glad to be back here, with all the Hassels and Bustles (don't think that was spelt the right way?) of everyday life.

Instead, like Amy Tan (1996), I speak 'a speech filled with carefully wrought grammatical phrases, burdened ..with the nominalized forms, past perfect tenses, conditional phrases, all the forms of standard English that I had learned in school, and through books..'.. It is not the 'broken' or 'fractured' English of my mother (p. 41). Like Tan, I was also 'ashamed' of the English my mother speaks and writes (p.42). And yet, unlike Tan, I did very well in the English of the school and the University setting. I was almost six when we arrived in Australia, in October 1951, and began school in late January of 1952 in another tongue. By the time I was in third grade, I had informed my parents that I would not be using German with them at home (!!), but German remained the private language between our parents, and it also remained the language I used to write letters to European relatives when my mother's persistence finally wore down the resistance I had to maintaining contact with her family, a family I felt increasingly less connected with even as a child.

I went on to major in English literature and British and European history at the University of Western Australia and, after graduating, taught English in Australian schools for 15 years, during which I also chaired two English Departments in two high schools before transplanting myself to the US in 1982, undertaking a doctoral degree with a specialization in applied linguistics/SLATE (second-language acquisition and the teaching of English) and later, teaching and coordinating programmes in English education at The Ohio State University. It really was not until I began writing my dissertation that I learned my English was not the kind of English that would 'do' for academic work. That discovery led me to an understanding about why I had chosen the topic I had selected for my dissertation research (Söter, 1986): *Writing: A Third Language for Second Language Learners.* I had thought it was an interest that had arisen from my teaching experiences during which I was concerned about the increasing numbers of students who came into our schools with various forms of 'broken' English affecting their writing. At the time, this was of critical concern since all secondary students were required to take written (essay) exams in five subjects at the end of their twelfth year in order to be granted their Higher School Certificate and to achieve entry into the universities. Five hours of writing in response to 'blind' questions about literature, writing, and language faced all students in English, whether native speakers of English or not.

But buried beneath this concern was another: had my own writing been shaped by thought patterns that were not influenced in their expression only by standard British English, but also perhaps by the residual impact of having first learned to read in German? Were the lengthy, multiply-embedded subordinate clauses that are still typical of the early drafts of my written discourse attributable to the influence of my mother tongue? That I have an instant connection with hearing and reading German is undeniable, although I no longer have the extensive vocabulary that would enable me to read literature or academic discourse without a dictionary. I can, however, intuitively sense what Goethe meant when he wrote *Uber allen Gipfeln* or his epic work, *Faust*, and I still prefer to hear Mozart's *Magic Flute* sung in German than in any other language. All this, even though when I decided to take two courses in German language and literature in my liberal arts degree, I found that my German was not 'pure' German but a variant that was looked upon with disapproval. Nevertheless, my early encounters with writing American academic discourse revealed that a natural form of expression that I had taken for granted as acceptable and indeed, had been a vehicle for success in Australian educational contexts, was suddenly a 'problem' and that in order to continue to be successful, I would have to 'clean up' my discourse, get rid of the embedding, become direct, get to the point, bare my thoughts and assert my views. Although I believe my situation was somewhat advantageous, compared to other international students at the University of Illinois in that I was not deemed a non-English speaker, the significantly different versions of 'standard academic prose' between the US and Australia highlighted a difference I had always intuitively suspected was there even in the Australian context, but which had not been so evident there because my serious academic writing did not begin until I began my dissertation and later writing.

I think it's also worth noting that, while taking German literature during my undergraduate years, I found I had to write papers in German about the novelists, playwrights and poets we read. Since I had not read criticism in German, this was a laborious task, and it was assumed that, because we were in the course, we could struggle through this on our own. I resorted to using English essay rhetorical structure (the kind that worked for me when writing papers in English literature classes) and using German vocabulary and grammatical structure. Fortunately, our enlightened professor graded the content of the paper though felt compelled to comment that my German academic writing left a lot to be desired! My colloquial German used in letters to my relatives in Austria was not adequate for my academic efforts. At the time, I remember sensing that there was more to writing these papers than just the vocabulary and the grammar. I also recall a sense of blankness in terms of rhetorical structure – the map for the argument was simply not there. However, all this preceded the writing research that was to come in the mid and late 1970s – research that made it clear that writing is a cognitive act (and later still, that it's also a social act) and that rhetorical structures are related to ways of thinking. We also did not understand the relationships between writing and cultural conditioning and the ways we are influenced in our perceptions and orientations as a result of that conditioning. My experiences throughout school and college, however, were very helpful later when I found that students I taught, many of them second generation migrants, also brought into their writing, strange stylistic phenomena despite their having been born and schooled in Australia. Closer inspection revealed that for many, the dominant language in the home was still the mother tongue and that many of them were bilingual although not necessarily bi-literate.

That's Not Reading

Children seem to retain memories that, at the time of the experience being recalled, have a pivotal impact on them although exactly how that experience was pivotal often becomes unclear in later life. Perhaps it spurs them on to proving someone wrong, or perhaps it inhibits further growth in some domain. My pivotal recollection of my first year of schooling was my teacher informing me that 'that's not how you read' and 'you had better forget what you learned because I'm going to teach you to read the right way.' I do not recall what prompted her remarks, but I have never forgotten them. She may have been annoyed at my eager 'I learned to read my dad's German magazines,' for that is how I learned to read. He had a habit of dropping them at the foot of the kitchen table after finishing each one in turn. I would often sit beneath the table and took to flipping the pages, connecting pictures and cartoons to text, and thus, over time, recognizing links between the two. At times, I know, I asked him what the words meant. Thus, in a rudimentary way, I had learned to sight read the German language. But whatever had been learned had to be put aside, and so I began again with English, learning the letters of the alphabet in the 'apple tree', and obviously survived the experience.

Growing up as a migrant in Australia during the 1950s and 1960s meant you were 'different'. As a consequence, we children all desired to merge as soon as possible with the descendants of the British Isles. If one had an anglicizable name, s/he changed to that version as soon as possible. If one did not, s/he remained marked. Perhaps, because of that, and because of my mother's insistence that we continue to write to our European relatives in German, I retained a sense of my Austrian-ness until I visited that country in my late twenties. And, perhaps because of that, I pursued the reading of various German poets, novelists and dramatists in my undergraduate years. At the same time, I became an avid reader of British literature while in secondary school and also in my liberal arts education and later, my Master's degree in English literature at the University of Sydney. I read Chaucer, Marvell, Dryden, Pope, Byron, Coleridge, Keats, Shelley, Worsdworth, Tennyson and T.S. Eliot among the poets; Shakespeare's tragedies and comedies; Austen, Andrews, Hardy, George Eliot, Dickens, Woolf, Joyce and Waugh among the novelists. Later, I taught all of them to senior high school students who were convinced I was 'looney' about them and used to regard my enthusiasm for these literary heavies with indulgent patience.

L2 Literacy and Professional Success

In retrospect, I see these writers as having compounded my inclination toward 'heavy prose' that I believe came from the early influence of German. Jane Austen, George Eliot, Charles Dickens and Thomas Hardy, in particular, seemed to enjoy the suspension of the final clause as much as I did. It was not good training for writing American academic prose! To this day, I cannot say I have American native-speaker intuition concerning the placement of commas in those convoluted sentences or native-speaker certainty about which preposition to use. To this day, I feel the desire to camouflage the essence of a statement with qualifiers, hedges and conditional modifiers expressed in the form of 'perhaps', 'one might say', 'it could be argued that', 'it is possible that', and so on. To this day, I lean toward the framing and statement-modifying adverb or adverbial phrase. Understandably, these habits are frustrating for American academic editors. And yet, I have learned to do what I call 'conscious writing' when writing academic prose. That is, I try to monitor what I write as I write to avoid the lengthy clean-up process that often interferes with substantive revision in subsequent drafts.

Although my second language has long been the sole language of my professional life, I find that I still occasionally resort to my L1 when seeking a phrase that aptly describes an emotion I want to capture in my creative writing (prose or poetry). I may not use the L1 term for that emotion or sense of experience but discover a better English alternative during the process. Perhaps this is the result of occasionally still writing to my Austrian relatives in German or reading a poem by Heine or preferring to listen to various *lieder* and arias in German rather than any other language. I do not believe we ever truly 'shed' our native tongue. The language we use at the very least reflects our thinking and, dare I say it, may even shape our thinking. My occasional resorting to German for a thought must reflect an orientation that suggests English cannot work for me on those occasions. The reverse applied when writing my papers in German literature. Given that I had not 'thought' about German literature in German, I found myself turning to English and even made attempts to 'Germanicize' English words because they expressed a concept that I had only thought about in English. Similarly, one of my Korean friends maintained his L1 as a parallel language in every aspect of his life but the academic one. When I asked him whether he would think about his dissertation subject in Korean and then write about it in translation, he declared he could not think about the subject in Korean. It represented an experience that began with English and for which he had only English words and syntactic structures. His dissertation was conceived of and written about totally in English.

In thinking back on what contributed most to my writing in English, I would have to say reading played a significant role. I had loved reading from the earliest years and was regarded as a bookworm throughout my childhood. My reading was mostly fiction, with an occasional biography tossed in, and essay collections during my high-school years. But I also loved reading history and during secondary schooling enjoyed reading books that addressed historical accounts of early settlements in Australia as well as historical events in Britain and Europe from the Middle Ages to the end of World War II. At 17, I won a state-wide essay contest run by the major newspaper in Perth, Western Australia. Perhaps the topic was already close to me – the fostering of positive international relations – but I also attribute some of my success in that instance to my reading of history. Research in schema theory seems to support my belief that our experiences, whatever they may be, provide us with the frames for our subsequent thinking about them. I had not read German criticism though I did know how to do 'lit crit' in English, and so I turned to the frames and maps I already possessed. The influence does not work only at the level of vocabulary and grammatical structures but, more significantly, at the subtle levels of thought structures which become expressed as rhetorical and logical structures. Spoken language, especially colloquial, daily talk, does not provide an appropriate frame for academic discourse, or any written discourse for that matter. The only medium that does provide this appropriate frame is written discourse. And so, in reverse, while I can spontaneously maintain a conversation in German, I cannot, without a great deal of work (reading and writing), maintain a line of unbroken thought, develop it, sustain it and appropriately express it in writing in that language. My dominant literacy experience has been in the English medium, my L2.

At various times throughout this essay, however, I have alluded to differences in standard English English vs. standard American English. I recall various ESL texts that are geared specifically for special purposes (ESP, or English for specific purposes) and find myself wondering if we should not include a modifier – 'American English for specific purposes' might be a more accurate descriptor. At the same time, a global variety of English may well emerge as more of us become E-mail communicators, so perhaps this is a moot point. Ironically, however, it was the realization that I came to the US, not with a foreign language so much as a 'foreign' dialect that ignited my research interest in writing across cultures, an interest that has been sustained both in my teaching as well as in my research. It was also this sense of 'difference' that awoke an interest in exploring the possibility that my native language may, too, have left a residual impact on how I think and write today. It cannot help but have left its mark because I believe, as does the Spanish writer Antonio Munoz Molina, that 'language is my homeland ... it is both the present and the past' (in Gazarin-Gautier, 1991: 216–227). If I have any advice to pass on to others, it is to accept the influence of one's mother tongue, embrace it and understand it, for in denying it, one denies a part of oneself.

References

Gazarin-Gautier, M-L. (1991) *Interviews with Spanish Writers.* Elmwood Park, IL: Dalkey Archive Press.

Söter, A. O. (1986) Writing: A third language for second language writers: A cross-cultural discourse analysis of the writing of schoolchildren in Australia. Unpublished doctoral dissertation, University of Illinois, Urbana-Champaign.

Tan, A. (1996), Mother tongue. In Shawn Wong (ed.) *Asian American Literature: A Brief Introduction and Anthology.* New York: Harper Collins.

How a Speaker of Two Second Languages Becomes a Writer in a Foreign Language

Born and raised in Lithuania, **Adina Levine** has been involved in language teaching for more than 30 years. She received an MA in English language and literature from Vilnius State University, Lithuania, and her Ph.D. in linguistics from the Hebrew University, Jerusalem, Israel. She is Assistant EFL Program Coordinator of EFL at Bar-Ilan University in Israel and has taught ESL and applied linguistics in Israel for the past 20 years. In addition, she has taught courses in applied linguistics in Brazil and the Netherlands. Her research interests include EFL reading com-prehension and foreign language acquisition, with a special interest in literacy. She has pub-

lished in journals such as *System, TESL Canada Journal* and *Reading In a Foreign Language* in addition to contributing book chapters to edited vol-umes. She is a frequent presenter at TESOL, AAAL and AILA conferences.

I was brought up and educated in post World War II Lithuania, which at that time was one of the Soviet Socialist Republics – an integral part of the Soviet Union. The school system in Lithuania, just like any other part of social, political and cultural life in Lithuania at that time, was under the complete control of the Soviet regime. There were two types of schools in Soviet Lithuania: schools where the language of instruction was Russian, and those where the language of instruction was Lithuanian. Although I grew up bilingual, as both Lithuanian and Russian were spoken at home, I was sent to a Russian school ('dues' paid by my parents to the regime?). Until fifth grade, Russian was the only language we were exposed to at school. Starting with fifth grade, all the pupils in Russian schools had to simultaneously start learning Lithuanian as their L2 (second language), i.e. the language of the environment (officially, the Ll of the Lithuanian Socialist Republic), and English as a foreign language. It should be noted that the syllabi in the school system of Lithuania were strictly under the control of the authorities: there was no room for any free choice or private initiative in any aspect of the educational system.

What contributed to my L1 literacy development? First and foremost, my home environment. Both of my parents were people with university education, literate in Lithuanian, the language of their schooling, and Russian, the language of the environment in the years prior to World War II in Lithuania as well as during the years spent in Siberia during World War II.

Since my early childhood, I remember myself surrounded by books: there was never a day without a book being read to me by my mother and later, when I learned to read myself, it was going to the library to exchange books or to the bookshop to buy a book that had been my greatest pleasure. My friends often called me a 'bookworm'. No wonder that my most favourite subject at school was literature. I was lucky to have a literature teacher whose knowledge of the works of the great Russian poets and writers was so deep that just by listening to her one could not help but fall in love with Pushkin's poetry, the novels of Lermontov, Turgenev, Goncharov and Gogol, as well as Chekhov's stories and plays. One of the biggest advantages of life in Lithuania at that time was the accessibility of books, theatrical performances, operas and ballets. I can say that this exposure to classical Russian literature and to the great works of classical music played an important role in shaping my literary tastes and enhanced my later infatuation with the arts generally, and with English literature specifically.

Were we taught how to write in our L1? Hardly so. The 'free writing' was supposed to be as close as possible to the text source, or to the lesson given by the class teacher. No training in writing skills was offered either in L1, L2 or FL. Concepts such as writing techniques, writing conventions, thesis statements, audience awareness, etc., were unknown to language learners.

Follow the patterns of authentic writing, imitate sentence and paragraph forms, keep as close as possible to the sources, these were the instructions to be adhered to. It is not clear to me to this day whether what we were told to do was not some form of 'plagiarism'. Having been encouraged to memorize long chunks of texts, we were then supposed to substitute the words in the text learned by heart with the words that would express our statements and ideas. In other words, we were expected to slot our words into a rigid text template.

I began reading and writing in English as a foreign language in high school, although the truth of the matter is that, while I could consider myself a skilled FL reader towards the end of my high school studies, I was hardly a writer in English as a foreign language.

I read short stories, mainly adapted for language learners and published in the Soviet Union, as there was hardly anything else available in the country, which lived behind the 'iron curtain.' But because reading in general had always been my greatest pleasure, I read anything and everything that I could put my hands on.

As far as FL writing is concerned, I have to say that during the eight years of learning English as a foreign language in high school, we were never required to write anything beyond syntactically and grammatically correct sentences. We were supposed to develop a wide range of vocabulary and be able to fit the words into syntactic patterns to express a variety of concepts. Foreign language instruction was based on drilling, on learning grammar rules, on rote learning of word lists. The tests we had to take both during the school year and at the end of every academic year were either oral tests or dictations.

There was definite progress in my development as an FL reader and writer during my university studies: I studied English language and literature at the University of Vilnius. For the first time in my life, I was exposed to authentic English writing; we studied works of Chaucer, Shakespeare, Dickens, Thackeray, Lewis Carroll, Bernard Shaw and Hemingway. The general philosophy of language instruction was almost the same as in high school: pay attention to the internal structure of the text, to the writer's choice of words, *follow the pattern* and *imitate*. To this very day I can recite pages upon pages from Lewis Carroll's *Alice in Wonderland* or from Charles Dickens' *David Copperfield* or *Oliver Twist*.

During the years of my studies at Vilnius University, the lessons in English language proficiency were aimed at developing our ability to form syntactically correct sentences and to link them coherently in order to generate suitable content. The emphasis was on the modeling of the linguistic features of written texts. The activities we were asked to carry out were: (1) reading and understanding the source text, (2) noting the language of the source text, (3) selecting relevant material (i.e. vocabulary and sentence patterns) from the source text, and (4) using the material for our written assignment. All of our teachers were non-native speakers of English, so it was natural for them – and us – to rely on written English texts and to extract as much information from sources as possible. I should note that the writing of seminar papers and dissertations followed the same pattern: we were supposed to collect a corpus of hundreds upon hundreds of examples from written English texts and use it in the development of our thesis. The thesis itself had to be written in either Russian or Lithuanian.

Did this type of instruction and learning experience prepare me to become an FL writer? Hardly so. I learned the language code, but had no sufficient knowledge in how to select *appropriate language* to suit *different* communicative tasks. I was familiar with text-internal features, such as syntactic patterns, but was not aware of the importance of linguistic conventions associated with different text genres, such as the choice of specific text forms dictated by communicative purpose, writer/reader relationship, or the medium of communication. In the best case, my FL writing could be defined as 'writing within one genre' (Caudery, 1998: 3). As part of my postgraduate studies, I wrote three articles, which were published in Russian in the university journal *Kalbotyra* (Linguistics).

My professional academic life underwent a complete change after my immigration to Israel. The new environment had two challenges in store for me (both of which seemed insurmountable at first): the need to learn (from scratch) the official language of my new homeland, Hebrew, and the need 'to compete' with native English speakers as my colleagues at work. English became the sole language of my professional academic life: I taught English as a foreign language to university students, I renewed my graduate studies as a Ph.D. student at the Hebrew University in Jerusalem, and I had to publish in English.

The first draft of my Ph.D. thesis on the subject of syntactic synonymy (written in Russian and brought over by me from Lithuania) had to be completely revised. Huge amounts of literature relevant to the area of my research were unavailable in Lithuania, which made my preliminary analysis inadequate and incomplete. It was at this stage that FL reading became an even more important resource for my writing than before, both in terms of ideas and in my development as an FL writer.

What had to be changed in my FL writing? Did it have to develop from incorrect to correct written English, from simple to complex written English? Which of the features of academic writing were most important for me to improve: formality, impersonality, explicitness, hedging, language complexity (Elbow, 1991)? Although the changes in my FL writing had to evolve along all of these features, the most important development had to be in the mastering of an *appropriate* written style. My previous educational experience had put me in a paradoxical situation. My speaking in the FL was in a register that was often too literary and sounded unnaturally 'like a book' (all those pages memorized in order to be recited!) while my writing was often done in a 'spoken' register (colloquial language). There seemed to be a marked imbalance between what Celce-Murcia *et al.* (1995) called grammatical and pragmatic knowledge, a disparity attributed to two key factors related to input: the availability of input and the salience of relevant linguistic features in the input from the point of view of the learner (Bardovi-Harlig, 1992). There was an obvious need to find a way to bridge the gap between the two types of knowledge: how to take care of mechanics, correctness and form, and how to communicate with the reader and not just put ideas down on paper.

Of the three linguistic problems: inappropriacy, inaccuracy and lack of linguistic resources, it was inappropriacy that I had to deal with as the most striking one. It turned out to be an achievable goal: variety differentiation was not much more difficult to acquire than grammatical accuracy. In order to develop audience awareness and a sense of purpose, to get practice in generating, organizing and revising ideas, I embarked on a long road of self-instruction, determining my own learning plans, materials and strategies.

The professional reading I had to do always involved a careful examination of the text. I read the text not only for meaning, but also for the features that made it suitable for its particular audience, purpose and medium. This kind of reading not only exposed me to authentic language in use, because it involved analytical reading, it also helped to increase my awareness of the factors that shape texts. Focusing on the communicative factors associated with genre taught me how the choice of language and text organization is determined by audience, communicative purpose and generic convention. Text analysis sharpened my awareness of the need to take into consideration more than surface-level accuracy.

There was basically nothing new in this type of analysis activity for me, since it was firmly ingrained in my mind during the years of previous learning. Two aspects, though, were radically different: the text types – research articles, manuscript reviews, grant proposals, instead of novels and stories of the eighteenth- and nineteenth-century writers – and more purposeful reading primarily aimed at text features associated with text style and genre rather than just at correct language use.

Can I anticipate the reactions of native speakers to my FL writing? I do not think so. There is always a strong element of suspense when a manuscript is sent off for review. And the reason for it is not just the content of the manuscript, but also its language and style.

References

Bardovi-Harlig, K. (1992) Pragmatics as a part of teacher education. *TESOL Journal* 1 (3), 28–32.

Caudery, T. (1998) Increasing students' awareness of genre through text transformation exercises: An old classsroom activity revisited. *TESL-EJ* 3 (3) [http://www-writing.berkeley.edu/TESL-EJ/].

Celce-Murcia, M., Dornyei, Z. and Thurell, S. (1995) Communicative competence: A pedagogically motivated model with content specification. *Issues in Applied Linguistics* 6 (2), 5–35.

Elbow, P. (1991) Reflections on academic discourse: How it relates to freshmen and colleagues. *College English* 53 (2), 135–155.

From L1 to L12: The Confessions of a Sometimes Frustrated Multiliterate

Andrew D. Cohen was born and raised in the US. After attending Phillips Academy, Andover, MA, he completed a BA in French history and literature at Harvard. After serving in the Peace Corps in Bolivia, he finished a Ph.D. in international development education at Stanford University, where he also obtained an MA in linguistics. He has taught ESL and applied linguistics for the past 30 years at UCLA, Hebrew University of Jerusalem, and at the University of Minnesota, where he is currently the director of the federally-funded National Language Resource Center. He also served as a Fulbright Lecturer/Researcher in Applied Linguistics in Brazil. His research has been

on language teaching, language learning, language testing, and research methods. His published books include *A Sociolinguistic Approach to Bilingual Education* (1975), *Language Learning: Insights for Learners, Teachers, and Researchers* (1990), *Assessing Language Ability in the Classroom* (1994), *Research Methodology in Second-language Acquisition* (1994) and *Strategies in Learning and Using a Second Language* (1998), He has just been re-elected for a second three-year term as Secretary General of the International Association of Applied Linguistics (AILA).

Through telling the story of my own multilinguistic literacy endeavors, my intention is to contribute even in a modest way to our understanding of how second language (L2) literacy can be achieved – in my case, differentially across a series of languages. The focus, however, will be on Hebrew, the language of much of my professional academic work for the better part of seventeen years.

First Language Literacy Development

My paternal grandparents were both from Russia and learned English when they immigrated to the US in the 1880s, but since my grandfather died before I was born and my grandmother died at the time of my birth, I was denied contact with them. My maternal grandfather also immigrated from Russia at the age of four, and lost his first language (L1) competence early on, as it was replaced by English. It is fair to say that I was born into a primarily monolingual family. My parents had both had a modest exposure to French in school and could read a little, and my dad had added a slight bit of Spanish in the navy, but their skills were limited. Neither could speak a foreign language. My older sister had also studied some Spanish, but did not develop any lasting control of the language.

With regard to English L1, both my parents were highly literate. In fact, my dad at the age of eight years old had been awarded a prize for having read an amazing number of books in the local library in Indianapolis where he grew up. At 15, he was already a college freshman, and he graduated from Harvard at 18, followed by Harvard Law School at 21. My mother also graduated college at 18. Their respective reading skills were phenomenal, and they both read voraciously on a host of topics – histories, biographies, novels, political treatises, religious themes, whatever. They also stayed on top of current affairs by reading the *New York Times* daily and in later years the *LA Times*. My older sister was also a reader, but more specialized, focusing on novels for the most part.

Written language played a large role in our family during my growing-up years. My dad was a lawyer and would leave my sister and me notes about everything, sometimes along with lists. Communication was often written, especially since he was a laconic person and preferred written to oral communication. When my dad was upset at some company over a consumer issue, he was quick to sit himself down at his manual typewriter and type out a lengthy letter to that company. Invariably he would get a reply and would engage perhaps in several exchanges until the matter was resolved. He preferred this 'paper trail' approach to that of picking up a telephone. In fact, he preferred not to talk on the phone, even to family members. My mom had serious rheumatoid arthritis, which made using her hands more of a challenge so, during my growing-up years, and especially later on, she was prone to use the phone and exercise her gift for gab rather than attempt to write more than a brief letter.

I was an active youngster and so did perhaps less pleasure-reading than many other kids my age. I preferred to be out doing sports – baseball, basketball, whatever. When I did read, it was Chip Hilton sports stories and other theme books. I enjoyed identifying with the young hero, who invariably came through in the end. In school, I read not only what was assigned, but volunteered to do projects where I needed to go to resources in the library or even send away for materials (to some foreign embassy or company). Then I would write lengthy reports based on the materials that I received. By fifth grade, I had developed a tiny handwriting I reserved for such reports in order to keep the number of pages down! Needless to say, this script most likely taxed the reading abilities and patience of my teachers, but they never said anything. I would sometimes accompany these reports with murals which I was granted release time from class to paint. So by late elementary school, I was already a report writer and crude artist (a skill I was not to pursue!). While I did not keep diaries in those years, I was a letter writer, with the main recipients being my parents. So, when my sister and I would repeatedly go to a sleep-away camp in North Carolina in the summers, I would write lengthy descriptive letters to my folks, detailing everything from baling hay to horse polo to long hikes up mountain peaks.

I remember having my TV-watching time restricted at home to a limited number of hours, and by the time I was 14 and a 'lower middler' (high school sophomore) at Phillips Academy, Andover, MA, I was watching no TV at all. I had to be in my room studying by 8 p.m. every night. I was expected to read extensively in my classes, especially in history, where the demanding assignments involving guided reading would take me to the library for hours on end. I also read novels, and sometimes in a most metalinguistic way: my lower middle English teacher, a man named Higgins (!), was not only a stickler for correct written grammar, but also most concerned that we learn about styles of writing. So he would have us read *All the Kings Men,* for example, and then write the opening portion of a novel on a topic of our own choosing, but imitating as best we could Robert Penn Warren's writing style. This was an activity I much enjoyed. Also, while at prep school, I filled many hours with sports, e.g. soccer, lacrosse, squash, ping pong, and billiards. I filled the rest of the time becoming literate in reading music – playing trumpet in a jazz band, marching band, concert band, and pit orchestra for Broadway musicals. Hence, there would not have been time for TV in any case.

When I first emerged as an L1 writer with published manuscripts was when I left college and went directly into the Peace Corps as a volunteer in rural community development on the High Plains of Bolivia. While I was still serving, I had an article of mine published in the Peace Corps magazine, entitled 'In the Andes, a Discovery of a Compromise Verb Tense.' It was a humorous description of the Aymara language that I was faced with learning on site. Also while on site, I wrote in English a description of the Aymara language (phonology, grammar, and dictionary) for internal use by Peace Corps volunteers in Bolivia, based on the work of a Bolivian priest that had appeared in Spanish. Then upon returning to the US, I produced a

115-page chapter entitled 'A Volunteer on Bolivia's Altiplano' for an edited volume published by the Latin American Center at UCLA. With these offerings, my writing career was officially launched. I guess I demonstrated to myself that I could write something that others would want to publish so that still others could read it.

Experiences with Literacy in Numerous Languages

While I am going to refer to Hebrew as my ninth language, it actually was my second in some ways that I am discounting, since all I learned to do was recode the Hebrew characters, without any comprehension of the meaning of the words. As I went through the ritual of bar mitzvah (i.e. becoming a man in the eyes of the congregation) in our Reform Jewish synagogue on Long Island, so I needed to learn how to *recode* Hebrew, that is, recognize the symbols adequately so that I could chant the appropriate text in Hebrew. Needless to say, this was an enormous challenge for a 13-year-old boy since I did not know what the words meant! At that point in time, I had not studied modern spoken Hebrew, but simply the language of the Bible and of prayer. I acquitted myself adequately enough only because I memorized most of the text so that I would not have to recode it on the spot. Then, as the years went by *after* my bar mitzvah, I watched myself become progressively inept at that recoding skill. I progressively forgot the Hebrew alphabet, since the words and phrases never had had any meaning for me.

While this article will eventually focus on literacy in this language, I need to point out right away that I am currently working on Japanese, my eleventh language beyond my native language, English. So I will briefly indicate the nature of my literacy endeavors as they concerned the other ten languages with which I had learning experiences. My second language was Latin (4 years in secondary school). I chose to study this classical language during freshman year in high school because various adults had suggested that it provided an important basis for later study of modern languages. I then pursued it for another three years at prep school primarily because Andover had a highly developed Latin program. I came to read Latin at a fairly advanced level, both expository texts (such as Caesar's wars), narratives (such as Cicero's treatise on old age), and poems (such as love poetry by Plautus), using mostly a grammar translation approach.

My third language was French, which I studied for two years at prep school – the first year focusing exclusively on aural-oral skills, and the second calling for the introduction of literacy. I was attracted to the language because French culture appealed to me and because the French program was well respected at my prep school. After graduation from prep school, I spent two months in the Experiment in International Living in France, living for a month with two French families and then traveling around France for another month with two of my French sisters from the second family. As an early sign of commitment to language learning, I informed my parents that summer that, if they wanted to hear from me, it would only be in French, and in fact, I wrote all my letters home in French – no English – as one way of developing fluency in written French. (How much they understood of what I wrote is still a mystery to me.) So, even at that young age, I practiced a French-only policy in written literacy, and it most likely served me well at that time. As an aside, I am still in contact with the first of those French families forty years later, and I continue to write letters in French to my French mom (though now I use the wordprocessing program *Systeme D*, with its easy access to accent marks and its on-line dictionary).

The summer after the Experiment in International Living program, I returned to France for two months to get further exposure to the people and the language, just prior to majoring in French history and literature at college. My intention was to study the language at the University of Grenoble, but after a class or two focused exclusively and monotonously on grammar, I chose to ditch the classes and improve my language by inter-actions with local French peers at the city cafes. This system worked extremely well and, in no time at all, I had different sets of friends in different cafes. It was also during that summer that I commenced the acqui-sition of Italian, my fourth language. The motivation was to date Italian women who were visiting in Grenoble during my stay there that summer. While I never studied the language formally in a classroom, I was to refresh my knowledge of Italian almost 30 years later through a Berlitz phrase book and a cassette tape, for a vacation in Italy. Given the solid base I had by that time in Spanish, as well as in French and Portuguese, Italian did not pose major problems, at least with regard to basic conversation. And the reading of signs, menus, and the like was not particularly taxing.

During the three years of my French History & Literature major at Harvard, I had ample opportunity to read in French, focusing primarily on French literature. I did a senior thesis on Marcel Proust's *A la Recherche du Temps Perdu*, and remember reading comfortably and insightfully in French most of this voluminous work. While I wrote the thesis itself in English, perhaps a quarter of my written output in this honors major was in French, including all of my papers for my tutor during junior year. As he was a Frenchman, it just seemed that the natural thing was to write for him in French. (My sophomore and senior-year tutors were English speakers, and I wrote for them in English.) Since the early 1980s, I have needed French for reading professional letters and documents, primarily associated with the work of the International Association of Applied Linguistics (AILA), since for the bulk of that period I have been an AILA officer and the association prides itself on being bilingual, with English and French as the official languages. I have also had cause to speak French at AILA professional meetings. I have also had interaction with French immersion schools over the years and have used French in this context. In addition, I have sprinkled in occasional visits to my Experiment family in Bordeaux, which gives my French a boost each time I do it.

I started my fifth language, Spanish, during the summer after junior year when I started Peace Corps training in an Outward Bound camp in the Puerto Rican rain forest, near Arecibo. My motivation for learning Spanish was simply that it was a useful lingua franca for me if I wanted to serve as a volunteer in an Indian community in South America. I continued studying the language for a semester during senior year, and developed literacy skills that were adequate for writing letters, notes, and other short pieces. I actually had cause to use my literacy skills in Spanish during the second year of my Peace Corps service, when, among other things, I became a teacher of Spanish speech and composition at a vocational middle school in the town of Ancoraimes, near Lake Titicaca (80 miles north of La Paz). I had Aymara pupils in grades seven and eight (ages 14–24) write me essays in Spanish and then present them orally. It was at that time that I displayed my total ignorance of dialects of Spanish, and assumed that all deviations from standard Spanish in their essays were the results of learner errors rather than reflecting what they were, dialectal variants of Spanish, based primarily on the influence of Aymara. I had not studied linguistics during my BA at Harvard, and was not to have my eyes opened to the reality of dialects until my graduate studies in linguistics with Charles Ferguson, Robert Politzer, and company at Stanford. It is fair to say that language experiences such as that one whetted my appetite for studying linguistics.

It was also during that Peace Corps stint that I translated a 20-page veterinary manual from English into Spanish for a Methodist Missionary veterinarian. It was only eighteen years after Peace Corps that I had my first cause to use Spanish professionally in the field of applied linguistics, when I was called upon to give a talk and a workshop in Spanish at the annual meeting of the Spanish Association of Applied Linguistics. In subsequent years I have had further occasions to present talks and workshops in Spanish, most recently in Colombia over the last several years.

During senior year at college, I not only studied Spanish but also started studying my sixth language, Quechua, on my own, because it appeared that our group of volunteers would be stationed in the Cochabamba area of Bolivia, where the particular tribe of Bolivian Indians (referred to as *campesinos*) spoke primarily Quechua. As it turned out, we learned towards the end of that year that we would in fact be stationed with the Aymara Indians on the High Plains. At that time, the Peace Corps was not yet ready to teach the Aymara language to prospective volunteers[1], so I found myself submersed in this, my seventh language, on a 'sink or swim' basis. I chose to swim and found that Aymara was far more important a language for me to know on a day-to-day basis in my work as a community development worker than was Spanish. The simple truth was that my work called for aural-oral skills in interaction with the local *campesinos* who did not speak Spanish.

I developed a modicum of facility with a transliterated version of Aymara – enough to assist me in learning some of the language and in preparing some instructional materials to pass on to other Peace Corps volunteers. The language was basically that of a non-literate people, though missionary groups were at the time making efforts to translate the Bible into Aymara, as well as numerous hymns. Suffice it to say that my contact with Aymara was mostly aural-oral but, as with Quechua, in order to learn the language I was studying from instructional materials which had been created using one of several systems for representing the spoken language. If I wrote either language, it was simply to write down an utterance that I was learning or practicing. The orthographic system involved a series of challenges. Only one such challenge involved the representation of the following phonemes as graphemes: the postpalatal simple *c*, aspirated *qh*, and glottalized *c'*, as well as the post velar simple *k*, aspirated *kh*, and glottalized *k'*. Some wrote them as *caya, qhaya, c'aya, kaya, khaya, and k'aya*, but unfortunately, others had other orthographic systems.

My eighth language, Portuguese, I started acquiring orally during two trips to carnival in Rio de Janeiro while I was still in the Peace Corps. A primary motive for wanting to gain a modicum of fluency in the language was to be able to interact with local Brazilian women – and to be able to enjoy the carnival celebration with them. In retrospect, it made carnival much more enjoyable! Upon my return to graduate school at Stanford, I took a one-semester course in Portuguese that relied heavily on the audio-lingual method and on spoken Portuguese and included extensive memorization of dialogs. While the course did not give me a grounding in Portuguese literacy, I did acquire sufficient oral skills to serve as a translator for a team of Stanford Research Institute-sponsored professors on a satellite television project in 1969.

Eighteen years later, I was to be a Fulbright lecturer and researcher in

Brazil for twelve months, and during that time I spent one semester teaching two courses entirely in Portuguese, one being a doctoral seminar on research methods and statistics in applied linguistics. While I developed considerable fluency in spoken Portuguese (thanks to both my earlier study of Portuguese and my solid grasp of Spanish), and came to read the language most successfully (both the morning paper and student academic work including theses), I did not develop more than a rudimentary ability to write since I did not sort out how the orthography of the language worked. I returned to Brazil the following summer to teach in a month-long summer institute in applied linguistics.

Then enter my ninth language, Hebrew, which is the main focus of this paper. As my wife and I chose to make Jerusalem, Israel, our home as of 1975, Hebrew became, by necessity, the language of my professional work for the next 16 years. Leading up to our move, we had informal Hebrew sessions with tutors and I audited Hebrew classes at UCLA, where I was teaching. Once we arrived in Israel, we were at about an intermediate level, and went immediately into special classes for university professors and their spouses; in order to protect our egos, the work in the course was not graded! The emphasis was on reading the newspaper and on oral communication, and hence we were not instructed in the reading or writing of academic texts. The closest I got to that was in the intensive summer course which I took after the first year in the country, where we had sessions once or twice a week with a doctoral student in one of several fields. I chose to be in the 'sociology' section. The TA was versed in sociology but was not a language teacher, so the focus was genuinely on the content theme, not on language form. I will return to Hebrew after rounding out the picture of my full set of exposures to literacy.

My tenth language was spoken Arabic, which I studied off and on over some ten years in Israel at a language center that primarily offered Hebrew classes. My motivation to learn this language arose only once I had been in the country for eight years and I saw the importance to peace in the region of having Israeli Jews know enough spoken Arabic to be able to interact with their neighbors in the language. At several points in time, I made an effort to read literary Arabic, but each time I quickly forgot the vowels and consonants of the language almost immediately after learning them. In learning spoken Arabic, I was in a class with Hebrew speakers and the vocabulary was glossed in Hebrew. The system for writing the spoken Arabic involved the use of a transliteration using Hebrew letters (written from right to left). When I speak Arabic today, I think partly in Hebrew (as Arabic and Hebrew share common words and grammatical structures) and partly in English. Interestingly enough, when I think in Hebrew, I think from right to left as I visualize words, and when I call up an English transliteration, it is from left to right in my mind even though I learned through Hebrew transliteration.

My eleventh language was German, and the occasion for learning it was to evaluate a method for language instruction emphasizing first and foremost the structure of the language. The gimmick for the approach is that the learner is eavesdropping (through audio-tape) on a series of lessons between the originator of the method and one or two students. I had no desire to learn that particular language since my association with the language was primarily concerned with my in-laws' suffering in Hitler's concentration camps. But when the author of this instructional system approached me with the request to evaluate his method, German was the only of his three languages of instruction that I had not already studied (French and Spanish being the other two). This was a highly intensive method that was exclusively aural-oral. For a week, I listened to the series of tapes and then had a private tutor who engaged me in conversation for another week. At the end of that period, I was able to carry on basic conversations in oral German, if I had time to translate between languages and if I kept the topic on something for which I had vocabulary. In addition, I was able to read what I was saying, as well as other basic textual material. I made no effort to write the language.

My twelfth language was Japanese. My motivation for learning the language was that I was spending time in Japan (by then about four months altogether) and felt that it was imperative to have some Japanese skills for these trips. In addition, as a linguist and language learner/teacher, I saw the learning of Japanese as a special kind of challenge since it was so different from any other languages that I had studied. So I started learning it by auditing classes at my current institution, the University of Minnesota. Then, during a six-month sabbatical at the University of Hawaii (1996–97), I took a one-semester accelerated course in beginning Japanese. The focus was perhaps more on literacy and on grammar than on conversation. We were taught the two syllabary systems, *hiragana* and *katakana*, and were also taught 140 *kanji*. The social setting for this case study in foreign-language learning was almost exclusively the academic setting of a classroom. At the end of the course, I could write Japanese utterances, such as diary entries, descriptions of hotel resort settings, and the like. I could also read basic communications, including those with *kanji* that I had already learned. While my literacy skills in Japanese have attrited almost entirely, I have from time to time resuscitated my speaking skills, usually with the assistance of native Japanese-speaking *tandem partners*. In these sessions, we spend half the time in Japanese to assist me in my learning and use of

Japanese and half the time in English to assist them with their learning and use of English.

Now let me return to my ninth language, Hebrew, and pick up the thread of the literacy discussion since Hebrew has been the only other language aside from English in which I have spent a considerable amount of my professional career working. As I indicated above, as of 1975, Hebrew became, by necessity, the language of my professional work, and was to be so for the next 16 years. The motivation that my wife and I had was to make our lives in Israel a success, and to raise our children bilingually. The position that I assumed at the School of Education, Hebrew University of Jerusalem, required that I teach all my courses in Hebrew, after the first year of grace when I was permitted to teach in English. Hence, I needed to shape up my non-existent academic skills in Hebrew, primarily in order to lecture in Hebrew, but also in order to read, evaluate, and grade student papers, and also to write handouts, comments on student work, and occasional short papers on my own or in consort with colleagues. This discussion will encompass a finite period of time because I was a professor in Israel for 17 years, before returning to the US to teach at the University of Minnesota in the Fall of 1991.

My Sojourn in Hebrew Literacy

Even though I learned how to recode in Hebrew in preparation for my bar mitzvah (as indicated above), I only started learning what words meant in Hebrew when I started studying Hebrew informally at the age of 25 or so, as a graduate student in International Development Education at Stanford University. My wife and I had decided we would go to live in Israel and that it would be imperative to know the language if we wished to succeed there. I started studying more formally when we graduated from Stanford and I took a teaching position at UCLA (*en route* to Israel). I audited Hebrew classes there for those with some limited background. While I was expecting conversational Hebrew, the focus was on Hebrew literature. So I found myself reading short stories and essays of a decidedly and exclusively literary nature. Whatever writing we did was limited to comments on those stories and essays, as I remember. So while at UCLA, I felt frustrated that I was not acquiring functional literacy skills, and did not see the relationship between the literary texts we were studying and the literacy needs I was going to have when living in Israel.

When I compared the learning of Hebrew to the learning of other languages, it was to my dismay that I realized there were many fewer cognates between English and Hebrew than between English and those other languages. Not only was Hebrew written from right to left, but the punctuation system was different and there were no capital letters. In addition, the language included pronouns and prepositions that were attached to nouns, adjectives, and even verbs. These and other major differences made it very difficult for me to transfer reading strategies associated with, say, skimming.

When my wife and I arrived in Israel with intermediate Hebrew skills, the class we took focused on refining our communicative skills and on reading about current events in the newspaper. Actually, much of the textual material that we read simply reflected spoken dialogs that were in written form. This training did not prepare me to read and understand students' term papers and theses, nor their short-answer and essay responses on exams. In short, I was not trained in either the receptive nor productive skills for dealing with Hebrew for academic purposes. I had a further embarrassing problem that my Hebrew handwriting was childlike in nature and I did not know how to keyboard in Hebrew. Furthermore, to add insult to injury, my sense of Hebrew spelling was so poor that anything I wrote had numerous spelling errors in it.

The summer after our first year in Israel, I took the intensive summer course along with students. The problem was that I was a good test taker so I placed in the highest level of Hebrew, which put me far, far below the average student in that class. In fact, some of my fellow students had just graduated from Hebrew high schools in New York City or LA, and spent their idle time in that summer class writing Hebrew poetry (which left me mesmerized). When the teacher called on students to read text aloud, I would do everything my body posture and eyes would allow to indicate that I was unavailable. I did find the study of one modern Hebrew play to be a sheer delight, even though the text was ostensibly well beyond my actual proficiency level. The roving literature teacher herself brought the text alive and just reminded me how only a portion of reading proficiency is 'level,' and how much of it is the quality of the teacher and the interest provoked by the content. That intensive summer course also offered subject-specific sections, so I chose the one closest to applied linguistics, namely, 'sociology' and, as I mentioned above, a doctoral student was our instructor. It was refreshing to have someone who was not at all interested in correcting our Hebrew language errors, but rather in getting us to discuss issues in sociology so that we would have an experience of using Hebrew in an academic area. This experience also contributed to my academic literacy somewhat and to my morale a good deal.

From my second year at the Hebrew University of Jerusalem, when I started teaching in Hebrew, I was at a distinct disadvantage in my role as a professor. I had a fair amount of difficulty understanding my students' oral comments in class, and an enormous amount of difficulty deciphering their written comments on course work. They were not expected to keyboard their work since at that time the society was still over a decade away from the microcomputer, and keyboarding was reserved for people in menial jobs such as secretaries. What this meant was that instead of spending my time decoding the students' messages, I first needed to spend an inordinate amount of time simply recoding them because some of the marks that they made on the page – especially downward strokes looking like an undotted *i* or an *l* in English – could be construed to represent one of perhaps five or six different Hebrew characters. Also, since Hebrew is written essentially without vowels, I was lacking clues to just what the words they were writing actually were. In English, this would be commensurate with being confronted with a phrase such as 'He was l-king s-x' and having to guess if the phrase was 'He was liking sax', 'He was lacking sox', 'He was lacking six', 'He was lacking sex', or some other combination. My mind needed to go through conniptions in order to determine what was being written. My powers of inference were called for in over-drive fashion.

It was not until a dozen years later that the microcomputer was in full swing in Israel and that a wordprocessing program emerged that provided Hebrew and English. Fueled by my intense embarrassment at distributing classroom handouts written in a childlike script left over from my bar mitzvah days, I quickly found myself software to learn Hebrew keyboarding, and within a week, much to my amazement, I was touch typing in Hebrew, a system that called on my fingers to move in entirely different ways. Even the punctuation marks were not placed in the same locations as on the English keyboard. From the moment I started keyboarding, my handouts for class, I distinctly remember feeling a huge morale boost. I now could write in acceptable print. But that did not solve my spelling problem. So for the next few years my handouts were typed, but not spelled correctly. Then finally the first spelling software emerged (not attached to a word processing program, but separate and expensive). The problem is that Hebrew spells the bulk of its words with simply three consonants and no vowels, so there are many look-alike words. Hence, I needed to teach my spelling software the words that I was likely to need checked in my professional language. All the same, there were still numerous cases where the program accepted as 'correct' certain words that were not the intended ones, and I would be oblivious to this fact!

During my sixteen years in Israel, I rarely read for pleasure in Hebrew. Although my wife and I would occasionally read a newspaper in Hebrew and were able to do so with relative success after six or seven years there, I tended to get the *Jerusalem Post*, which was in English, rather than make the effort to read in Hebrew. In my early years in Israel, I found and devoured a few novelettes prepared through a series that subsequently went out of business, called the Gesher 'bridge' series. They did just that. They presented adult content for those at a low level of reading proficiency, and what is more, vowels were included, much as they are for school children until third grade. In addition, a glossary was provided at the bottom of each page. I thrived on that kind of spoon-feeding while it was available.

It was during my first several years in Israel that I did something else that would succeed in jump starting my reading skills, which were far from adequate. I would purchase and read prurient novels that I was able to find at the bus station (also for a brief period of time until they were discontinued). These had clearly been translated from some other language, such as English. At first, I needed to use a dictionary to determine what parts of the body they were referring to, but after a while I was able to read them rapidly. While undoubtedly these novels were far less engaging and alluring in Hebrew than they might have been in English, the very fact that I was reading through them at what amounted to a fast pace for me produced a shift in my reading. I realized that those many years after my bar mitzvah when I progressively forgot the Hebrew alphabet and became more and more a disenfranchised member of the Jewish congregation had a profound effect upon my psyche with regard to the Hebrew language. I saw myself as an incompetent, and as someone who simply would not succeed at cracking the Hebrew code. Of course, I was reading texts that I had not been trained to read for comprehension. The English translation was often provided for the prayer book rituals, but the translations were always figurative and the language invariably flowery and certainly not conversational. Well, reading the prurient literature got me over the psychological barriers and beyond my emotional baggage into an experience of success at moving rapidly through text. Needless to say, this was not academic text, but still it was text.

Some years after these earlier breakthrough experiences, I do remember reading a modern, full-length novel or two, such as *The Lover*, by Aleph Bet Yehoshua, a well-known and respected writer who was also a professor of literature at Haifa University. The novel was made into a successful movie, in fact. Yet mostly I found that unsimplified novels had too much vocabulary that I did not know, and so I was discouraged from attempting to read them.

In addition, I came to learn that I was not going to achieve any great success with skimming in Hebrew, that is, reading rapidly through text and slowing only at particular moments to attend to some point in greater depth. I found that the Hebrew language was simply too compact in its structure to enable me to skim over it, the way I would in English and in the various Romance languages that I knew and in which I could read comfortably. Especially with academic texts, I invariably needed to unpack considerable grammatical information from inflections attached to the content words. In addition, I needed to learn a host of new vocabulary since there were so few words in Hebrew that were cognates of English words. I certainly did my best to start with the cognates but that list ran out far too rapidly for my taste.

Another thing I did was to create a glossary of applied linguistic terms in English and Hebrew, because I simply did not have the vocabulary I needed in order to teach courses in first and second language acquisition, language processing, language teaching, and language assessment, without having terms on which I could rely. I made the mistake initially of thinking I could simply show up in class without the appropriate terms and let my students provide them for me. Given that modern Hebrew was and still is undergoing development on a daily basis, my efforts at asking students how to say, for example, *transformational grammar* or *semantic feature* in Hebrew resulted in ten or more minutes of hassling among students who failed to agree on an acceptable term. It was then that I pre-empted these student altercations by calling my colleagues on the phone the evening before class to get the terms from them. And sometimes they did not even agree! It was then that I went to Igal Yanai, the Secretary of the Academy of the Hebrew Language, based in Jerusalem. I learned that the Academy had stacks of computer print outs with terms in various states of approbation. While the Academy represented a respected coterie of experts who met regularly to determine the lexis that the developing nation was to be using, many of their deliberations led only to computer output without any of the material ever being published.

So with Dr Yanai's assistance, and that of another colleague in applied linguistics, Raphael Nir, I co-authored a *Dictionary of Applied Linguistics Terminology*, which was published by the Hebrew University of Jerusalem in 1986. That was another milestone in my efforts at literacy because it gave me far more of a sense of comfort when I used terms in class. If students took issue with my use of terms, I would refer them to the glossary and indicate to them that the terms were approved by the Academy itself.

My one other publication in Hebrew was an invited article on the topic, 'What is Psycholinguistics?' for publication in a local Israeli journal. A native-speaking Hebrew teacher corrected or reconstructed the essay thoroughly, and suggested numerous changes in the areas of vocabulary, syntax, cohesion, rhetorical functions, and paragraphing (one change every seven words on average). Three of my colleagues in applied linguistics (Rafi Nir, Shoshana Blum-Kulka, and Elite Olshtain) were then asked to *reformulate* the essay so that it reflected the way that they would write the same article, rather than editing my writing. Each made on the average 50 stylistic changes, as well as some grammatical changes overlooked by the Hebrew teacher. This procedure provided me some rich insights into my deficiencies in Hebrew. With respect to vocabulary, it was found that I tended to use the same vocabulary in writing that I used in speaking. Register difficulties were particularly noticeable in my use of conjunctions and adverbs. In other words, I learned that while I had a working knowledge of technical terms in writing, I did not have a similar working knowledge of function words in writing – largely because they differed from ones used in speech. For example, in Hebrew speech, 'also' is expressed by *gam*, whereas the results from the reformulation research would suggest that the preferred expression in academic writing is *k'mo-xen*.

With regard to syntax, several rules that I had heard in passing in one class or another were underscored by the fact that the reformulators heeded them. For example, there is a rule in Hebrew that calls for inverting the order of the subject noun phrase and verb phrase following an adverbial phrase with sentences in the past tense. I used the NP + VP order (e.g. 'the researchers investigated...') which is generally acceptable except after an adverbial phrase (correct: *Ad lifney eser shanim, xakru haxokrim...* 'Until ten years ago, investigated the researchers...'). This violation in written syntax was not dealt with in the thorough correction or reconstruction of the essay by my Hebrew teacher, but it was eliminated in the reformulation conducted by all three of my colleagues in the field. With respect to cohesion, the reformulators provided me with a breakthrough: seeing that Hebrew does not tolerate as much use of pronominal reference as does English. In Hebrew, lexical substitution would be more appropriate. Thus, after writing 'the second language learners,' the next mention in Hebrew might be 'the language learners,' and then 'the learners,' and perhaps then 'they,' while in English the writer might jump immediately to 'they' in the second mention. I had read about this stylistic difference in the literature contrasting English and Hebrew discourse, but had not applied it in my own writing. This exercise demonstrated to me that reformulation by a native has the potential of pointing up important matters of style, vocabulary, and syntax that often lay outside the realm of traditional teacher feedback on essays. Needless to say, I felt very comfortable publishing this article after sifting through and integrating the rich reformulated feedback that I had received. While I did gain those insights into the writing of academic text, it did not motivate me to publish in Hebrew, especially since the payoff was so slight. I received much more academic mileage out of publishing in English, which, thank goodness, was not difficult for me, given my rich background in English-language literacy.

Along with my inability to skim text – something that made the reading of a 450-page draft of a doctoral thesis a less-than-desirable undertaking – there was the further frustration at not being able to determine whether material submitted by students was rightfully theirs, or plagiarized from some more knowledgeable source. Whereas I was and am able to spot plagiarism in English almost instantly, I realized that I had no such skills in Hebrew. I felt lucky if I understood what was being written, not whether the student was the actual writer or not. I never resolved this dilemma, though I frequently admonished students to write material in their own words wherever possible and if not, to cite their sources. In addition, I always continued having difficulty determining whether my Hebrew-speaking students were well versed in what they were writing about or whether they were just putting words and phrases together that would have a ring of coherence to them for a non-native reader such as myself. If the text seemed padded, a bit empty, or somewhat incoherent, I usually assumed that it was due to my deficiencies rather than theirs. In English, I am quick to spot when a writer does not have much to say, or at least, is not saying very much at a given moment.

Despite my difficulties in reading, as the years went by I gained a certain comfort level in my ability to plan course work in Hebrew and to generate handouts that were moderately competent. In addition, I was continually writing memos in Hebrew, almost invariably handwritten, since this is what others did. I was also reading adequately enough that I no longer had major qualms before assigning a given grade to a term paper or exam. There were still two things lacking in my Hebrew that were not going to find their way into my language for the remainder of the years in the country. One was the ability to move from register to register. In fact, I was largely oblivious to whether a given vocabulary word or phrase was higher or lower register in Hebrew. I distinctly remember after a plenary address I gave at the annual conference of the Israeli Association for Applied Linguistics, having a native Hebrew-speaking colleague point out to me that my address was an excellent example of a mixing of registers. One example she gave was that I had used the term *migvan* 'variety' when I should have simply used the English loan word *variatzia*. Here I thought I was being properly academic, and in reality I was being recondite!

The other thing lacking in my Hebrew was the ability to use the language, whether spoken or written, in a humorous way. Most of my oral and written text came out as straight or serious. Even after so many years, I had not learned how to play with the language, whether through puns, innuendoes, or other forms of humor. It was probably fair to say that I was not that versed at perceiving humor in the writing of others, depending on the topic and situation.

So when the Gulf War erupted, Israel was threatened by it, and for various reasons, I started exploring jobs back in the US, the prospect of returning to an English-language environment for the remainder of my academic career looked surprisingly appealing to me. It would allow me to read and respond to drafts of student term papers and theses far more quickly. It would allow me to focus exclusively on *what* I wanted to teach in the upcoming lesson, without having to preoccupy myself initially with *how* I was going to say it. It would also mean that if I needed to send a memo to a dean, I would be able to compose that memo rather effortlessly instead of having to deliberate at length to make sure that it would communicate tactfully what it was I wanted to communicate. It would also mean that I could build humor back into my use of language in a way that I never achieved through written or even spoken Hebrew. It would mean I would be back into a language where I had more control over the terminology needed to get a message across, the register of language, and the connotations behind the words.

I have now been back in the US for over eight years and I must admit that all of the advantages of being a professor in an English literacy context ring as true today as they did when I was contemplating the return. And I intend to return to live in Israel some day – but not to function there as a professor in Hebrew, I would imagine.

Notes

1. Several years after I left the Peace Corps, they were to hire linguists from the University of Washington, Seattle, to come down, do field work, develop materials, and then teach the language to volunteers. The approach that they used was the audiolingual one, with pattern practice drills galore.

My Experience of Learning to Read and Write in Japanese as L1 and English as L2

Ryuko Kubota was born and raised in Japan. She received her Ph.D. in education from the Ontario Institute for Studies in Education of the University of Toronto. For the past twenty years, she has taught English in Japan and Japanese in North America. She has also been involved in teacher education for ESL and foreign languages in the US. She is currently an assistant professor of foreign language education at the University of North Carolina at Chapel Hill. Her research interests include issues of culture in second language teaching, second language writing, multicultural education and critical pedagogy. She has published articles in the *Canadian Modern Language Review, Education about Asia, Foreign Language Annals, Japanese Language Education Around the Globe, Journal of Second Language Writing, TESOL Quarterly, World Englishes,* and *Written Communication.*

Introduction

As a college professor, reading and writing constitute an essential part of my daily professional life. Yet it is puzzling how I first acquired these skills. Writing this essay provided me with an opportunity to review the pile of my writings I kept from my childhood in Japan. Doing so made me realize how much I have accomplished over many years. Before I present my experience of learning to read and write in Japanese as L1 and English as L2, I will briefly describe my present reading and writing activities. My current position at a university in the USA requires me to engage in teaching Japanese as a foreign language to American students, training second/ foreign language pre-service teachers, advising students, conducting research, writing academic papers, serving on committees, and corresponding mostly by e-mail on job-related matters. As such, my present reading and writing activities gravitate more toward English than Japanese and more toward academic than non-academic texts. Currently, I have little time for reading for pleasure and I do not write to close friends as much as I used to. Although the predominant language that I use now is English, I am more skilled in and comfortable with reading and writing in my first language. This is perhaps because all my reading and writing activities from childhood into adulthood were in my first language, and I did not develop advanced skills in English literacy until later in my life.

I received my primary, secondary and tertiary education in Japan. My educational background may not be largely different from what most other peers of mine experienced in the 1960s and 1970s. I engaged in various reading and writing activities at school, and I was surrounded by a rich environment for literacy at home. I began to study English as a foreign language when I was in the seventh grade, and I continued to take English courses until I graduated from a four-year college in Japan. However, it was not until I graduated from college that I immersed myself in an English-speaking environment and began to develop advanced oral and written skills in English. Although this was a late start to develop advanced L2 proficiency, I believe that the L1 literacy I developed at home and in school served as a foundation for my acquisition of L2 literacy. I will begin my recollections by introducing my family and their background in literacy.

My Family and Literacy

I grew up in a small extended family with my parents and grandmother but without any siblings. Although none of them received higher education, reading and writing have always been an important part of the family life. My father is a retired white-collar local government employee. He was born in 1926 and received ten years of public education. His father was a businessman, and his mother was an elementary school teacher before she had children and later became a leader of a women's organization after World War II. I grew up seeing my father often bring work home. He would write reports and speeches by hand, since at that time there were no wordprocessors for Japanese. After he retired from the local government about fifteen years ago, he worked for a private college for nine years and now he volunteers for the local community. He has been writing reports, business letters and personal letters using a wordprocessor and a personal computer for the last ten years.

My mother has been a housewife and an *ikebana* (flower-arranging) instructor. She also received public education for ten years, but her final two years of schooling were interrupted by World War II. Her father received ten years of education and business training, and opened a retail store selling fabric for *kimono*s. I remember him as an intellectual and a great master of calligraphy. According to my mother, her father was unable to receive education beyond the eighth grade because a fire destroyed his family business. He learned business-related skills as an apprentice and taught himself calligraphy, literature, history, and so on. Wanting his children to receive a proper education, he bought many books for them, which most parents at that time were unable to do. My mother has been reading literature as a member of a *dokusho-kai,* a reading group that her ikebana instructor initiated. According to my mother, the ikebana master believed that beautiful works of ikebana are created by cultivating one's knowledge and appreciation of art and literature. My mother still participates in dokusho-kai and discusses reading with her peers. She also appreciates and writes *haiku.*

Another family member I lived with was my grandmother. She was actually not related by blood with either of my parents. Since she and her husband had no children, they adopted my parents as a married couple in order to maintain the family line. Born in 1905, my grandmother received public education for eight years and then went to a sewing school for a few years. She taught *sado* (tea ceremony) at home when I was growing up. While her mind and vision were still clear, I often saw her read books that my mother brought home. Reading a newspaper continued to be her daily pastime until she died in 1993 at the age of 88. Her husband attended a private Japanese institution of higher education in Shanghai, China, and studied business and economics in the USA and the UK during the 1920s. He passed away soon after I was born.

None of my family members was literate in English, except for my grandfather, whom I did not know. When my parents attended public schools, English was excluded from the curriculum because of the war. While there were no opportunities for me to learn English from my family members, my family provided me with a rich environment for L1 literacy.

My L1 Literacy Development

One of the ways to trace back one's reading and writing experiences would be to examine actual materials that one read and wrote while growing up. I have kept many of the children's books, textbooks and notebooks that I used during my childhood in Japan. These records reveal a very rich print environment both at home and in school.

My experience in reading began before I entered a public elementary school (from the first to the sixth grade) in Nagano[1] in 1964. When I was a child, my mother and grandmother used to read children's books with colorful illustrations to me. When I was in kindergarten and lower elementary grades, my mother used to read bedtime stories to me. My favorite one was *Winnie the Pooh* translated into Japanese. I remember asking my mother to read my favorite lines again and again.

While I attended a kindergarten for two years, there was no formal instruction in reading and writing.[2] According to my mother, however, I was already reading *hiragana*[3] before I entered elementary school, perhaps because my mother and grandmother regularly read to me. My first formal instruction in reading and writing was given when I was in the first grade. My first-grade notebooks contain many hiragana-writing exercises. Some of the notebooks have diaries, one of which describes several things that I did one afternoon, all connected by *te kara* ('and then'). Diary writing was an important part of language learning. My teachers[4] made us keep a diary during long vacations. As I proceeded to the second and third grade, the volume, complexity, and sophistication of my writing increased. My writing started to include various conjunctions, direct quotations, and a title for each diary entry.

The kinds of writing done in school can be found in anthologies called *bunshu* ('collection of compositions'), such as *gakko bunshu* (a school anthology of students' written work), *kojin bunshu* (a personal anthology), and *sotsugyo bunshu* (an anthology made by a graduating class). Once every year, my elementary school published gakko bunshu in which the written works of several students from each of the twelve classes (two classes for each grade) were published. The one published in my fifth-grade year (1969) was 81 pages long and contained *seikatsu-bun* ('writing about life' – topics on one's lived experiences), diaries, poems, letters, book reports, travel reports, and scientific observation reports. My diary on a night-watch walk with my father was selected and printed in this issue. My sixth-grade personal anthology was bound with cover pages that I painted myself and contained six seikatsu-bun, two poems, one travel report, one letter, three book reports, and one essay. The graduation anthology of my elementary class contains personal essays on memorable experiences, each student's future dreams, and personal profiles.

It is worth mentioning here that seikatsu-bun, one of the genres that I mentioned above, reflects the instructional approach for writing called *seikatsu tsuzurikata undo* ('the movement for writing about lived experiences') that seems to have still been used when I was growing up. Influenced by the democracy movement during the *Taisho* period (1912–1926), this movement began in the 1920s and was particularly popular in poor farming communities in northern Japan. It placed an emphasis on realism and encouraged students to describe their lived experiences and express their feelings and opinions as authentically as possible. Opposing the traditional teacher-centered conformist approach to teaching, it promoted a student-centered, experiential, self-advocacy and emancipatory approach based on the philosophy that writing about authentic lived experiences would help students become aware of the social reality and their own experiences objectively, develop empathy and solidarity among students by sharing writing with each other, and transform the social reality for the better (cf. Murayama, 1985; Ogawa, 1980; Sasai, 1981). In a way, it is quite similar to the Freirean pedagogy of conscientization and emancipation. Seikatsu tsuzurikata is not only personal narratives; it also includes report writing for science and social studies as well as opinion essays. By describing precisely what is observed in human experiences in a society and by abstracting and drawing generalizations from observations, seikatsu tsuzurikata builds a foundation for scientific inquiry which contributes to transforming human experiences and the society (Ogawa, 1980).

Japanese language learning in the elementary school also included mechanical exercises. My teacher sometimes made us copy some stories and poems in the textbooks as homework assignments. This exercise is still common in elementary schools and sometimes in secondary schools. The current Course of Study (national curriculum guidelines) for elementary school includes *shisha* (sight copying) and *chosha* (dictation) as one of the activities for first, second and third-grade Japanese language instruction. My friends who are school teachers in Japan recently told me that they sometimes require their students to do this exercise because they believe that copying allows practicing *kanji* (Chinese characters) in contexts rather than in isolation and it helps students become aware of effective expressions and text organization. This approach is apparently based on the idea that repeated practice of established forms builds a foundation for self-expression.[5]

The notebooks I used in upper grades contain summaries and outlines of the stories in the textbook. The outline is often divided into a few categories; for example, a story outline (things that the author/character did, saw, or heard) and the feelings of the author/character in the story. The Japanese language textbooks for upper grades begin to contain report writing on trips, scientific observations, and so on. A scientific observation report includes (1) motivation of the research, (2) observations, and (3) conclusions. I observed a water lily one day and wrote a report following this format. Also, self-editing was encouraged in the process of writing, as evident in some of my composition drafts with insertions and corrections. All these activities seem to have contributed to building academic language skills.

As can be expected from my family background, I was surrounded by books when I was growing up. My parents bought series of children's books, many of which were translations of stories written by American and European authors of children's literature. During the upper grades in elementary school, I was a compulsive reader. When I was in the sixth grade, my teacher made the class do a competition of reading 10,000 pages. I checked out many library books of mostly world literature. The essay in my sixth grade personal anthology discussed the importance of reading to me. In the essay, I mentioned *Sherlock Holmes* and *Daddy Long Legs*, and stated that I had jotted down things that struck me while reading rather than just reading mindlessly only to reach the goal of 10,000 pages.

When I was in junior high school (from the seventh to the ninth grade), writing increasingly became a support skill for learning the content of subject matter such as social studies and science. My social studies notebooks are filled with definitions of terms, summaries of historical incidents and so on. I remember I often used the encyclopedia to learn detailed information on certain topics in social studies. While reading explanations, I used to take notes and summarize what I read. The records that I kept include a large piece of paper with a summary of the city of Kamakura (an old capital of Japan). I probably made this summary with other members of my group and posted it on the wall right before a school trip to Tokyo and Kamakura. Group work was a popular instructional strategy when I was in junior high school. The homeroom class, which studied most subjects together for three years, was divided into seven groups, each of which engaged in collaborative learning and peer-monitoring of behaviors in both classroom and extra-curricular settings.

When I was in junior high school, writing was not only for academic but also for social purposes. The graduation anthology for my class demonstrates this point. To publish this 193-page anthology, students in the class formed an editorial committee and decided on the content and the format. I was one of the members of the committee. The anthology, which was a product of a truly student-initiated project, includes not only personal narrative essays and opinion essays,[6] but also the goal of the class, an essay from the class leader, essays from teachers, school/class events, profiles of classmates, profiles of the seven small groups, excerpts from class newsletters, and excerpts from the class journal.

The class newsletter and the class journal represent writing for social purposes. The class newsletters were written by students on topics such as class reform, current topics in the news, suggestions for the Student Council, and so on. The class journal was kept by a secretary during a brief homeroom meeting that was held at the beginning and at the end of every day. It included the daily schedule, events of the day, minutes of the homeroom meetings, and comments reflecting on that day. All students in my homeroom took turns in pairs to serve as a chair and a secretary for the short homeroom meetings. During the discussion, students would raise issues such as problematic behaviors of their classmates during class or other school activities, and the whole class would discuss solutions. The secretary would record the discussion in detail – sometimes almost verbatim.[7] One of the examples is the discussion of an incident in which girls were noisy during singing practice for the music competition and a boy made an insulting comment about the girls' singing skills. The journal entry for this day includes a summary of the discussion followed by three pages of quotes. Writing of this kind was clearly not for academic purposes, but served for building a community as a social unit.

When I was in high school, I do not remember any specific writing assignments we were given in Japanese language class, but I remember that writing was an important aspect in essay tests such as world history, ethics and philosophy.[8] Also, writing became an increasingly important part of socialization. I exchanged with my peers what we called *kokan nikki* ('exchange diary'), which was written casually in a notebook and circulated among a specific group of friends. Members of the group took turns to write a diary, expressing anything that they wanted to share with other members of the group. It was an open discussion forum in which we expressed our feelings and opinions, creating solidarity and a sense of belonging. There were at least three kokan nikki; one for the high school band to which I belonged, one for girls of the same age in the band, and another for girls in our homeroom class. Some of these notebooks were circulated very frequently, and we would write from one to ten pages for each entry. Common topics among girls were, of course, boys and human relationships, but we also wrote about school, family, the future, and life.

In college, unlike most of my classmates who were more interested in socializing than studying, I tried to take advantage of the academic opportunities that I had. I read textbooks, other related materials, Japanese novels, and Russian, American and English novels in translation. In college, I wrote papers and exams each term, although there were no courses offered on academic writing in Japanese. The reason I was able to write papers successfully was perhaps because I already had a strong foundation in writing. Reading related materials also helped me figure out what kind of format I should use. During college, I also wrote to my pen pal very frequently.

After I graduated, I taught English at a public junior high school in Nagano. Most of the writing I did was job related, such as report writing for school committees. I read fiction and non-fiction for pleasure. As I will describe below, I began to develop advanced English skills for academic purposes after I graduated from college. English has become my predominant language for daily use since I started my academic work in an English-speaking environment.

My Experiences of Learning English as L2

The English language instruction that I received from the seventh grade in a public school through my undergraduate program was probably no different from what most other students experienced during the 1970s. As a seventh grader, I had already developed a significant level of L1 literacy and metalinguistic awareness, which I think facilitated my learning of L2. However, since the instructional emphasis in English classes tended to be on grammar and vocabulary and there were only a few opportunities to use English for real purposes, my English proficiency developed very slowly during ten years of secondary and tertiary education. It was during the post-undergraduate immersion experiences in English that I experienced several big leaps in the development of my literacy as well as my oral skills in English.

In 1970, I was in the seventh grade in a public junior high school in Nagano. This is when I began to study English. At that time, I was interested in popular songs in English and was eager to learn the subject. I was a very motivated student who every morning used to listen to a radio program that introduced English conversation, grammar, and vocabulary for junior high school students. However, unlike today in Japan, there were no native speakers of English in English classes throughout my secondary education, nor was the impact of English on everyday life as great as it is today. Thus, there were hardly any opportunities to use English for real communication. I was fortunate to have good teachers, one of whom was a fluent speaker of English and often talked to us in English in class. However, immediate purposes for using English were usually absent from my learning experience. Reading, grammar and vocabulary were the primary focus, and writing was mostly practiced through translating isolated sentences from Japanese to English. In our high school, we were required to do extensive reading using graded readers. We read abridged versions of *The Arabian Nights, The Adventures of Tom Sawyer, Animal Farm,*

Grimms' Fairy Tales, etc. This experience definitely helped me develop reading skills, but a real purpose for reading was still lacking.

I went to a private university in Tokyo. For the first time, I took some English classes conducted entirely in English. It was also the first time I had native English speakers as instructors. However, most classes were very large with forty to sixty students. I took a few English composition classes, one of which was, as I recall, mainly focused on translating sentences from Japanese to English. Another class was taught by a British teacher who gave us composition assignments. The writing we practiced in that class was on immediate topics from personal experiences, and I do not remember receiving any substantial training in academic writing. The English Department in which I was enrolled offered students an option of either literature or linguistics as a primary focus of study. Since I was interested in analyzing language, I opted for linguistics. I took some seminars on syntax and semantics, and wrote my undergraduate thesis in English on a topic in linguistics. Although my writing ability at that time was quite limited, what helped me produce a significant piece of academic writing in English without any formal training was perhaps reading related materials in the field. Reading articles on the topic of my research helped me discover patterns of arranging materials at the sentence as well as at the larger discourse levels.

To my disappointment, however, my four years of college experience were not enough to develop substantial skills in English. I was still unable to converse fluently or to express myself naturally and fluently in writing. Extensive reading of authentic materials was a struggle for me too. When I began teaching at a junior high school, I wanted to continue learning English. Then I experienced one of the significant leaps in developing my confidence and proficiency in English during a summer workshop for Japanese teachers of English that was held at a language institute near Tokyo. The workshop offered a one-week immersion experience for the participants to develop their English proficiency and gain knowledge and skills in teaching English as a foreign language. The workshop required all participants to interact in English all day. This was my first experience immersing myself in English for academic purposes for such an extended period of time. After the workshop, I was motivated to study more, and began to read English newspapers in order to expand my vocabulary and reading skills.

Another big leap was achieved when, after teaching at the junior high school for three years, I joined a program that offered Japanese citizens the opportunity to teach Japanese culture at US public schools while living with a host family. Thus, in 1983, at the age of 25, I went for the first time to live in an English-speaking country. The first three months of this one-year stay in Washington state were, in a way, my silent period. I was able to carry on daily conversation on a one-on-one basis, but participating in group conversations was difficult because it required a great amount of concentration for listening and fluency in speaking, both of which I lacked. I started to keep a diary in English because I found it easier to write than to speak. Speaking in English made me feel pressured and frustrated because I was still groping for words and struggling to put them together in a sentence within a limited amount of time. Writing, on the other hand, allowed me to express myself at my own pace and to feel relaxed. Diary writing eventually helped me develop not only fluency in writing but also confidence in my oral communication.

In Seattle, I audited some courses in TESOL at a university for one academic quarter. The professors were kind enough to offer their feedback on the papers that I wrote for their courses. This was my first experience of engaging in writing for academic purposes outside of Japan. Here again, I did not receive any formal training in writing, but my reading of research articles provided me with a model for expressions and patterns of discourse that I emulated in my papers.

My experience of being in a master's program in TESOL in Vermont during the 1986–87 academic year also provided an experience of using English for real purposes. Because of my previous experience of living in the USA and auditing university classes, and perhaps because the program was more geared toward experiential and reflective learning than abstract research, I did not experience much difficulty with required course work.

After I came back to Japan, I published an article in Japanese based on my master's thesis in a peer-reviewed journal. This project turned out to be a struggle for me. For many years, I had been motivated to develop my English proficiency by forcing myself to think in English. The English mode of thinking that I was using while writing my master's thesis in English seems to have negatively influenced my writing of the paper in Japanese. A Japanese reviewer commented on my manuscript and said that there were many parts that sounded like English. My paper was eventually published (Kubota, 1989), but this was a time when I became acutely aware of the importance of using an appropriate form of discourse for the language one is writing in.

By the time I started my Ph.D. work in a Canadian institution in 1989, I felt more comfortable with academic writing in English. Reading related materials continued to facilitate my writing. However, it seems to me that my writing at that time still needed much improvement in the area of style and tone. In retrospect, my professors and fellow students were very tolerant with the stylistic limitations of my writing. They were usually concerned with the content of my writing and rarely corrected stylistic aspects. Perhaps influenced by the stereotype that English discourse is direct and straightforward, I did not pay enough attention to politeness strategies, which are commonly used among academic writers (Belcher, 1995). It was not until I started to publish academic papers that I became more sensitive to the tone of my writing.

Now I read and write in English mostly for research and work-related purposes because I work in an English-speaking institution of higher education in the US. However, reading and writing in English are often arduous tasks for me, partly because the pace is considerably slower than when I read and write in my native language. When I look at print in Japanese, characters sink into my brain in meaning units with little effort, whereas this immediacy is often lacking in English. In writing, although idea generation and organization are always time-consuming aspects for me in both L1 and L2, writing in English usually requires more time on syntactic and lexical manipulation than writing in Japanese. Using a computer certainly makes it easier for me to revise as I write. Yet, I seldom feel confident about the lexical and syntactic accuracy of my English writing. Although I had experienced difficulty in writing that paper in Japanese based on my master's thesis in English, I realized how quickly and effortlessly I was able to write in Japanese when I worked on another paper a few years ago (Kubota, 1996).

When I write in English for public purposes, I almost always have my writing proofread by someone. I sometimes regret the fact that I feel restrained from expressing my authentic voice (i.e. unedited writing of mine), and I often wish the audience would treat the written texts with non-native features the same as texts written by native speakers. However, I am aware of the power of writing that conforms to the conventions of the target discourse community. This awareness comes from my experience of teaching Japanese as a foreign language. As a teacher, I come across my students' L2 texts with obvious errors, awkward expressions and unnatural discourse structures. Although the levels of naturalness of written discourse vary, the more natural the text sounds, the more effectively the content communicates. To me, however, this does not mean that all L2 texts should be perfectly native-like; it seems that there is a certain threshold level for L2 texts to communicate effectively. Beyond this level, the author has a free choice for syntactic, lexical, and discursive usage. When I receive feedback from proofreaders, I occasionally notice some stylistic alterations. If I know for certain that I have a choice, I go for the way I want to express myself. Most of the time, however, I feel that I need to follow the feedback that I receive.

Conclusions and Implications

As a child who grew up in Japan during the 1960s and 1970s, I had a rich experience in L1 literacy, both at home and in school. I was always surrounded by books and was given ample opportunities to express myself in writing for both academic and social purposes. A foundation for academic literacy skills was built through language activities in the elementary school such as extensive reading, report writing, making an outline of a story, separating facts from opinion or feelings, and editing. Even the elementary school training of copying from textbooks might have helped me develop metalinguistic awareness for analyzing structures of written language and discourse.

In theory, I would have been able to transfer my L1 literacy skills to L2 while I was growing up. However, I did not develop my advanced literacy skills in English until later in my life, because of a lack of immediate needs for using English. What helped me develop fluency in L2 reading and writing were immersion experiences in the target language where immediate needs were present. Keeping a diary in English, which I did in order to ease the frustration caused by my lack of oral communication fluency in English, definitely enhanced my fluency in writing. The development of my academic writing skills in English was also facilitated by reading English articles in the field that I was studying. In my experience, practicing a large volume of reading and writing helped me develop these skills. At the same time, different skills interacted with each other; for instance, reading helped writing and writing helped speaking, enhancing the overall development of language proficiencies.

As a reader and writer of English as a second language, I feel that learning to read and write in English will be a life-long project. I doubt that I will attain a native-like level of proficiency, but I am learning little by little. I always appreciate candid feedback on my writing from proofreaders, since I can only learn from mistakes. Just like some of my students of Japanese as a foreign language, I would be making the same errors again and again if they were not corrected. Like my students, I might still make the same mistakes even if they have already been corrected, but I need to be reminded whenever there is a chance.

It is important to note that my experience is located only at a certain time and location, and should not be over-generalized. Although Japan has a uniform educational system with nationally approved curriculum guidelines and textbooks, there are some regional differences (Smith, 1995) and the curriculum has been revised several times since my childhood. Influenced by the discourse of *kokusaika* ('internationalization'), writing instruction seems to be shifting from seikatsu tsuzurikata to an emphasis on expository writing with logical expressions of thoughts. Also, my experience in the 1970s must be quite different from what today's children experience. When I was growing up, there were only three TV stations available in our area. I did watch some popular animation and adventure programs for children, but I would say that the amount of time I spent in front of a TV thirty years ago bears no comparison with the amount today's children spend. Also, there were neither computer games nor cellular phones, which many of today's youngsters have. A continuous investigation of questions such as 'What are the instructional emphases in teaching reading and writing in L1 and L2 in Japan?' 'What kind of teaching approaches are used?' 'What types of genres are taught in school?' 'What kinds of texts do Japanese students write in L1 and L2?' 'What is the impact of today's technology on literacy?' and 'How has instruction for literacy changed in the history?' would provide insights into the development of literacy among Japanese students, and implications for teaching a second language to these students.

Notes

1. Nagano Prefecture has been known for its emphasis on education with very active professional development among teachers. Whether this had any bearing on my experience in developing literacy would require further investigation.
2. The Japanese kindergarten is independent from the elementary school and it generally emphasizes socialization through free play rather than academic instruction (cf. Lewis, 1995).
3. Hiragana is a set of characters that represent syllables in Japanese. Children usually learn hiragana first and then proceed to learn *katakana* (another syllabary to represent mostly loan words) and *kanji* (Chinese characters). For detailed information on the Japanese writing system, see Taylor & Taylor (1995).
4. In Japan, the same teacher usually teaches the same group of students for more than one year. In my case, I had two teachers during six years: a female teacher from the first through the third grade, and a male teacher from the fourth through the sixth grade.
5. For related discussion, see Lewis (1992).
6. The topics of the opinion essays include philosophical ones such as 'Friendship' and 'On courage' as well as sociopolitical topics such as 'Pollution' and 'Opposition to the "Plans for Reconstructing Japanese Archipelago"'.
7. In fact, the homeroom teacher wrote a message in the journal:

   This is the record of our history. You are now writing one of the pages of our history. Let us write everything that happened each day. Have you written down about the marvelous things that your friends did? Have you written about friends who looked sad or were in trouble? Have you documented our history?

8. One of the entrance examinations to a national university that I took had two essay questions on world history:

(1) Take into consideration the establishment of Confucianism as a national religion (philosophy) since the Han Dynasty and explain the historical significance of the criticism of Confucianism seen in the Literary Revolution in the beginning of the Republic of China; and

(2) Explain the relationship between the Religious Revolution Movement and the establishment of modern nations in the case of England and France.

The test required applicants to write 400 characters in Japanese for each essay (an equivalent to a little shorter than one page, double-spaced in English) within 90 minutes. To my surprise, even though I applied to English, I was admitted to the social studies strand in the School of Education, perhaps because I did better in world history than English(!).

References

Belcher, D. (1995) Writing critically across the curriculum. In D. Belcher and G. Braine (eds) *Academic Writing in a Second Language: Essays on Research and Pedagogy* (pp. 135–154). Norwood, NJ: Ablex.

Kubota, R. (1989) Analysis of English learning problems experienced by Japanese students in the U.S. and suggestions for global bilingual assessment (in Japanese). *Bulletin of the Center for Education of Children Overseas* 5, 1–25. Tokyo: The Center for Education of Children Overseas, Tokyo Gakugei University.

Kubota, R. (1996) Critical pedagogy and critical literacy in teaching Japanese (in Japanese). *Japanese-Language Education around the Globe* 6, 35–48. Saitama: The Japan Foundation Japanese Language Institute.

Lewis, C. C. (1992) Creativity in Japanese education. In R. Leestma and H. J. Walberg (eds) *Japanese Educational Productivity* (pp. 225–266). Center for Japanese Studies, the University of Michigan.

Lewis, C. C. (1995) *Educating Hearts and Mind: Reflections on Japanese Preschool and Elementary Education.* Cambridge: Cambridge University Press.

Murayama, S. (1985) *Seikatsu tsuzurikata jissen ron* (Theories of Implementing Seikatsu Tsuzurikata). Tokyo: Aoki Shoten.

Ogawa, T. (1980) *Ogawa Taro kyoiku-gaku chosaku-shu, Dai 3 kan* (Written Works on Education by Taro Ogawa: 3). Tokyo: Aoki Shoten.

Sasai, H. (1981) *Seikatsu tsuzurikatu seiritsu shi* (A History of Seikatsu Tsuzurikata). Tokyo: Ayumi Shuppan.

Smith, H. W. (1995) *The Myth of Japanese Homogeneity: Social Diversity in Education and Socialization.* Commack, NY: Nova Science Publishers.

Taylor, I. and Taylor, M. M. (1995) *Writing and Literacy in Chinese, Korean, and Japanese.* Amsterdam/Philadelphia: John Benjamins.

An Introspective Account of L2 Writing Acquisition

A native of Japan, **Miyuki Sasaki** received her BA from Hiroshima University. In addition to her two MA degrees, one in English education from Hiroshima University, the other in TESOL from Georgetown University, she has a Ph.D. in applied linguistics from UCLA. Her dissertation was published as a book entitled *Second Language Proficiency, Foreign Language Aptitude, and Intelligence: Quantitative and qualitative analyses* (1996). Currently an associate professor in the Faculty of Foreign Studies in English and Applied Linguistics at Nagoya Gakuin University, Seto, Japan, she has published in the areas of language testing and second language writing

behaviours in journals such as *Language Learning, Language Testing, International Review of Applied Linguistics, Journal of Second Language Writing,* and *JALT Journal.* She is the mother of two young children.

One fall day in 1989, I received a letter from the editor of *Language Learning* stating that my paper had been accepted for publication (Sasaki, 1990). I was delighted, but surprised that my first attempt to submit a paper to an international journal was rewarded in such a way. Of course, the acceptance was under the condition that I revise it according to the reviewers' comments. But considering that I later received a number of other discouraging rejection letters, it was truly a lucky start for me as an English as a second language (henceforth, L2) academic writer. I was then a graduate student at the University of California, Los Angeles (UCLA), and the paper was one of the qualifying papers I had to submit for advancement to Ph.D. candidacy. In the paper I tested several hypotheses related to Japanese students' construction of English existential sentences with a locative topic (e.g. There are twenty-seven students in Taro's school.). The hypotheses were based on the results of the master's theses I wrote for Georgetown University and Hiroshima University.

Since that sunny fall day, I have written several papers in English, some of which have been published in professional journals (e.g. Sasaki, 1991a, 1991b, 1993a, 1993b, 1997, 1998a, 2000), but I can't judge whether people should call a person like me a 'successful' L2 writer. I only write an average of one paper a year in English, which is not always published. Moreover, although in the end those papers are written in English, all the other matters related to the writing process are conducted in my first language (henceforth, L1), Japanese. In order to overcome the disadvantages of an L2 writer, I often select topics that require full Japanese proficiency. That means that I usually conduct research in Japanese using Japanese participants. I also read background literature in Japanese, which English native speakers may find difficulty getting access to. Throughout the entire research process, I think in Japanese, take notes in Japanese, and write the first rough drafts in Japanese because I can't think thoroughly about any complicated matters in English. It is not until the last stage of the research process, when I put everything together into the form of a paper, that I start to use English. This may not be the most efficient way of writing an English paper (especially because I translate most of my ideas from Japanese into English when I write a second draft), but this is the only way I can write in English.

As a result of many fortunate encounters with wonderful mentors, in addition to my own efforts, I have become reasonably proficient in writing in English. I have also come to like writing in English (although not as much as in Japanese). However, if I can be allowed to be honest, the only reason for my writing the final draft of academic manuscripts in English is that it is almost the only means of communicating with other scholars in applied linguistics, the field where I work professionally. If I could choose, I would be happy to write everything in Japanese. In that sense, my motivation as an L2 writer is purely instrumental. Should we still call such a person a 'good' L2 writer? I don't know. I only hope my story will encourage some other L2 writers by explaining how a person like me has come to gather enough courage to keep writing in an L2.

Before I explain my development as an L2 writer, I should begin with the story of my development as an L1 writer because it has formed the most important basis of my L2 literacy. I was born in Kita-Kyushu, a middle-sized city in southern Japan, in 1959, as the second child in an ordinary middle-class family. My father was an office worker, and my mother was a nurse. If there was something special about my family regarding my L1 literacy development, it was my parents' love of literature. Not only did they enjoy reading all types of books and magazines, but they also enjoyed writing poems. My father wrote (and still writes) modern poems, and my mother wrote haiku, a type of classical Japanese poetry. They belonged to different local literary societies, and sometimes had their poems published in the society magazines. From them, I learned how literature could make a person's life happy and meaningful. In addition to their regular jobs, they seemed to take great pride in their literary work.

Thanks to my parents, I came to enjoy reading and writing in my L1, and this has contributed a great deal to my life as a student, and later as a teacher and researcher. I have enjoyed reading all types of texts including novels, mysteries, documentaries, and poems. I have also enjoyed writing letters, reports, essays, and poems. My readiness to read and write in my L1 has not only helped me gain new knowledge and think analytically, but also has consoled me and brought me great joy. For example, when I was studying in the United States, reading books and magazines from a local Japanese bookstore had a great soothing effect on my homesickness. Even now, I sometimes 'take refuge' in reading and writing in Japanese when I get tired of working in English too long.

With such a positive orientation toward literacy in my L1, it was natural for me to like Japanese best of all the subjects during my elementary and high school years. Because Japanese language education in those days tended to be focused on literature appreciation (Kinoshita, 1981), I learned to enjoy novels, essays, and poems written not only in modern Japanese but also in classical Japanese. When I was a senior high school student, I was especially fascinated by novels, diaries, and essays written by women writers in the eleventh century. I thus read *Sarashina Diary* (by Sugawaranotakasueno Musume), Izumi Shikibu's Diary (by Izumi Shikibu), the *Tales of the Genji* (by Murasaki Shikibu), and *Makura no Soushi* (by Seisho Nagon), enjoying the beautiful sound and rhythm of the original texts alongside their modern Japanese translations. If there is one thing I now regret about my Japanese classes, it is the fact that the teachers never taught us how to use the Japanese language for more practical purposes than literature appreciation. The Japanese texts in those classes were always only a target to be analyzed and appreciated, and they were never used as examples of texts written for communicative purposes. We never learned how to write effective letters, reports, or research papers in systematic ways. The only occasion we had to write was for 'Kansoubun,' personal impressions of the literary materials we had read. On such occasions, those impressions were always written only once, and then only to be graded by the teachers.

In 1978, I entered Hiroshima University to major in teaching English as a foreign language (TEFL). I didn't choose Japanese literature as my major then because I felt a sort of moral resistance against making my living out of something I could enjoy so much. Instead, I chose English, the subject I liked second best. Although I could not like English as much as Japanese, my story as a learner of English is also a happy one of a person blessed with many wonderful opportunities. As is typical with other Japanese learners of English as a foreign language, I started to study English when I was twelve. I was taught English three to six hours a week for six years by Japanese teachers in junior and senior high schools. Those English classes focused mainly on grammatical details and intensive reading. We had very few chances to speak English during those class hours. Because of the way English was taught, I always felt that studying English was similar to studying mathematics, in that it presented me with logical problems to solve. But I still liked English better than mathematics because English made me imagine foreign people and countries I had never seen. I dreamt that some day I would go to one of those countries and talk to the people living there. This dream later came true when I became a junior at Hiroshima University: I passed the exam to go to the University of Michigan in the United States as an exchange student for one year.

In that one year at the University of Michigan, I, for the first time, met people from different cultures, as I had dreamt, but I also learned a lot about using English for communicative purposes. This was my first step toward becoming a full-fledged L2 academic writer. Because I had not learned to write more than a paragraph in English before, I had much to learn in the freshman composition class I took during the first semester. In the first class, the teacher told us that there are some rules in English composition we have to follow, but that if we follow the rules, anybody can write a reasonably good composition. The teacher's statement sounded like God's blessing to me, as I was already struggling with the quantity of the writing requirements in the other classes. The 'rules' I learned in the composition class included the concepts of unity and cohesion, which have since helped my English writing a great deal. I also learned several effective patterns of paragraph development such as 'cause and effect' or 'comparison and contrast.' Although I later learned that not all writers of English follow such rules and patterns, these rules were truly helpful for a new writer like me. Another important thing I learned in the freshmen composition class was the idea of writing as a process. I learned that a good end product can only be achieved through a long revising process. I had never learned such things either in my previous English or Japanese classes in Japan. The knowledge I gained in the freshman composition class at the University of Michigan made me realize that writing can be treated as a 'skill' you can improve if you are provided with proper training. Until then, I had believed that writing ability was a natural talent that could not be developed through training.

Although the freshman composition class was helpful, it was not sufficient to enable me to write 'reasonably good papers' in other content
courses. I was always asked by the professors to explain more. This was
partly because I lacked sufficient English proficiency, but I also felt it was
because writers are expected to 'explain more' in English than in Japanese. I
noticed that leaving it to the readers to infer my intentions or making them
'read between lines,' a strategy I used in writing Japanese, is not desirable
in English academic writing. When I wrote in English, I tried to make the
relationship between sentences as clear as possible, even if it appeared too
obvious to me. I also lacked writing fluency. I often got stuck while writing
because I couldn't think of good expressions for my ideas. I tried to cover
this lack of knowledge by doing as much reading of the given topic as
possible. The big (three inch thick!) Japanese–English dictionary I brought
from Japan was also helpful for finding appropriate expressions. I wrote
and rewrote my drafts of term papers many times before I submitted the
final draft. I went to a 'composition house' where advisors helped the
undergraduate students cope with their writing assignments. When I spent
a lot of time on a paper, the quality of the end product was relatively good (I
actually got an A minus for the first term paper I wrote for my English literature class!). But when time was limited, such as in an in-class written
examination, I tended to do very poorly. I always ran out of time, and often
received the lowest score in the class. I realized that I could never compete
with native speaking peers if I did only the same things. Consequently,
whenever I could choose, I looked for some aspects of the given topic where
I had more knowledge than American students did.

After I went back to Japan and graduated from Hiroshima University, I
spent a total of eight years studying TEFL and applied linguistics in three
graduate programs both in Japan and in the United States. When I became a
doctoral student at UCLA, I further specialized in the areas of language
testing and second language acquisition. During these eight years, I basically wrote papers in Japanese in Japan, and in English in the United States.
Several things I learned during these years could be applied to writing in
both languages, and other things to writing in only one language. One
example of the things that have been useful for writing in both languages
was my learning the K–J Method (Kawakita, 1967) just after I started my
graduate program at Hiroshima University in 1983. The method was developed by Prof. Jiro Kawakita for collecting, classifying, and synthesizing
necessary information for doing academic research. The method had originally been developed for getting insights from data obtained in fieldwork,
but it was later revised to be applicable to other research activities. Thus, I
learned to jot down whatever ideas came to my mind regarding whatever

research topic I was working on, and later sorting them out on cards so that one card would represent only one idea. Then I would spread all of these cards on the floor, and organize and reorganize them until these cards formed several meaningful groups. Finally, I would decide the sequential order of these groups to appear in my paper (this is a greatly simplified version of the actual procedure). I was especially inspired by Prof. Kawakita's idea underlying the K–J Method that the entire act of doing research can be treated as a collection of skills that can be learned by *anybody* given proper training. His idea encouraged me whenever I became skeptical about my ability to become a professional researcher. I faithfully followed the K–J Method for some time, and then gradually revised it so that it would best fit my research style (for example, Prof. Kawakita suggested using a certain type of card for taking notes, but I came to use regular notepaper simply because it was easier to obtain).

There were also other things I had to learn that could be applied to writing only in English or in Japanese. While reading books and papers published in journals in my field, I noticed that there are several typical ways of writing successful academic papers (especially ones based on quantitative studies) both in Japanese and in English. It was actually easier for me to learn the English ways of writing because the basic rules are similar to the 'rules' I had learned in the English composition class at the University of Michigan. I had much more difficulty learning the Japanese ways because I had never taken any academic writing classes in high school or at the university in Japan, and because there were very few 'manuals' for academic writing available for Japanese university students at that time (Kinoshita, 1990). I had to read a large number of published papers to find general patterns or 'rules'. This situation reminded me of the Japanese proverb 'skills should not be taught, but they should be *stolen* (by the disciple closely observing his/her master) to be successfully acquired.' I felt that this proverb could also hold true for the Japanese academic society I was in.

In contrast to the situation in Japanese, I found numerous manuals for academic writing in English. Some of them were especially useful for researchers in applied linguistics. For example, most of the professional journals in applied linguistics required the contributors to follow the *Publication Manual of the American Psychological Association*. It is quite a thick book (the present fourth edition is 368 pages) which provides the details of what should be included in a good and understandable research manuscript. As an L2 writer, I was happy to know that there existed such 'rules' that I could follow. Those rules reminded me of what my freshman composition teacher at the University of Michigan said: 'When you follow these rules, anybody can write a reasonably good paper'. This was still good advice. As in the case of general English writing, I have since found that not all researchers necessarily follow such 'rules' for writing good papers, and that the rules are somewhat different from subfield to subfield (e.g. second language writing, language testing, interlanguage pragmatics), but I still appreciate the fact that the field of applied linguistics appears to be tolerant of L2 writers' writing as long as it follow these 'rules'.

I also learned a great deal through actually writing papers. When I was studying in the United States, I had to take three or more classes a semester/quarter, and I usually had to write at least one paper for each class. Because the themes of those classes sometimes varied greatly, the topics of the papers I had to write also varied a great deal (although they were within the range of classes given for applied linguistics students). For example, in one language testing class I took at UCLA, I wrote a paper entitled 'A comparison of two methods for detecting differential item functioning in an ESL placement test', while at the same time for another class, I was writing a paper analyzing Americans' use of non-referential 'there' in spoken English. When I wrote those papers, I tried to look for some aspects of the topics for which I would have an advantage over American students, remembering the lessons I had learned at the University of Michigan. I thus used Japanese participants whenever possible. Being able to use the participants' L1 freely was especially helpful when I conducted case studies of children learning English as L2 (e.g. Sasaki, 1986, 1987), but even when I conducted experimental type studies, the qualitative data I could obtain in Japanese (e.g. through interviewing the participants after the experiments) provided insightful qualitative data to supplement the quantitative results (e.g. 1990, 1991c).

In addition to using such 'strategies,' I also rewrote my papers as many times as time allowed. When the final drafts were completed, I often asked a native speaker to proofread them. The papers always contained many grammatical mistakes even after I had made several revisions. At Georgetown University, I usually asked the advisors at the Study Skills Center for Foreign Students to help me. At UCLA, I was fortunate to be able to often ask Bob Jacobs, a colleague in the graduate program, to read my drafts. As a fine graduate student in applied linguistics himself, Bob checked not only the linguistic surface of my drafts, but also the overall organization and coherence. His comments were sometimes critical, but always constructive. After receiving his comments, I often spent a sleepless night before I was able to complete the corrected version of the final draft, but such efforts were often rewarded by good grades. Finally, when the professors returned my papers, I also learned much from their comments.

Their comments ranged from grammatical corrections to suggestions for better content and organization. Most of the comments were so encouraging that I sometimes further revised the papers even after the classes were over, and submitted them for publication in professional journals (Sasaki, 1991a, 1991b, 1997 are three course papers that were eventually good enough to be published after many such revisions.)

And that is the process that led to that lucky fall day in 1989 when my paper was first accepted by *Language Learning*. After the first happy feeling faded, I was overwhelmed by the quantity of changes I had to make. I went to Evelyn Hatch, the professor who supervised my writing for that particular paper, and showed her the reviewers' comments. She encouraged me to resubmit the paper, saying that it is very common to make many revisions before one's paper is published. On a computer screen, Evelyn showed me a detailed sample letter responding to each of the given reviewers' comments. She then tailored the letter so that it would better fit my case by adding some sentences that would 'sell' my particular revisions to the editor (winking as she explained this to me). Subsequently, the letter guided me throughout the entire process of resubmitting the paper. Without Evelyn's help and encouragement, I might have given up going through such a troublesome procedure. I have treasured that sample letter, and still refer to it when I have to resubmit my papers.

After such a long period of apprenticeship, I started to teach English and applied linguistics at a Japanese university in 1991. As a researcher, I have continued to work in the areas of language testing and second language acquisition, hoping to bridge the gap between these two areas. Thus, the topics of the papers I have written since 1991 include comparing two methods that measure English L2 students' speech act production ability (Sasaki, 1998a) and development of an analytic rating scale for Japanese L1 writing (Sasaki & Hirose, 1999). I have also become very interested in L2 writing (probably because I have had such difficulty acquiring English writing skill myself), and have conducted several studies on the product and process of Japanese students' writing in English (e.g. Sasaki & Hirose, 1996, Sasaki, 1998b). Based on these studies, I have written an average of one paper a year to submit for publication in professional journals.

Because I have sometimes been puzzled by journal editors' decisions (both their rejection and acceptance), I once wanted to know more about the publication processes in my field, and in 1997 took a weekend seminar at Temple University, Japan, on 'Writing for Publication' taught by Professor Sandra McKay, then editor of *TESOL Quarterly*. In the seminar, I learned more 'rules' of writing academic papers such as 'read and follow closely the specific guidelines for submission usually given in the front or back page(s) of each issue', or 'read the articles in at least several back issues of the journal you want to submit your papers to, and look for its "tastes" (what types of papers it tends to publish) as well as the quality of the papers published there'. I was impressed by Professor MacKay's efforts to teach the students the most efficient way to publish their papers. The knowledge we gained in her seminar may be difficult to get access to unless explicitly taught at such seminars, because such knowledge usually remains tacit and exclusively the property of those who are successful. I have never heard of such a course given to Japanese L1 writers in Japan. Here again, Japanese researchers may think that such knowledge should be 'stolen' rather than given, as the old Japanese proverb goes.

One last thing I would like to add regarding my growth as a professional L2 writer is my recent experiences as a reviewer. For the past several years, I have been given opportunities to be on selection committees for journal publication or research funding. Being on the selecting side, the other side of the coin, has shown me yet another perspective. The most important thing I have learned is that even the most established researchers' papers are not perfect when they are first submitted. Just like my own manuscripts, they are often revised many times before they become the final refined products. Furthermore, I have learned that manuscripts or proposals can be accepted in spite of apparent shortcomings if they have a point (or points) significantly appealing to the readers. I have been amazed by some of those researchers' efforts to complete long and thorough revisions if their papers have the slightest possibility of being published.

Such experiences as a reviewer have not only encouraged me as a researcher, but also have taught me an important lesson for teaching L2 writing. As with my own experience, L2 learners are often shown only the almost-perfect-looking end-products of writing in their textbooks. Unless the teacher points out that those end-products can only be achieved through many hard-earned revisions, and that the first drafts are usually far from perfect, learners tend to make the mistake of assuming that those writers (especially native speakers) can write perfectly from the very beginning. Because L2 learners (as well as L1 writers) cannot write so perfectly from the beginning, this misunderstanding can have negative effects. I therefore think that L2 teachers should show their students the entire process of a good piece of writing, so that their students can see that the final product is actually the result of many drafting stages. If the text is written by a non-native speaker, and if the final draft looks as good as the ones written by a native speaker, it would be even more encouraging. Knowing that they can start with a rough, imperfect draft, L2 learners will surely feel less hesitant to write in L2.

Although I have now been studying English for as long as 28 years, I still have great difficulty putting my thoughts into acceptable English. I often get stuck because I cannot think of appropriate expressions. Because I don't read anything in English except academic papers, my vocabulary stock is still quite limited. In short, it takes me a long time to complete a refined final draft in English. On the other hand, when I write papers in Japanese, I am often surprised by the speed. I can finish one paper in about one fifth of the time I need for finishing an English paper. The time difference is quite shocking. Is it still worth the effort to write papers in English? I sometimes wonder. But then I think of the comments I have received from researchers around the world after my papers have been published in international journals. Those are the people I could not have reached if I had not written in English. Their comments have inspired me, and have sometimes opened a whole new world of research to me. Meeting those researchers at conferences is always fun and rewarding. All those things cheer me up, and so, I gather up all my courage again, and try to write another first draft in English.

References

Kawakita, J. (1967) *Hassouhou* [Abduction: Ways of Producing New Ideas]. Tokyo: Chuoukouronsha.

Kinoshita, K. (1981) *Rikakei no Sakubun Gijutu* [Writing Techniques for Science Writing]. Tokyo: Chuo Koronsha.

Kinoshita, K. (1990) *Repooto no Kumitatekata* [How to Write a Report]. Tokyo: Chikuma Shobou.

Sasaki, M. (1986) Second language acquisition: A case study. Unpublished master's thesis, Georgetown University, Washington, D.C.

Sasaki, M. (1987) Interlanguage development: A case study of a child. Unpublished master's thesis, Hiroshima University, Hiroshima, Japan.

Sasaki, M. (1990) Topic prominence in Japanese EFL students' existential constructions. *Language Learning* 40, 337–368.

Sasaki, M. (1991a) An analysis of sentences with nonreferential *there* in spoken American English. *Word: Journal of the International Linguistic Association* 42, 157–178.

Sasaki, M. (1991b) A comparison of two methods for detecting differential item functioning in an ESL placement test. *Language Testing* 8, 95–111.

Sasaki, M. (1991c) Relationships among second language proficiency, foreign language aptitude, and intelligence: A structural equation modeling approach. Unpublished doctoral dissertation, University of California, Los Angeles.

Sasaki, M. (1993a) Relationships among second language proficiency, foreign language aptitude, and intelligence: A structural equation modeling approach. *Language Learning* 43, 313–344.

Sasaki, M. (1993b) Relationships among second language proficiency, foreign language aptitude, and intelligence: A protocol analysis. *Language Learning* 43, 469–505.

Sasaki, M. (1997) Topic continuity in Japanese-English interlanguage. *International Review of Applied Linguistics* 35, 1–21.

Sasaki, M. (1998a) Investigating EFL students' production of speech acts: A comparison of production questionnaires and role plays. *Journal of Pragmatics* 30, 457–484.

Sasaki, M. (1998b) Toward an empirical model of L2 writing process. Paper presented at the third Pacific Second Language Research Forum, Aoyama Gakuin University, Tokyo.

Sasaki, M. (2000) Effects of cultural schemata on students' test-taking processes for cloze tests: A multiple data source approach. *Language Testing* 17, 85–114.

Sasaki, M. and Hirose, K. (1996) Explanatory variables for EFL students' expository writing. *Language Learning* 46, 137–174.

Sasaki, M. and Hirose, K. (1999) Development of an analytic rating scale for Japanese L1 writing. *Language Testing* 16, 457–478.

Writing from Chinese to English: My Cultural Transformation

Jun Liu was born in a small town in Jiangsu Province, China. Growing up during the Great Cultural Revolution, Jun came very close to pursuing a career in Beijing Opera. After teaching college English at Suzhou University for ten years, he went to the US to obtain a doctorate in Foreign/Second Language Education at The Ohio State University. He is now an assistant professor of English at the University of Arizona. A recipient of the 1999 Newbury House Teaching Excellence Award and author of more than two dozen publications in ESL/EFL teaching and classroom research in both Chinese and English, Jun is currently completing a book on Asian

students' classroom communication patterns in US universities, to be published by Ablex. He is also co-authoring another book, on peer response in the L2 writing classroom, to be published by the University of Michigan Press.

I was born in a family of four in a little town in southeastern China. I don't know whether this is the family trait or fate, but all four of us, my parents, my sister and I, make a living by teaching, and all of us, except for my mother, are associated with the TESOL profession. My father is a retired teacher who taught high school English in China for more than 35 years. My mother is also retired from teaching, having been a physical education instructor for more than twenty years in the same school as my father used to teach in. My sister has been teaching English in a local teachers' college for more than a decade, and my own first English-teaching experience was in a teachers' college in China. I am now teaching both ESL composition and teacher training courses in a major research institute in the United States.

I grew up in a critical historical period in China – what is called the Great Cultural Revolution. All the intellectuals were supposed to be cultivated through working in the countryside and living with farmers and peasants. Criticism and self-criticism were the regular practice to show good will, and the intensive study and memorization of political slogans and quotations from Mao Zedong, then the Chairman of the Communist Party, were a daily routine. Anything related to Western culture had to be abandoned, and anything coming from abroad had to be confiscated. A sense of security was always absent while sleeping at home as once in a while the Red Guards (those left-wing high school students with their left arms wrapped up with red cloth on which *Hong Wei Bing*, Red Guards, was written) would stop by without notice for revolutionary inspection. Their disturbance, aimed at searching for proofs of ideological and spiritual pollution, was sanctioned by the Communist Party. As my father was an English teacher, he was one of the suspicious targets who were thought to be poisoned by Western thoughts and by being in possession of Western books. I remember helping my father remove from our bookshelves many, many English books he had purchased in second-hand bookstores when he was a student in East China Normal University in Shanghai in the late 40s and early 50s. As we did not have a basement, we strategically hid those books underneath our beds, and covered the books with sheets. I also remember how much fun it was to display on the bookshelves as conspicuously as possible all sorts of works by Marx, Lenin, and Chairman Mao – almost all in red and golden colors. I found the days when I was excused from school due to sickness particularly fascinating as I could be left alone at home with the doors shut and concentrate for hours and hours on going through all the books underneath our beds, looking for the portraits of long-bearded Westerners like Ben Jonson and John Milton. I began to be acquainted with the names of Lord Byron, Percy Bysshe Shelley, William Shakespeare, John Milton, Charles Dickens, and Jack London.

One day when I mentioned some of these English names in a family conversation, my father was genuinely shocked. While warning me of the 'danger' of these books, my father encouraged my sister and me to start reading 'Rip van Winkle' from Washington Irving's *Sketch Book*. It was indeed a challenge, as it was so different from what my sister and I were taught through the radio or in school slogans such as 'Long Live Chairman Mao', 'A long, long life to the Communist Party', and quotations from Mao Zedong translated from Chinese into English. My father was very patient, and used to tell us that, even though the story was difficult for us to read, once we understood it and committed it to memory, our school work would become a piece of cake, a theory very unlike Krashen's Comprehensible Input. But it worked well because we trusted our father and we did understand and enjoy the story of the Catskill Mountains, although we filled the book with notes, Chinese characters, and phonetic symbols. My sister and I were very competitive. She obviously had a better memory and I still don't know why, but I was proud of having more dramatic, if not better, pronunciation as I amused myself in varying my intonation to sound different from my reading of Chinese. When both of us were eventually able to recite the first few pages of the story, we were all amazed, and we began to lay our hands on more books, such as Charlotte Brontë's *Jane Eyre*, Charles Dickens' *David Copperfield*, and Emily Brontë's *Wuthering Heights*. We started practicing retelling chapters, but found it too difficult to write them. At that time, I was fourteen.

I was one of the top students in all the subjects at junior high school, and especially outstanding in Chinese and English. I remember that my Chinese compositions were usually displayed in class as good models simply because I followed the good models from textbooks. In Chinese language classes, we usually wrote four or five compositions per semester, practicing different rhetorical modes, such as narrative, expository, and argumentative essays. Each assignment was given after studying a model essay in a Chinese textbook, and one of the criteria for evaluating our compositions was to see how well we imitated the style of the model essays. As the Chinese language is full of four-character idioms, the proper use of idioms is highly regarded as a symbol of success in writing. This was partially the way that reading and writing were connected – identifying and understanding the idioms in reading and using them appropriately in writing. As I recall, we did not do multiple drafts for our composition writing, as it was too labor-intensive for teachers owing to the fact that there were at least forty or fifty students in a class. In addition, as neither computers nor typewriters were available at that time, I had to give a lot of thought to each essay before I actually wrote it down to save time in copying and recopying, and also to save paper. That formed my habit of sketching and outlining many times to compensate for multiple drafting. I also recall that there were no peer review activities because of the nature of competitiveness coupled by the emphasis on independent writing without consultation with others in class. We had to be critical of our own writing through self-criticism, a skill acquired as the result of numerous cultural and political movements in China. When I wrote in Chinese, grammar was never an issue. What distinguishes a good composition from a not-so-good one seems to be the richness of language and vocabulary and organization. I know I was often constrained by model compositions; any difference in style and organization between what you were supposed to write and what you actually wrote was discouraged. The philosophy is clear: the teacher knows how to make you a good writer, and obeying the teacher and following the instruction is what you are supposed to do. Any variation is a violation of proper student behavior and thus the consequence of little learning is blamed on the students themselves.

Although I consider myself a good writer in Chinese, I wish I could be better. I always feel the lack of variety in my writing as a result of the lack of extensive reading. Reading Chairman Mao's works over and over again until I could automatically recite them did not help me a lot in expanding my vocabulary in writing, and the fact that reading ancient poems and essays was not encouraged at school because of the political climate also denied me the solid foundation of ancient Chinese writing abilities. This was debilitating to many people in my generation who grew up during the Cultural Revolution.

Nevertheless, my family environment had a great impact on my abilities in reading both classic Chinese literature and English novels and essays. My father always got up early in the morning and, with a cup of tea, he sometimes read aloud ancient Chinese poems with a special tone he acquired in the early 30s when he was a school kid, or novels like *Gulliver's Travels* and *The Scarlet Letter*, in the tiny courtyard where we could only see the sky if we sat in the center of the yard. I woke up many times amidst his enthusiasm in reading and I remember being challenged to read aloud a paragraph or two of whatever he was reading before I had breakfast. Gradually, I found I had a talent in reading aloud both Chinese poems and English novels, which must be associated with my interest and practice in Peking Opera and stage performance. As I recall, in order to play the major role, Li Yuehe, in one of the model Peking Operas, *The Red Lantern*, I had to try hard to compete in the audition with the other candidates at school. I used to climb up the mountain in my hometown to practice singing early in the morning. In this way, no one could notice me in the midst of the woods and rocks before sunrise, and I could try all sorts of voice variations without feeling inhibited or noticed. I always carried an English book with me, as my father would not allow me to go without it, and I thus practiced reading aloud an English essay or a poem, and this, I believe, had a great impact on my expressiveness in both L1 and L2 writing. I often jotted down from whatever I was reading the expressions and sentences I was amazed at, and particularly those I would never have thought about using in Chinese. Owing to the lack of the language environment, communication in English through either the spoken or written channel was almost impossible. Practicing writing in English, therefore, was also hard as there was no source of instrumental motivation. So my focus was on accumulating what I would call idiomatic English by reading and note-taking, and thus this was my 'silent period' in English writing.

I was fortunate to escape from settling down in the countryside upon my graduation from high school, as the first-born in a family, my sister in this case, was forced to live among peasants in a suburban area outside my hometown. She was adrift and confused as to what to do in the future as many other young people were at that time. I, meanwhile, went to help her on summer vacations and during weekends. While she was out in the field cutting rice or spreading manure with bare hands and feet, I went fishing and cooked meals with the catch of the day to reward her. We spent many days like that, and sometimes we switched positions when she badly needed a breather. Upon graduation from high school, I was assigned to work in a city hospital and was trained to be a lab technician, taking blood samples of patients and analyzing the blood under a microscope. After six months, I was bored and also aimless. My sister and I did not know what the future would hold for us, and we lost all our interest in learning English. I started playing violin, and became a comedian, indulging myself in making people laugh without laughing myself, and was very active on the stage in my spare time. My sister applied for a substitute teaching position in a local elementary school, trying to escape from the manure-filled farm-lands. My parents were busy working, and none of us was optimistic about the future. Going to college and university was something we could not hope for, as only those who were politically outstanding would be recommended by the Communist Party. That was the toughest time in my life. I remember my parents argued many times. While my father insisted on my hard work in English and math, my mother wanted me to develop my interest in becoming an actor. I, too, was confused.

In 1977, with the downfall of the 'Gang of Four', the college entrance examination system was restored. It was the first time in a decade that fair competition for university enrollment was in effect. Both my sister and I tried and, though we were very rusty in our knowledge about many subjects examined, both of us made it. I was enrolled in a provincial Teachers' College, and majored in English. The ratio of college enrollment was one out of a hundred as we had accumulated ten years' of high school graduates. This was also the first time I left my parents. After the diagnostic tests upon enrollment, I was placed in an intermediate-level class – which was quite a blow to me. I thought I could have done better, but I accepted the fact. Extremely competitive, I was determined to make it to the top as I always did.

Learning a tune should be done through daily practice, just like learning to box, as an old Chinese saying goes. So should the learning of writing. I felt so awkward in writing my first English composition at college, 'My favorite teacher'. In this essay, I featured my elementary class master, Yi

Shen, who, believing that one day I could become a mathematician or engineer, always argued with my music teacher for taking too much of my time in practicing Beijing Opera. I started with an introduction and a thesis stating that she had the greatest impact on my early school life. Then I provided three examples to show why Yi Shen was my favorite teacher. The essay ends with a classic tone that she was one of those teachers who would always be in my memory. It was an OK paper, but I later realized that if I had been asked to write this paper in Chinese, I would have written in exactly the same way. So, what's the rhetorical difference between Chinese and English? I was puzzled. I felt very uncomfortable in the initial stages of English writing, not because of a lack of ideas to write about, but because of a lack of knowledge of what constituted a good paper in English. Unfortunately, we did not have English composition courses *per se* while I was at college, partly due to the lack of faculty, and partly due to the fact that many faculty members in that department believed that literature courses and grammar lessons were more important. Composition should be secondary. Therefore, I had no formal training in English composition while at college.

I had neither opportunities nor motivation to write in English upon graduation with a BA in English language and literature. Fortunately, I was recommended to remain at the English Department to join the faculty to teach methodology courses and supervise student teachers. In fact, my acting skills through years of Peking Opera and experience in stage performance as a result of the Cultural Revolution helped me a lot with humor and poise in class, and I was later told that my demonstration class in a junior school got me the job. One of the challenges I set for myself as methods instructor was to deliver the content in English. Although I was quite fluent in English at that time, to explain second language acquisition theories and teaching strategies in English was artificial to me as I sounded like I was repeating what I read from the books. I wished my L2 writing were strong enough to synthesize what I had read in the same way as I could in my L1. But I have to confess, I was teaching Chinese students English Methodology in English in China, and therefore, I could never get past a sense of artificiality and comedy in facing a large group of homogeneous students who shared an L1 and culture with me. I regurgitated in English what was known to the students: teaching principles set up by the Chinese Ministry of Education.

I started practicing English writing once in a while, but I was not motivated enough to keep it up. First, there was no instrumental motivation for me as language teaching journals in China only accepted articles written in Chinese, and secondly, there was no sharing of my writings, as I felt uncomfortable asking my colleagues to read my papers since I was afraid of losing face. Revealing my mistakes to those I worked with in China was indeed an embarrassment. The lack of the need as well as a sense of self-protection through avoidance had a negative impact on my L2 writing.

Quite frankly, by the time I came to the United States as a Ph.D. student in foreign and second language education at a major research institution in 1991, I was not competent in L2 writing. Although I had no trouble expressing myself in English, I was not familiar with the standards of academic writing. I remember the first assignment I had in an education course I took – an essay introducing myself as a language learner. I spent hours and hours composing the essay, and yet, with great disappointment, the paper turned out to be a Chinese composition in English, although the instructor did not comment on this. It did not read how I had hoped though I used lots of idiomatic expressions. I was so frustrated with this experience, which was aggravated when I was placed in an advanced ESL composition course the first week I started my Ph.D. program. I was quite embarrassed and even felt humiliated to be placed in the same class with those whom I could have taught. It was excusable for the majority of the students whose majors are not English to take ESL composition courses at various levels, but the fact that my ten years of English teaching did not make me a good L2 writer made me feel sad and disappointed. However, I went through this course and was given ample opportunities to practice academic writing. I benefited from multiple drafts, tutorials and peer reviews, which we never did in China. Although, because of my professional sensitivity, I sometimes disagreed with the instructor in his handling of the class, I did see the need to take ESL writing courses even for advanced learners like me. Exposing my weaknesses in writing, and being helped, are learning in themselves.

When I write in Chinese, I tend to concentrate on the organization and the presentation of the ideas I want to convey logically and idiomatically in the paper. However, when I began to write in English, I intentionally tried to focus on syntax and structure, and thus lost a lot of the spontaneity and creativity a good paper needs. It took me a while to forget about grammar in my L2 writing when I started writing my personal journals, several times a week, and tried to express myself without worrying about grammar. I also tried to practice writing in different genres, from narratives to critiques, and from argumentation to research proposals, which enabled me to become more sensitive in reading and more careful in writing.

As I reflect on my L2 writing experience, I tend to associate it with the use of computers. I find it fascinating how composing on a computer affected my way of thinking and way of writing. Using a computer was a totally new experience for me when I came to the United States, and I remember one day spending hours and hours in a lab typing a three-page essay and yet losing everything before I could print it out. What fascinated me most was writing on a computer screen, which not only made me feel at ease in controlling and revising what had been written through 'cut and paste', but also satisfied my ego as everything written was 'beautiful' in font and 'professional' in format, thus adding aesthetic appeal to the composing process. I was often amazed at how much more I could write and how fast I could compose on the computer screen as compared to handwriting on Chinese square sheets with each character taking a square.

One of my goals in ESL writing is to publish. Publishing in English is much more challenging than publishing in Chinese. I remember when I was a second-year Ph.D. student, I wrote a review about a methodology book in TESOL which was written by a well-known scholar in the field. Encouraged by a professor, I was very enthusiastic and submitted it to one of the leading journals in the field. Unfortunately, it was immediately rejected simply because I was a student. I was told that only peers who are faculty members could have the status to write book reviews for that journal. However, this discouraging experience did not prevent me from submitting it to another journal. To my surprise, this time it was accepted. This inspiring experience of my first English publication marked the beginning of my professional career in the US, and I also gained the confidence in L2 writing which I had obtained long before in my L1 writing.

It was the third year into my Ph.D. program, and after I had completed my Ph.D. general examinations, when I decided to apply for a TA (teaching associate) position in the ESL Composition Program. Thanks to the program director's global vision and open-mindedness, I was immediately hired. Going through the hiring process did provoke moments of anxiety, but I felt empowered to be in a position where I could encourage those ESL students who had not yet experienced how important and rewarding it was to be competent L2 writers. For the first time in my life I felt that I was accepted as a member of the target community. Needless to say, in order to live up to the expectations, I started teaching ESL composition with great enthusiasm and effort, believing that I could uniquely contribute to the program by sharing my pains and gains as an ESL writer with my ESL students. In the ESL composition classroom, I encountered both suspicion and admiration from my students. The suspicion usually came from those who walked into my classes with presumptions that their English teachers in the US should be native English speakers, which is quite understandable. When the reluctance and indifference shown on the students' faces in the first few classes were greeted with smiles and understanding, when their names carrying more than ten syllables were pronounced distinctly, when anecdotes of my experience in learning English and my own struggles in writing were shared with them, and when their first assignment was returned with my constructive comments, suggestions and encouragement, their suspicion about me was soon replaced with comfort, trust, and admiration.

It is true that I am not a native speaker of English, and never will be. But the quality of teaching a language is not determined by whether you are a native speaker or a non-native speaker, assuming sociolinguistic competence is achieved. I believe that the language I speak and the way I teach could make a difference in the students' perception of me as a Chinese teaching English in the US. I remind myself constantly that I am teaching English in an English environment. The only way I can make up for my lack of nativeness is by being aware of my non-nativeness, which will keep me aiming high. To me, a journey of self-cultivation and refinement usually ends when one no longer feels such needs. The success of a non-native speaker ESL professional lies more in his/her modesty than in dignity. My students liked me because I did not hesitate in assuring them that I needed to consult my native-speaker colleagues about a word, a phrase, or a sentence in question. My students liked me because I would give them opportunities to share their dilemmas in class, their difficulties and their actual procedures in completing a certain writing task as compared with mine in doing the same task. My students liked me because they felt comfortable in commenting on summaries and papers including mine. In my ESL composition classes, I encourage peer review, peer editing and collaborative writing, in which I am usually a part. I do peer reviews with my students as one of them, doing the same task and participating in discussion without dominating it. To me, empowering our students through empathy is the beauty of being a non-native speaker teacher – sailing with our students to the shore instead of summoning them from the shore. Although my experience indicates that peer review as well as open class discussion might not appeal to many ESL students who come from cultures that do not encourage these activities, I feel that keeping these activities in ESL classrooms will not only help student writers, but also create supportive communities through which ESL students could build their new identities to cope with the target culture. To me, teaching L2 writing to ESL students without helping them establish their L2 social identities is a disappointing endeavor. Reading students' papers constantly reminds me of my own struggles in searching for an L2 identity through writing. Being able to discuss and share with my students the dilemma and conflicts in the process of writing academic papers also convinces me that the key to improving one's L2 writing lies in the willingness to observe L2 writing conventions, the persistence in writing what has not been practiced before, reliance on multiple feedback, and the confidence built up in the course of publication.

In teaching L2 writing as a way to facilitate ESL students' cultural transformation and establishing their L2 identity, I encountered many dilemmas. Would my prescribing to my students what to write restrict their thoughts and expressions? Would my upholding academic standards do a great disservice by inhibiting them in reflecting on their own cultures and ideologies? Would my required dense assignments of reading and writing for the course burden them to such an extent that they become resistant in learning? Would the use of my earlier writings as samples to reveal my writing experience reduce their opportunities of reading a greater variety of articles? Would my emphasis on their discourse in writing discourage them from concentrating on eliminating grammatical errors? As I kept on thinking about these questions, I became clearer about my own source of motivation in learning L2 writing and in establishing myself as a good L2 writer. It is the establishment of my own L2 identity that makes me a good L2 writer. Likewise, it is the constant practice in L2 writing that helps me establish my L2 identity. Therefore, the L2 writing experience and the L2 social identity co-exist and they reinforce each other. Admittedly, my Chinese way of thinking has a great impact on how I compose in English, but I realize that in order to maintain my L2 literacy and L2 social identity, I have to understand the fundamental thinking processes of the target culture, and the way that my L1 culture can be accepted. I gradually become accustomed to American discourse and rhetoric through constant reading and writing, and the efforts I have made in adapting my writing style to fit the general preference of the American audience has been rewarded by a few publications. But that does not mean that I have lost my Chinese writing style. I still see the legitimacy and beauty of Chinese writing even though I do not practice it in US academia.

I believe that writing is a skill: the more you practice it, the better your writing is. I have been in the United States for almost seven years: five years as a Ph.D. student and two as a TESOL professional. I have published more than ten papers and reviews in English and given more than a dozen presentations at professional conferences. I have enjoyed my L2 writing experience as much as, if not more than, my L1 writing experience. Writing for me has become a pleasurable activity as I see it as a channel to communicate with other TESOL professionals about my research findings. I feel so lucky that my colleagues are very supportive and collaborative, and constantly discussing professional issues with them has sharpened my vision in academic writing. I feel I have so much to write about, and I also feel the more I write, the better I can write. Whenever my students ask me how they can improve their L2 writing skills, I would say, keep on writing in English every day, and your writing will take care of itself.

I won't say that I am an excellent writer in English, because you can tell that I write in English with a shadow of Chinese, but I know I have the confidence in communicating what I wish to express. If everyone conforms to one style in academic writing, then where is the richness of writing?

Part II: Crossing Cultures Across the Disciplines

Learning Is a Lifelong Process

Ming-Daw Tsai received his B.Sc. in chemistry from National Taiwan University, Taipei, in 1972, and his Ph.D. from Purdue University in 1978, working with Heinz. G. Floss. He is currently Professor of Chemistry at The Ohio State University. The honours he has received include Alfred P. Sloan Fellow, 1983-1985; Camille and Henry Dreyfus Teacher-Scholar, 1985–1990; The Ohio State University Distinguished Scholar Award, 1992; and Elected Fellow, American Association for the Advancement of Science, 1992. He has served in the following national panels: NIH Physical Biochemistry Study Section Member, 1988-1992; Co-chair, Gordon Conference on  Enzymes, 1993; NIH Training Grant Study Section, 1997-present; Nominating Committee, American Chemical Society Division of Biological Chemistry, 1997-1998; Board of Consulting Editors, *Bioorganic & Medicinal Chemistry*, 1998-present; Board of Consulting Editors, *Bioorganic & Medicinal Chemistry Letters*, 1998-present. In 1995, he became Director, Campus Chemical Instrument Center, and took on the role of program director of Ohio State's Chemistry/Biology Interface Training Program. His primary research interest lies in the interface between chemistry and biology, specifically, the structure-function relationship of enzymes and proteins

Chemistry is an experimental science. Thus, one would think that a chemistry professor should spend most of the time in the laboratory. However, for right or wrong reasons, I now spend more than half of my time writing in my office. The proportion of writing in my daily work has been increasing throughout my career. At first it was only recording experimental procedures. Then you need to write a thesis and research papers. Upon becoming a professor, writing research proposals became an important responsibility since the first step of doing research is to obtain funding. As more and more students and postdoctoral researchers joined my research group, it became impractical for me to work in the lab since there were more proposals and research papers to write. Editing the writing of students also became an important part of my job.

The need to do writing is further enhanced by the progressing of computer technology. For many of us, writing e-mail messages has gradually substituted for telephone conversations. E-mails are free in most cases. They are instant. You write and send them whenever you want, and no one will put you on hold.

Of course I am talking about writing in English, which is my second language. My native language is Chinese. Writing in Chinese is almost like an art. I don't know what fraction of the entire population speak and write English, but I do know that English is the international language in science. I have written well over 100 scientific papers in chemistry and biochemistry. Not a single one was written in Chinese.

Writing in a second language is not easy. However, it is no more difficult than writing in your mother language, if you consider that the most important aspect of writing is to communicate your thoughts or your research finding to a specific audience, in an effective way. In other words, language skill can be learned, but it is only one of the skills you need to learn to write well.

I grew up in Taiwan and completed my college education and two years of military service there, before going to Purdue University to pursue my Ph.D. degree. We spoke Taiwanese at home, and learned Mandarin in school. Taiwanese and Mandarin are two of the numerous dialects of Chinese, but they are different enough that you would not understand the other unless you had learned it. Fortunately there is only one written language in Chinese, which we learned from grade school through college.

I also understand a little spoken Japanese, mainly because my parents used to talk to each other in Japanese. They were educated in Japanese when Taiwan was under the occupation by Japan. They, of course, also learned Taiwanese and Chinese, and later English as well. They immigrated to the US about a decade ago and have been surviving well in this large melting pot. In fact they are a melting pot by themselves: they were told they were Japanese under Japan's occupation; then they thought they were Taiwanese after Japan left; shortly thereafter, the Nationalist government of the Republic of China moved to Taiwan and my parents soon learned that they are Chinese. And now they are Americans.

While studying chemistry at Purdue University, I married my wife, also a graduate student from Taiwan. However, she could not speak Taiwanese since her family moved to Taiwan late, around the time the Nationalist government moved there. So Mandarin became my daily language at home, and our children learned Mandarin at home and in a Sunday Chinese school. As much as we have tried to enforce Chinese speaking at home, my children gradually switched to English when they reached their teens. At some point, they would rather not speak if they were forced to speak in Chinese, so we gave up and my family became dual-lingual again. I say dual-lingual instead of bilingual because they are different. Bilingual people are good at both languages. Dual-lingual means there are two languages being used because part of the family are more comfortable in speaking Chinese and the other part in English.

Even though I am familiar with at least two languages, I never think I am good at language – writing, reading, or speaking. From elementary school to high school, there was only one goal in the minds of most students: to get into a good college. This is hard to understand for American people, since almost everyone who wishes to attend college can do so here. In Taiwan and many other Asian countries, there is only one chance in a year – a joint college entrance examination – to get into college. You fill out your priority for various colleges and departments and then take a two-day national examination. On the basis of your total score you are assigned a school and a department. Only 30–40% of students at any time can get into a college, and far fewer can get into one of their top choices.

I succeeded in getting into the top university in Taiwan, and a highly ranked department (chemistry) at the time. My examination score must have ranked in the top 1% if not better. This one-time success determined that I would spend the rest of my life in chemistry. Everything looked great, but not so in terms of my reading and writing skills. The entire educational curriculum was designed so you can do well in the college entrance exam. Since I chose science to be my field, literature reading and writing was hardly emphasized.

English was a required course throughout middle and high schools. It was also one of the subjects in the college entrance exam. Thus English was highly emphasized, perhaps more so than Chinese. Many of us continued to take English classes throughout college, since many of us considered college a 'preparatory school' to graduate school. Since there were very few graduate programs in Taiwan at that time, we had to, and also wanted to, go abroad – to pursue American dreams. We studied hard for TOEFL, which was almost like the entrance exam to the US.

Then came a shock – after ten years of intensive study in English and a successful TOEFL, you couldn't speak when you arrived in America. The shock is felt both ways. The academic institutions that admitted the students on the basis of their outstanding record in science and English find that some of the students can hardly speak or write. There are numerous stories related to this experience, one goes like this: A foreign student met his advisor for the first time. At the end of the meeting the advisor said 'see you later' and left. The student sat there for hours waiting for the advisor to come back later and continue the meeting. Of course, not all stories are amusing. The academic institutions face serious problems because many of these students are supposed to serve as teaching assistants. They constantly have to deal with complaints from students that their teaching assistants could not speak English.

There are various reasons why so many of us did not learn English well. Learning a second language in your native country is never easy because you have few chances to practice. You can study science or practice the violin alone, but you can't really converse in English with yourself. The quality of teachers is another problem. At the time of my education, going abroad was uncommon. Most people who had the opportunity to study abroad would probably be teaching in colleges, not in middle schools. Thus our teachers learned English the same way – without practice. Thus we learned grammar in depth and performed well in exams, but had no real experience in speaking and writing. Reading is better since many of the scientific textbooks were written in English.

You would think that, once you live in a foreign country, you will quickly become fluent in the second language. This is true for some, but not others. Most foreign students, including myself, struggled because we were in a real world – all lectures were given in English. One major obstacle to English learning at this stage is that, since we were a hemisphere away from home, we tended to live and play with our fellow friends from Taiwan and speak Chinese. Another major obstacle is the pronunciation. Even if you can listen and can speak English fluently, your speaking may not be easily understandable because your pronunciation is incorrect. This is the most difficult to fix, since it has to do with fundamental differences between English and Chinese.

One thing I found most useful during my graduate school at Purdue is that my advisor recommended me to attend an 'English speech clinic'. This is not a regular English class for foreign students. Instead, the program trained students for skills in teaching children or adults with speech difficulty, and we were recruited as their training objects. This may sound a little insulting since I did not have a speech disability. However, because the program got into the very fundamental way of pronunciation, it turned out to be extremely useful.

The biggest progress I made during my graduate studies was in writing – from nearly ground zero to being able to write research papers and Ph.D. dissertation. The experimental procedures and results are usually not too difficult to write because they can just be plain statements of what happened. The discussion section, however, is very difficult. There are two separate but related issues in writing the discussion. One is to interpret your results to the maximal significance without overstating the significance; the other is to use proper wording for your statements. The first lesson I learned was not to say that I have 'proven' something. The word 'prove' is far too strong in most chemistry papers unless you are Newton or Einstein, while it may be very appropriate in mathematics. Chemistry results are based on experiments performed under a set of defined conditions. While the results can 'suggest' or 'indicate' something, they are usually not sufficient to prove a theory – which usually requires very extensive experiments under many different conditions. Another difficulty in writing discussions is that, while scientists are encouraged to be imaginative and to propose novel ideas, an inexperienced writer can often mislead readers into thinking that what he or she proposes are facts.

Then came the next shock: when I started looking for a faculty position in chemistry, I realized that I was far away from being well prepared to perform the major parts of my job – teaching freshman chemistry to a large audience, and writing research proposals and papers independently without the assistance of my advisor. The teaching problem was compounded by my lack of natural ability in public speaking. Even to speak in Chinese to a large audience would be difficult for me. However, everything takes practice. After so many years I now enjoy giving lectures – what can be better than having a large number of people listening to you? Isn't this the dream of all musicians? Just prepare yourself and perform.

Writing, after all, is the most important part of what I do now. I am willing to admit that I am now a good writer for research papers. However, it does not come easy, even now. Each paper or proposal has gone through at least ten rounds of revision before submission. Some of the revisions are scientific; some are language. To write a good paper, you need to integrate English skills with scientific ability. In some cases, the results are to be published in a short communication and there is a limit in length. Most proposals also have limited page numbers. In these cases you need to work on every sentence or even every word. Conciseness and clarity are two of the important criteria.

In addition to scientific papers, I also have to write correspondence. Someone taught me that you should always keep your correspondence to one page, no matter how important and complicated it may be. Anything longer could become less effective. Thus I have learned to write short and effective memorandums and letters.

After you have mastered the technical aspects of English, the challenge will be to reach the next level of sophistication – to think in English or dream in English. This level is very difficult to reach unless you learn English from childhood. As an outsider to linguistics, my understanding is that this is a criterion that determines whether a person is truly bilingual. I know what it means because I can think and dream in both Taiwanese and Mandarin. However, I still think in Chinese most of the time even though I have lived in the US longer than in Taiwan. When we speak or write, we need to go through a translation process that slows us down. This is an important point that should be recognized by teachers and friends who deal with international students.

So what is really the level of my English proficiency? On the one hand, I write scientific papers better than most of my native American students. I don't mean scientifically; I mean using English to communicate scientific results. On the other hand, I still make mistakes in tenses and articles. How about writing outside of scientific fields? I don't want to admit to my children, but their papers in high school English classes are better than what I can write. Their reading speed and vocabulary are far better than mine are. Their speaking ability, of course, is something I will never reach in my life. I will always speak with a Chinese accent. My tongue is Chinese, after all.

In closing, I'd like to say that learning a language is inseparable from 'learning' – I mean learning everything. Language is the major means through which you learn. If you live or study in a different country, your language skill will determine how quickly and how much you learn from the world surrounding you. For those of us who immigrated to the US from Asia and settled here permanently, there is a potential trap in our lives – that we stop reading broadly because reading in English requires extra effort. If this happens to you, then your life will likely fall into a pattern of *ping-yong* (mediocrity). According to a well-known Chinese literature scholar, Chio-Yu Yu, ping-yong is a passive but opportunistic life attitude. Those who have it are not seriously lacking anything, but they are hardly moved by the fascination of the outside world, the profundity of human history, the nobleness of ultimate truth, and the richness of life. Thus, learning English to me is a constant process, the process through which I express myself and learn from the outside world. Learning is a lifelong process; so is learning English.

Linguistic Experiences of a Mathematical Career

Born in France, **Louis de Branges** moved to the US at the age of nine. He attended Saint Andrews School from 1944 to 1949, received a BA from the Massachusetts Institute of Technology, and a Ph.D. in mathematics from Cornell University. His academic career has been spent almost entirely at Purdue University, Indiana, where he began in 1962 as an associate professor, was promoted to professor in 1963, and to distinguished professor (Edward C. Elliott Professor of Mathematics) in 1989. He is known for the solution of difficult mathematical problems, of which the most famous is the Bieberbach conjecture, solved in 1984. He has received a number of academic prizes including a Sloan Foundation Fellowship (1963) a Guggenheim Foundation Fellowship (1967), and an Alexander Ostrowski Prize (1989). Bilingual in French and English, he is also fluent in German and Russian.

It may appear that a professor of mathematics has no use for language other than a special language of symbols and formulae. Mathematical arguments are indeed written in a distinctive language that obeys a rigid logic of its own. But this mechanical use of language detracts attention from more essential applications that it is my purpose to describe.

The language of my birth was French although both of my parents were Philadelphians. They emigrated to France in 1931 with a common desire to use French as a language. My father spoke French because it was the language used at home by his parents. My mother spoke French because she had studied it at the Agnes Irwin School as a natural supplement to English. The move to Paris permitted my father to earn a living through language skill at a time when unemployment was a major social problem. He also maximized the purchasing power of dollar income from inherited capital. My father sold steamship tickets to wealthy Americans in the Paris office of the Compagnie Générale Transatlantique. A benefit of such work was free passage on the *de Grasse*, the *Normandie*, the *Champlain*, and the *Ile-de-France*.

The German invasion of France caused an abrupt change in my childhood. Although our family remained together in Paris during the first year of the occupation, a separation occurred when my father stayed there while my mother brought my two sisters and myself to the United States. The four of us spent the war in a seashore cottage at Rehoboth Beach, Delaware. I had spoken French at home and at school until I was nine. Suddenly there was no one with whom I wanted to speak French – not even my mother, who was unable to maintain her French character in an English-speaking environment. I acquired a language of my own, which was used for thinking and for reading but rarely for speech. I learned English from an instructive exterior point of view.

Ideal learning opportunities were created when I was admitted at age twelve to St Andrew's School, Middletown, Delaware. Education requires purposeful organization. The school day was divided into seven forty-minute periods of study or instruction by teachers specialized in each subject. Homework was assigned and collected at each class meeting. It was read and commented on in a meaningful way by the teacher. Additional study periods were held in the evenings after scheduled sports in the afternoon. I realized that my education was considered valuable not only to myself or to my family, but also to society.

Five years of boarding school were sufficient to give me an acceptable mastery of written English. The language was more difficult for me than French because it is less supported by grammar. English is, however, comparable to French in the great variety of available words. I quickly came to respect good writing in any language as a major achievement. I eventually came to consider the principal obstacle to good writing to be the difficulty in good thinking. I learned to be stimulated in good thinking by the search for good expression.

Others share with me the exciting experience of learning a language. But my learning experience had an unusual effect because it stimulated me to learn mathematics. This was possible because I had learned through reading French to read independently of instruction. Coherent sources of mathematical information were then found not only in university libraries, but also in school and public libraries. Interesting mathematical reading was even found in those home libraries that offered the *Encyclopedia Britannica*. Books of that time were solidly bound and clearly printed on paper of good quality. Mathematical articles were addressed neither to a professional mathematician nor to an ignorant layman, but to an intelligent, or even talented, amateur. The good taste and high quality of this written English permitted a step into mathematical maturity which otherwise only occurs in graduate school.

My four undergraduate years at the Massachusetts Institute of Technology consolidated the progress made in both French and English at St Andrew's School. Courses of linguistic interest acquired importance for being an exception in the curriculum. In the one semester of a course in scientific German I acquired the intention to learn this third language. The one semester of a course in world literature allowed me to make twelve selected readings in French. My acquaintance with the works of Molière, Voltaire, Rousseau, Stendhal, and Flaubert dates from that time.

My four graduate years at Cornell University contained significant linguistic experiences. Since I had then chosen mathematics for a career, I had committed myself to a lifetime of teaching, which began with the duties of my assistantship. Teaching is a challenge in the use of language. A good teacher communicates in words supplemented by simple pictures. The challenge of teaching mathematics consists of decoding a technical language of symbols and translating it into a verbal pattern with sufficient repetition to impose itself on memory. A good teacher finds the essence of a complicated situation and sends the student in the direction he must go to master it. A good teacher does not reach that goal himself in teaching since so doing is unnecessary for good students and confusing for poor ones. Furthermore, the teacher needs to use his voice to create the emotional strength necessary to sustain action. Humor is an effective teaching tool when it is varied.

What a teacher has to say is never less important than how he says it. To convey a message, a teacher needs an honesty, which requires courage because it can be dangerous. I will illustrate this with an event that occurred in my first years of graduate school. A girl who came to my calculus class on the first day of a semester asked my advice about how to learn the course. We must have talked for some time as I was persuaded to give a frank answer. I explained my method as an undergraduate student of reading the book, doing the homework, and attending class only for examinations. I saw her again only five times during the semester. Since she obtained a perfect score on every examination, she was by far the best student in the class. This is an instructive example of good teaching because a minimal use of words is made. Yet the value of the instruction given surpassed a semester of lectures. Brevity is the essence of good expression.

The valuable experience obtained in the use of English occurred simultaneously with a valuable experience in the use of French. A series of graduate texts in mathematics had been written by a Professor Nicolas Bourbaki of the University of Nancago. I was attracted by the masterly use of French language for the presentation of mathematical arguments. This encyclopedic source became a principal reference for my graduate education. The theories that most attracted my interest were discoveries of Stefan Banach in Warsaw, Marshall Stone in Chicago, and Mark Krein in Odessa. Of these, Banach had died and Stone had left research to become head of the department of mathematics at the University of Chicago. Bourbaki is a pseudonym for an association of French mathematicians, established in Nancy, who were frequent guests in Chicago. I decided to learn Russian because it was the language of the remaining active contributor.

When I had submitted my doctoral thesis, I packed my belongings in a wooden box and took a Greyhound bus to Aberdeen Proving Ground, Maryland, for six months of active duty in the United States Army Reserve. Before leaving, I bought a small book similar in appearance to a military manual, which had, however, been published in Moscow. My reward for eight years of university education was promotion to first lieutenant, a rank of significance among those who are only second lieutenants. And I quietly learned Russian from the book during classes on military procedures. At the end of basic training, I obtained the lowest grade in my class on a written examination. This came to the attention of a superior officer, who could not understand that someone with the best education in the class should obtain the lowest score. I could not explain that I was learning Russian for fear of being thought a communist, something which had to be avoided when Sputnik had made its appearance so soon after the end of the Korean conflict. This was unfortunate, as the major was an accomplished linguist with whom I spoke French. I may have been spared failing the course by the high score that I obtained on a test of English writing ability.

The first ten years of my career established the pattern of research and teaching which has been maintained in the subsequent thirty years. In my first academic positions, I taught undergraduates at Lafayette College and Bryn Mawr College. I also obtained visiting research positions at the Institute for Advanced Study and the Courant Institute of Mathematical Sciences. The subsequent years at Purdue University continued an association with the Philadelphia area as long as my mother had her home in Wayne, Pennsylvania.

In these first ten years, I produced a graduate text on a subject that had been inadequately treated by Bourbaki. Mathematical analysis is a product of that flowering of culture that characterizes Europe of the seventeenth and eighteenth centuries. A significant date is the discovery in 1650 of the differential and integral calculus by Isaac Newton. Integration is the process by which the whole is assembled from its parts. Differentiation is the process of decomposing the whole into its parts. A calculus is a science of computation. Of these three words, the most important one is integration. I would like to explain integration with an example borrowed from Archimedes.

The problem is to determine the quantity of wine in a given round tub. For this measurement, you might choose a cup, carefully fill it to the brim, and empty it into another tub, and continue until the original tub is empty. The quantity of wine is then measured by the number of cups of wine emptied. This method is, however, often inaccurate because a quantity of wine which is less than a cup is left over. The inaccuracy can be reduced by repeating the procedure with a smaller cup. But it cannot with certainty be eliminated.

The solution, which was already implied by Archimedes, is that the process of measurement is continued indefinitely until an answer without error is obtained. Undergraduates who are unwilling to accept this explanation are penalized in examinations. But the explanation has subtle philosophical, if not religious, implications that were noticed by Gottfried Wilhelm Leibniz in the first publication of the calculus. This is that the solution presumes a procedure that can be implemented by no person. It lies beyond human verification.

A majority of students will answer that they do not care as long as it works. But the point is that a hypothesis has been made that it does work. The hypothesis is unjustified since not everything that has worked in the past will work in the future. Hypotheses need to be identified and examined for weaknesses. They sometimes need to be corrected. For these reasons, the mathematical progress made in the eighteenth century did not close the subject of integration. New insights that were obtained in the nineteenth century culminated in the work of Thomas Stieltjes.

Stieltjes was a Dutch mathematician who died of tuberculosis in 1894 after obtaining a position at the recently-founded technical university in Toulouse. Although he was only 38 years old, his integration theory is the basis of spectral analysis in the twentieth century. The principal applications appear in quantum mechanics and in signal processing. I became interested because of their importance in science and engineering.

My graduate text on integration applies the same principles of expression as Bourbaki except that it is written in English. Words and ideas dominate over symbols and formulas. Calculations, of which there are many, are compressed into exercises for the student. Major assertions requiring demonstration or proof are stated as theorems. There are 68 theorems and 355 problems. The book is a treasury of information on integration as it applies to spectral theory.

The book went out of print after an initial distribution to all major mathematical libraries. Since the undergraduate market for mathematical texts was more attractive to the publisher, he closed his graduate series. But, before doing so, he sold the copyright to Masson for translation into French. The translation was made by a Canadian mathematician whose work is distantly related to mine. I was informed of the project only when I received the galley proof for correction. I then made a second translation from a language that is called Franglais into French. The French edition remains available in an attractive format at a low price. But it has attracted the attention of few readers in French. The principal readers are Russians who can read English.

The first twenty-five years of my career were difficult because the recognition accorded to my book on integration was insufficient to maintain research funding. Since I could not afford to travel abroad, my use of languages was restricted to the reviewing of mathematical publications in Russian and the reading of international editions of newspapers. The *Manchester Guardian Weekly* attracted my attention because of the lively English used by Alistair Cooke. Then I was attracted to *Figaro Hebdomadaire* because of the excellent French of Raymond Aron. Eventually, I became a faithful reader of *Die Zeit* because of the wonderful articles in German by Marion Gräfin Dönhoff. Insights on the teaching of mathematics came through exposure to the European cultural sources of this academic discipline.

A historical example of a successful mathematical education deserves attention. When the mother of Blaise Pascal died, his father assumed responsibility for his education instead of sending him to school. The child received careful instruction in reading and writing and in related subjects such as languages, literature, history, and religion. The nature and uses of mathematics were explained without any encouragement to pursue the subject. But the information he received was sufficient for him to reconstruct plane geometry. His understanding of Greek mathematics was superior to that of those who had read Greek texts because the logical arguments that he applied were his own. Since some of the results he discovered were new, they attracted the attention of learned societies in Paris which specialized in mathematics. Although Pascal is known primarily as a philosopher, he is equally deserving of fame as a mathematician.

An instructive account of his education as a child was written by his sister in the preface to Pascal's *Pensées*. The precision with which she describes her brother's progress demonstrates that she was as competent a teacher as her father. Her portrait as a Jansenist nun, painted by Philippe de Champaigne, hangs in the French national museum built on the site of the

Abbée de Port-Royal des Champs. This center of the Jansenist movement near Paris was destroyed in 1710 under the orders of Louis XIV.

The ideal conditions for a mathematical education cannot be produced in a modern university. But Purdue University has permitted me to conduct teaching experiments with that aim. My involvement in undergraduate teaching occurred in the years before my research received international recognition. My teaching aim is to have students think rather than to acquire knowledge. Since logical thought depends on words for the expression of ideas, students should be required to write solutions of mathematical problems in essay form. The function of the teacher is to assign appropriate problems and to correct solutions even to details of punctuation and grammatical structure. In no case should a student be given a solution since his difficulty will then recur at a higher level.

The ideal conditions for learning mathematics cannot be realized without an appreciation, first on the part of the teacher and then on the part of the student, of why the study of mathematics is necessary. The reason for this is not obvious since the numbers 1, 2, 3, ..., for example, are presented without justification or explanation. The properties of numbers are either learned in childhood or can be found in books when they have been forgotten. The student needs his attention called to the three dots which are always used when the numbers are listed. These dots indicate that there are too many numbers to write on any page or in any book. For this reason, no verification of the properties of numbers is possible by any person, even with the help of the most sophisticated computing equipment. All work with numbers is based on the unverifiable hypothesis that the number system in its entirety exists and obeys consistent rules. A student of mathematics must therefore learn what these rules are and how they are logically related. He has to acquire a respect for the immensity of the mathematical universe, which is rare among those without mathematical training. Mathematical issues cannot be decided without hypotheses, which are not subject to proof. A student who appreciates the logic of this structure is already a mathematician.

The success of my undergraduate teaching was interrupted when my research contributions finally received recognition. The first invitation to visit Paris in the summer of 1980 was followed in succeeding summers by invitations to Lancaster, Amsterdam, Groningen, Stockholm, St Petersburg, Heidelberg, Regensburg, Vienna, and Tel-Aviv. I list these cities as they are viewed from a center in Paris. My teaching effort was accordingly shifted to the graduate level. My knowledge of the principal European languages greatly augments the benefit of sustained European travel. I am well received in European universities, where my closest colleagues are found.

Should these colleagues read the present account of linguistic experiences, they will wonder that any learning effort should be deliberately expended on a language other than the universal language of mathematics, which is English. This is certainly the language that they use for any publication which is to be widely read. Their education would have been greatly simplified without the major effort that they have expended on this language, an effort that has often been made at the cost of other European languages.

I agree with the general evaluation of English as a language. And I consider myself fortunate to have received my principal education in that language. But I would not have used English so well if I had had no experience of other languages. Without that experience, I would have underestimated the value of language as opposed to symbols and formulas for the expression of mathematical ideas. I cite a remaining mathematical experience that has a linguistic significance.

I am myself the best student of my teaching of the foundations of analysis and the best reader of my integration theory. I have discovered after forty years of professional experience that alternative approaches are deficient or erroneous. Because of the high standards of publication, substantial errors seldom occur in mathematics. But disturbances in the mathematical community that originated in World War II have permitted such an error to occur. The error is not an error in the use of logical reasoning, but an error in the hypotheses on which that reasoning is based. Thousands of pages have been published and millions of dollars have been expended on the properties of quantities that do not exist. No error of comparable magnitude has previously occurred in the history of mathematics. The discovery and correction of the error is one of the major achievements of my career.

I propose a linguistic explanation of how the error was made and how it was corrected. It seems to me that the cause of error was the use of Lingua Mathematica for the expressions of mathematical ideas as opposed to a language of words such as, for example, English. By Lingua Mathematica I mean a precise language of symbols which precludes the possibility of error in mathematical arguments. Some dialects of this language are programmed on computers and dispense entirely with the use of words. The possibility of human error is eliminated in tests of consistency of mathematical theories. Surprising conclusions are obtained, since plausible statements have been found that can be neither confirmed nor refuted using generally accepted principles of mathematical argument.

These achievements of Lingua Mathematica have earned a praise that overlooks a weakness of mechanical language as compared with a language of words. The cultural traditions of word usage encourage a closer examination of hypotheses than do the traditions of mechanical language. Lingua Mathematica is excellent for the implementation of ideas that have been conceived of in words. But it is disastrous when applied to goals that have been insufficiently examined in the language of words. Entire mathematical careers have been invalidated by such errors.

Taking the Best from a Number of Worlds: An Interview with Hooshang Hemami

Hooshang Hemami received his B.Sc. in electrical and mechanical engineering from the University of Tehran. He studied with R. L. Cosgriff at The Ohio State University, where he received his Ph.D. in electrical engineering. Currently a professor of electrical engineering and biomedical engineering at The Ohio State University, he is also a Member and a Fellow of the Institute of Electrical and Electronics Engineers and has published numerous articles in journals such as *Biomechanics and Biomedical Engineering*, the *Journal of Biomedical Engineering*, and *Autonomous Robots*. His primary research interests are control, animation and dynamics of robotic and  biorobotic systems, marionettes and human movement. His personal interests include soccer, oil painting, creative writing and classical music.

Belcher: I think you said earlier, the last time we met, that you got your bachelor's degree at the University of Tehran in engineering.

Hemami: Electrical and mechanical engineering in 1958.

Belcher: And then you came to the United States to attend — [a leading research institution]?

Hemami: And then I came to the United States, yes.

Belcher: Was there any special reason for going to —?

Hemami: Well, I got a scholarship, and they gave us a list of universities where you could apply, and I just applied there. That was the only place I applied, and they accepted me, so I just went there.

Belcher: You had heard a lot or at least something about it?

Hemami: Yes, we knew some things about it. Of course, some of the other universities are also well known, like Stanford and Michigan, and so forth.

Anyway, I came to the US, and I started graduate school. I wasn't sure of the area that I would like to go in. — at that time had a lot of military supported activities, and I didn't want to do any of those, so I had a hard time coming to an area where I could do something myself. At the same time, I also was sort of disillusioned. You know, a lot of the propaganda, what I had learned about the United States and the Western world in general, started to come apart you see. What I had been told didn't hold.

Belcher: What was happening in Iran then?

Hemami: The Shah was in power, with the help of the CIA and the United States. Well, I was disenchanted with the Shah's regime and the whole system in Iran. I ostensibly came here to maybe not only scientifically, but also perhaps philosophically and intellectually, have something to hold on to. Since my system of beliefs sort of collapsed, I had a hard time. I had to start to reconstruct my philosophy. I think we have talked about this before.

Not long after I arrived, I decided I was not going to speak Persian anymore, even with my Iranian friends, and I told all of them so. They would all be at parties, or whenever we were together, they would laugh at me. I do the same still with any Iranian that works here. I just converse in English, for several reasons. In my case, if I speak Iranian, it interferes with my English; it starts to introduce into my psyche a whole bunch of old memories and reflections and feelings and so forth. I don't find that very helpful. I am prone to be melancholic sometimes, and it doesn't help.

Belcher: What were you looking for when you tried to reconstruct your philosophy?

Hemami: Something that would be, you know, based on what good things I had learned in Iran, and I had thoughts there from my background which I couldn't run away from, and then also, that would allow me to live in the West at some comfortable intellectual level. So that took some time. Really, I thought that would be my higher priority, rather than just go and get a Master's and Ph.D. and go back to Iran. So I started to read. I was always interested in human behavior and the psyche and so forth, so I started to read some psychology, which I didn't understand, you know. Finally, it cost me getting a Ph.D. there. I got my Master's, but I finally sorted things out. The main part of it was that I had to stand on my own feet. Really, there was nobody to help me with magic words or sentences or doctrines or something. What I came up with was to try to be unbiased and take the best of what the East and the West could offer and go from there.

Belcher: You have an interesting passage from Bertrand Russell on your website about scientific thought.

Hemami: Yes, that's right; I quoted him. I did a lot of reading in those days, in history of Western philosophy or civilization, and at that time, it impressed me very much that you have to have roughly this – that's the sentence that's very important that he said – 'In anything one believes, the degree of intensity of that belief has to be proportional to the evidence'. That had great influence on me, in my normal life, and also in my scientific life, because I realized that there's no point in having these dogmatic beliefs if one cannot objectively and scientifically prove them.

Belcher: I think you said, when we talked earlier, that at — you were working on your Master's in electrical engineering, but you also took some non-engineering courses?

Hemami: Right, I had to take some courses in, so called, humanities. We had to read *Confessions of St Augustine,* some Greek plays, some of Dante.

Belcher: I remember you were saying that you felt really constrained by your English because you had language to refer to concrete things but not abstract things.

Hemami: That's correct, and we had to write a final essay on one of the exams, and they asked us to write why St Augustine had picked up an apple from his neighbor's yard and eaten it. The only way I could communicate to the instructor was using concrete English, so I wrote something about that he was hungry; the apple enticed him.

Belcher: I think that's really interesting because I've heard a number of faculty talk about ESL students, and some of them have said one of their biggest problems is that they're not good critical thinkers, and I always wonder when they say that to what extent what they're really responding to is limited English.

Hemami: Yes, and, of course, really, it will take a lot of reading and some time for a person to be able to think in another language, to express himself or herself. At least for me, it has taken an enormous investment, which I'm not unhappy about. But I also was fortunate because I enjoyed reading, and I read all these nice passages. I wish I had collected all the passages that excited me, but I didn't, and now I sometimes go back to try to find those books and stories, but I don't remember what they were.

Belcher: Yes, it can be hard to recapture those things. You had also talked earlier about working with your advisor and how high his standards were, how he made you write draft after draft after draft.

Hemami: I had never written a technical report in Iran, and to write a technical report and write it also in English, it was a double challenge. I had to write twelve drafts of my thesis, and I wouldn't get help from him. He'd just look at me and say, 'No good', and just throw it in the wastebasket. After that, I decided I was never going to do that with my students, because if you say it's no good, then maybe perhaps some parts of it were very right and some parts were very wrong. I was not able at that time to judge which part was proper and which one wasn't. Some feedback at some level would have helped

Belcher: Not every student would be as determined as you were. Some would just be completely devastated by that kind of experience.

Hemami: I also didn't get much encouragement in some ways from him or from the head of the group.

Belcher: So you decided you wouldn't be that kind of advisor.

Hemami: Yes, yes, well maybe that was at least a start. A person has to be on his own. Maybe the students that they get there are that way, more independent, but certainly our students here need help, not only in the writing and formulation of their ideas, but also in the topics of their theses and dissertations. I didn't get any help there. What was more discouraging was that the head of the group, and I respected him very much, he tried to continuously discourage me. 'Why do you want to get a Ph.D.? Why do you want to do research? Why don't you go back to Iran?'

Belcher: That's terrible.

Hemami: But, you know, those times one needs a little more, perhaps, encouragement and support than like that.

Belcher: So you ended up leaving, and then you worked. You went to Dayton?

Hemami: Yes, I left, and I worked for National Cash Register for two years.

Belcher: You described that before as a sort of dark period. You were struggling to figure out what you believed in.

Hemami: Yes, and I had mundane things to do. I realized at that time that some of this repetitive industrial work, I would not be interested in. That was good in that sense for self-assessment or realization that there were certain kinds of engineering jobs that were boring and I wouldn't want to do them. So that was also in some ways good again, to set me straight, because after that, when I finished my Ph.D., I knew definitely that that kind of industrial environment was not for me.

Belcher: So you came to Ohio State from Dayton?

Hemami: And I finished my Ph.D.

Belcher: I remember your saying that it was more, not exactly laid back, but there was a slower pace at Ohio State that you felt was more helpful for you as a student.

Hemami: Yes, and also as a professor later, because I have set my pace and have followed my own schedule, more or less, rather than be pushed around by requirements of government and where the money was, so it has given me a way to do my long range plans.

Belcher: You were saying you also felt you didn't have a very fast paced research schedule or publication schedule for yourself, but yet you still have something like 200 publications.

Hemami: Yes.

Belcher: Which seems pretty impressive to me.

Hemami: Yes, that's with a slow pace, you know.

Belcher: With a slow pace *[laughing]*. So that's a fair number every year.

Hemami: Yes, and I have had good support from the department, I should say. Also, I've had a whole bunch of good students. It's like sports. The difference between a good coach and a bad coach sometimes is not so much in the coach but in the players he has to work with .*[Laughs]*

Belcher: So you collaborate a lot with your students?

Hemami: I collaborate a lot with my students, and I also work with a whole bunch of people on campus because my area (electrical and biomedical engineering) is interdisciplinary, so I look for help wherever I can get it.

Belcher: Do you work with people in the College of Medicine?

Hemami: Some, yes, in different levels, in different departments, like orthopedic surgery, physiology, anatomy, and there are others.

Belcher: Well, that's a lot of departments.

Hemami: Also mathematics, mechanical engineering, CIS, and some of the industrial engineering faculty.

Belcher: You said earlier that you sometimes have as many as fifteen students, or advisees.

Hemami: This was a long time ago. In the early 80s, I had about eight or nine MS students and six Ph.D. students. It was a heavier load. I have a much smaller number of students now, and I also do a lot of work myself.

Belcher: Well, it probably gives you more time to work on your own projects. Another thing you talked about before that was really fascinating to me was the role that other aspects of your life played in your being successful as a scientist, the fact that you had all these other interests.

Hemami: Yes, I remember that I have said this. I have made four other investments, and I can tell you what they are. One was to read in psychology, which I have done in the last 30 to 40 years continuously. I have been lucky these last ten years. Either I have more experience or maybe the realms of psychology, psychoanalysis or human studies have progressed a lot, so I have understood a lot more. As a child, there were a lot of things in Iran I did not understand, and also in the US, and now I understand them better. This worried me until five, ten years ago because I still didn't understand any of those things. You know they say that when you get older you get wisdom, and this is perhaps true, but maybe one doesn't really get wiser – or maybe one gets wiser in some ways and more foolish in other ways – so the center of gravity just remains. *[Laughs]* Another investment I have made was in classical music, in Western music as a whole. I haven't progressed much beyond classical music, but that has had great influence on me; it has been more or less a spiritual or emotional support for myself.

Belcher: Mozart especially?

Hemami: Mozart, Beethoven and Bach, I guess. I thought about this and realized that Bach wrote music for God, Mozart wrote music for Angels, and Beethoven wrote music for man. Yes, and I have had experiences with Mozart's music in terms of conveying emotion that in itself is something that I cherish.

I also play soccer, particularly the last fifteen years more intensely than before, and that has kept me in shape, not only physically but also intellectually. When I have had physical activity, I think better, I see better, I make less programming errors. Speaking of programming errors, you know, the soccer season ends at the end of October. I have been working on a project, simulation, a computer program, for four weeks, and it was just not performing well. I had wasted four weeks to try to determine why this was not running. *[He gets a printout of the program]*

Belcher: Is this another computer terrestrial?

Hemami: Yes, along the same lines, yes, and I was going to show you, the major mistake was I had a typographical error. I had written a little ..*[flips through the pages]*. This is one of the pages and pages of code. This 'd' should have been a capital 'D.' Four weeks! So what I'm trying to say is I think if I had been playing soccer this month…

Belcher: It wouldn't have happened. *[Laughs]*

Hemami: Yes, maybe I wouldn't have made that mistake. The fourth area that I felt I had to have was escape from all of this *[gestures toward office]*, and that is my painting. In some ways, I don't know why I got drawn to it. In the last fifteen years, I have been painting, and that's very good, you know, because I don't follow any styles. I don't follow anything; it is anything goes, absolutely unconstrained: colors, shapes, reality, unreality, abstract. Will it please anybody? It doesn't matter. So that has been a sort of complement in my work, because my work is very directed; things have to work, make sense, be stable, be believable, but I don't have to have any of these constraints when I paint.

Belcher: I know that you also write poetry.

Hemami: Well, it comes on its own. I don't know the dynamics of this. I think – this is my theory – I think my right side of the brain is in charge and drives the left side, which is scientific and articulates. I think that poetry is my left side trying to tell the right side, don't push too hard, let's go away from this mathematics and hard science. See what good things I can do if you just let me. And you know the more interesting thing is that I wrote about five or ten beautiful pieces of poetry in Persian with new stanzas, new shapes and forms. What I'm trying to say is, it's nothing that I remember from what I had written before. I haven't read anything really seriously in Iranian for forty years, but suddenly this stuff flows out and it is beautiful, nice shapes and allegories and images. The only reason I can give for it is that the left side doesn't like to do this kind of work anymore and is trying to bribe the right side – if you leave me alone, see what I can do? *[Laughs]*

Belcher: You had mentioned something earlier about sometimes reading Persian poetry now.

Hemami: Yes, yes, I have thought about this along the lines of I have to get the best of my Persian education and my Western education. I feel Iran has something that we don't have here, and that's what I call a mixture of vision and being at peace with the world and animals and perhaps poetry and philosophy all mixed up. I think some of this is beginning to come to the West through Rumi and some of the Persian philosophers or writers. Actually Rumi means from Rome, but that was his last name. He was a Turk, but he wrote all of this stuff in Iranian. I think he's being appreciated more in Europe.

Belcher: When did he write?

Hemami: Perhaps, seven, nine hundred years ago. There are books of his now that I see in the bookstores. It's Sufi philosophy. I see now they have these dancers come and play music and twirl around; they think with this they can get to a state of nirvana.

Belcher: You mean dervishes?

Hemami: Yes. Now to my knowledge, they don't use drugs, the ones that are genuine. They are somewhat also in Pakistan, Turkey and so forth. There's a counterpart to this in Africa and perhaps the islands off the United States: Puerto Rico, Trinidad, Jamaica, and so forth.

Anyway, Rumi's work is getting to the West, and that's the part that I don't think the West has a counterpart to: to be detached from the physical world and consider an equality among races and animals and leave space for the animals. Perhaps the Indians here practice some of this. Some of this also goes back to Zoroaster. You know Zoroaster was a Persian prophet prior to Islam and one of his teachings was that you have to keep the land, the water, the fire and the air clean. So that's the part that I think perhaps the West or the rest of the world could benefit by learning more about from Iran.

On the other hand, there are three things that the West has: freedom of the individual and this incessant study of the human mind – why we do things the way we do, what we are made of, and how we think and how we behave. The third one is, of course, music. Music, for whatever reason, has developed in the West a lot. Maybe because people in the West and in Europe are more intuitive, more right-sided in their brains. Maybe there are emotions and processes that are developed and need to be articulated and understood. I have tried to be aware of all these gifts, more or less, that are available now in the West.

Belcher: I think you also mentioned before that you like Western literature.

Hemami: Yes, yes, I try to read literature if I get a chance. This summer I read some work by Carson McCullers. I have two of her novels. The one that I really think is wonderful is *Reflections in a Golden Eye.*

Belcher: Yes, I read that many years ago.

Hemami: Very interesting writing. I am trying to read now Herman Hesse's *The Glass Bead Game.*

Belcher: I've never read that one.

Hemami: You know, I may not have to read more of his work because I came to some of his conclusions earlier. Hesse thinks that we all go through three stages of development. The first one is when a child is told that he can be wonderful and have all these wonderful things in life: virtue and truth, compassion, altruism, and so forth. The next stage is when he realizes that the world is not actually like that, and neither is he, so he rebels. Hesse thinks most people remain in that second stage of cynicism, rebellion, and no belief. Then he thinks that there is a fortunate group that says, well, I have to live in this world and contribute to it and be sensitive to mankind, so I will utilize all this good and bad in me. Although Hesse doesn't talk about it in this particular way, this is my way of understanding, the essence of this.

You can see examples of this, for instance, in Picasso, and perhaps Van Gogh, though not so much because he died young, but also Rembrandt tried to come to terms with the perhaps savage or bestial or however one wants to describe it and the good side. And there's the psychologist Carl Jung. I think one of the crises of this time for humans is that we are drawn to too many things and there is so much to do. We are fragmented, and this didn't exist in former times. One has to somehow deal with alienation and fragmentation. You can see this sort of thing in Rembrandt's later paintings, where they are disjointed and rearranged and convey in a sense what is not there.

Belcher: So, all of these interests help you with your writing?

Hemami: Yes.

Belcher: To talk more specifically about your writing again: how do you usually write articles? For instance, do you collaborate with a lot of people on the actual writing? Do you sometimes write the first draft of something and then share it with other people, or do you divide the article up?

Hemami: I try to utilize people's help. For example, I'm doing one article with my brother now, in Iran. He has had interest in impact because he's a mechanical engineer; he studied at Stanford. I have had an interest in impact in robotics and human movement and sports. So we have been sort of collaborating on a low level with notes back and forth for three years. Finally, I went to visit him, and I said I was close to doing some work, but he said he didn't think it was possible. So I have worked on it this summer and this fall and these last four weeks more or less to convince him that this simple understanding of the process of kicking the ball in soccer helps us. So we're going to start that as a beginning of our collaboration on impact processing, and I have promised him that I will have a draft for him by January 1. But now I selectively work on parts of a problem. You know, I had to work the four weeks on this simulation in order to run it, and finally yesterday it ran. Again because of that 'D,' I wasted four weeks, but still I was able to narrow it down and find it. I will send a draft to him on January 1. Then we can do a more theoretical version of this. I told him maybe I'll have another draft for him by the end of March, and a third one we can do on another wider formulation by June. Now whether I will deliver on this on time or not, I don't know, but that's my plan to work with him. Now I have a another project with one of our students here and a professor in electrical engineering, and I have a third project. I have to selectively work on pieces of these and somehow it works.

Belcher: What about editors and reviewers in your field, are they sometimes hard to work with?

Hemami: Editors – I try to do the best that I can in terms of English as well as the technical part. Now we may also make mistakes in our simulations. Maybe a number, instead of 2, it is 1.5, so the things that come out may not be accurate. That we cannot control, but the last five years also we have had a lady here who teaches part time and is an editor, so I have utilized her services. She reads our papers and corrects them. I have paid her $25 an hour, and I insist that I pay it or the project pays it or the student pays it, because I think a minimal quality is absolutely important. Now the reviewers don't so much quarrel with our writing for that reason, but sometimes they like things to be added or subtracted or they try to belittle and ridicule the work. My aim has been to use whatever they say constructively to make the paper better. Some other things, I cannot, you know, I cannot do anything about. Sometimes one journal doesn't accept a paper, so we do all the things we have to do and submit it elsewhere. Sometimes what I think is outstanding work gets rejected, while something that I think is mundane and not very important gets published right away. But I have tried not to repeat things, and everything has been, at least to my way of thinking, a new contribution or something added to the state of knowledge. This paper, how to kick a soccer ball, is a completely new paper; it opens a new field. It has taken a lot of time, but it will be a worthwhile effort, and others can build on it. I do this sort of thing sometimes, begin something, and my own students also start to do work on it with me, and then they can go further. If I give them the original problem to work on alone, they may get stuck and not be able to continue.

Belcher: Can I ask about your collaboration with your brother again? Will what you are working on together be an article in English?

Hemami: Yes, it will. My brother's English is very good. You see, he reads and is a mountain climber and a nature lover, so he photographs and travels and reads a lot. He gets *Newsweek* and *Time* and other English journals he subscribes to. So his English is excellent, perhaps, in some ways, better than mine is. Also, he would probably scientifically scrutinize the paper. He's a little more of a perfectionist than I am, so it would help, because when I put that draft together, if it is 80, 90% good, I'm ready to send it out. So our paper will be submitted here and published in a respectable journal. That's what our hope is in the whole sequence.

Belcher: I can't remember if I asked you this question before: When you work with your students, do you encourage them to develop other interests as you and your brother have?

Hemami: I do. Actually, I have given students books to read, sometimes literature. Of course, some read them and some don't. I had one student whose English was so poor that I tried to tell him that he has to move up to this realm, that he has to read more. He finally revolted – just dropped me and went elsewhere. He told me that everybody had told him that his English was wonderful. So he considered that I had something, some vendetta against him, some prejudice. But that's the only case that was like that. The other ones, I help them to try to come to terms with themselves. Unfortunately, a whole bunch of our foreign students, and this is a shame, don't try to understand this culture and take advantage of it. They just get so carried away with their thesis and research.

Belcher: In my field, there's even a term for that – 'instrumental motivation'. There are different categories of motivation that people who teach ESL talk about, but often graduate students, international graduate students, are seen as having solely instrumental motivation; they are just so focused on that degree.

Hemami: It's unfortunate also that they sort of mix together all the time only with themselves and don't try to venture out and learn something. I find that somewhat unfortunate, but it may be just financially or economically driven. I was faced with this too when I first came here.

Belcher: I know that I've already taken a lot of your time. It's just so interesting talking to you because I think a lot of us don't realize that people who do scientific writing will have a lot of other interests that actually contribute to their productivity as scientists and writers.

Hemami: Any time, as much time as you like, any time. It's wonderful to have an opportunity to talk about these things.

Growing up Trilingual: Memories of an Armenian/Arabic/English Speaker

Anahid Dervartanian Kulwicki received her bachelor's degree from the American University of Beirut in 1976. In 1977, she emigrated to the United States, where she earned a master's degree in pediatric nursing from Indiana University in 1980, and a doctorate from the Indiana University School of Nursing in 1987. Now a professor of nursing at Oakland University, she has been a Fulbright Scholar and research director of several grants at the Arab Community Center for Economic and Social Service. She has conducted research on cardiovascular risk factors and diabetes, and on honour crime among Jordanians in Amman, Jordan. She has also directed research and developed programs for Arab American communities on teen health, woman empowerment, prenatal care, family planning, sexually transmitted diseases, cultural self efficacy and values and beliefs. Her program on Arab Domestic Violence Prevention was selected as a model program by AYUDA Inc., a legal aid organization serving immigrant women and supported by a grant from the Department of Health and Human Services.

I grew up in a family of seven children in a small Armenian village in Lebanon with a population of just 400. There were no libraries or bookstores when I was young. Later, while I was in high school, a library was built, and we were able to have access to books. My family actually had the first television in our village, which gave us countless hours of entertainment in Arabic, English, or French (often with subtitles for the last two). Of course, we did not have computers, and even toys were not very important when I was growing up.

My primary language is Armenian. Almost all my childhood and school friends were Armenian. My parents, who are trilingual, are both literate in

Armenian, but my father also reads and writes in Arabic. The members of earlier generations of my family were, for the most part, illiterate, with the notable exception of my paternal grandmother, who read the Bible to my father quite frequently during his childhood. My own most vivid memories of the Armenian language almost always involve literacy in some way: reading Armenian poetry and novels, acting in plays sponsored by school, singing in the choir, and attending Sunday school. As a teenager, I even wrote several poems in Armenian.

I was very fond of the Armenian language while I was growing up, and I now feel that it has played an important role in shaping my Armenian identity. Being Armenian during my youth meant being part of a minority in a predominantly Arabic country. Studying the Armenian language and culture and being involved in both intellectual and social activities in Armenian helped me feel Armenian, which was very important in my early life.

Second/Third Language Literacy and Professional Success

At the school I attended in Lebanon as a child, the study of three languages – Armenian, Arabic, and English – was mandatory. Most other Lebanese schools taught Arabic and French. Since the official public language of Lebanon is Arabic, it naturally became my second language. English was my third language, used mainly in schoolwork until I graduated from high school and attended the American University of Beirut, an English-language university.

I have no recollection of the difficulties of learning any of the three languages, which we were taught beginning in kindergarten. It was a given for us as children to study all three languages. We did not think of it in terms of choice. I do remember, though, preferring Armenian during most of my primary school years. During the last three years of high school, however, I became very attracted to Arabic, mainly for two reasons. One had to do with the beauty and richness of Arabic, especially its romantic poetry. The second reason was that my father was very knowledgeable about the Arabic language and very curious about our Arabic class assignments, especially those related to composition and poetry. I should add that my father also used to read to us and to our relatives almost every night during the winter. The novels he chose were usually famous novels translated into Arabic, such as *Les Miserables*.

English became my primary focus after I started attending the American University, where all my academic work had to be in English. Although I had begun to do some pleasure reading in English while in high school, reading classic books by authors such as Charles Dickens, Shakespeare, and Emily Brontë, I did not particularly like English. It seemed much less romantic and more restrictive than either Arabic or Armenian. I was much better as a writer in Arabic and Armenian, and whenever I wanted to write, English was not my preferred language.

My advanced proficiency in English developed in two ways: basically as a product of my academic work, but also as a result of social contacts. When I was in college, I dated an American exchange student, who currently is my husband, and also boarded with an American family for three years, which greatly helped my proficiency. Nevertheless, since my academic work at that level was always in English, I generally associated the English language with work rather than with anything pleasurable.

When I was attending the university, my first assignment for the introductory course in English was to read *Catcher in the Rye*, which I remember not enjoying. My grade in that course was a 'C,' one of the lowest grades I received in college. Now, twenty-five years later, my daughter has written a paper on the same book, and now I realize why I did not like reading it: I never understood the culture of that book.

Writing in English, however, was always more of a challenge for me than reading in English. Even today, despite the fact that English is my professional language, I still do not greatly enjoy writing in English. Once I started graduate school, I worked much harder on developing my skills as a writer, which improved largely because of my husband's willingness to read and edit my work. I now write grant proposals, articles, and lectures, and even edit others' work, something I truly enjoy, but my own writing I still do not find very pleasurable. In fact, I try to avoid writing as much as possible.

I am so busy now teaching in the School of Nursing, doing research on topics such as AIDS, smoking, infant mortality, and the health care beliefs and practices of Arab Americans – always working in the English language – that I rarely have time to read anything in Armenian or Arabic. I do not write in Armenian now at all. English is not just the sole language of my academic life now; it is my main language of communication.

Writing for Publication

As a writer, I am driven more by topic than by audience but, because of the American audience I have, I do try to be as clear as possible. I think that individuals who communicate in a language other than their own are much more sensitive in making sure that they communicate clearly with their audience. This is probably why I frequently ask my colleagues to edit my work. My chief source of editorial feedback, though, is always my husband, the only person I regularly turn to for help. He has played a major role in my success as a professional academic writer.

Others have helped my writing in a number of ways too. I collaborate with as many people as I can. Collaborating with people who are good English writers is important for me. One of the many valuable lessons that working with my American colleagues has taught me is that some of them have as hard a time with writing as I have.

Something else that has improved my writing is reading. It is definitely a resource for my writing, especially in terms of style. The Internet, on the other hand, has not been helpful to me as a user of the English language and writer. I am actually finding out that the Internet is making my writing skills poorer because I pay less attention, especially to spelling and punctuation, when I use it.

Looking at my academic life overall – the various journal articles, book chapters, and reports I have published, as well as the editorial work I have done – there are many success stories I could tell and no real horror stories. However, I want to mention that I still find that some of my American colleagues correct me because of their perception that my writing or communication style might be poorer than theirs. In fact, I did my own little research about my colleagues who take every opportunity they can to correct my English. Twice I gave them documents that were published in textbooks without letting them know that they were from a book rather than drafts by me. Both times, my colleagues sent me back the documents with their corrections, thinking that I had written them!

Finally, I cannot emphasize enough how important it is to find someone to read your work whom you can trust and who genuinely respects you, but I realize how difficult it can be to find that someone. I feel that I have been very fortunate.

How Can I Help Make a Difference?
An Interview with Robert Agunga

Robert A. Agunga received his diploma in agricultural extension and farm management from the University of Science and Technology, Kumasi, Ghana, and his bachelor's, master's, and doctoral degrees in journalism and mass communication from the University of Iowa. He is currently Associate Professor of Human and Community Resource Development at The Ohio State University. He has served as a consultant in Ethiopia, Namibia, South Africa, Zambia and elsewhere. In addition to having published numerous journal articles and book chapters, he is the author of *Developing the Third World: A Communication Approach* (1997). He was an Ameritech Faculty Fellow in 1997–1998 and received the Outstanding Research Paper Award from the Association for International Agricultural and Extension Education in 1996. In 1990, he was chosen as United States Peace Corps Black Educator of the Year.

Belcher: OK, actually I'm starting to put together a book, and what I'm trying to elicit from people are narratives of their language learning and literacy experiences. I'm going to people who are highly successful writers in different fields.

Agunga: I don't know if I qualify. *[Laughs]*

Belcher: Yes, you do!

Agunga: That's scary. That is very scary. *[Laughs]*

Belcher: I'm especially interested in people who are speakers of different languages, and who are in different disciplines. I'm trying to find out how they became so successful. This is the question that students in my program are asking all the time. You know, 'How can I become a successful writer?' or 'I struggle as a second-language writer so much; what hope is there for me?'. I can point to people like you. But what students would really like to know is how it happens: what kinds of strategies you've used, what kinds of help you've had. So basically, I'd like to ask you questions about your development, even starting as far back as your childhood. In fact, the first thing I want to ask you about is what it was like in your family at home. Do you feel that your family gave you some advantages or encouraged you in ways that pushed you in the direction that you eventually moved in?

Agunga: OK, I'll try my best. But first, I just wanted to show you our magazine. This is part of our third writing course, and we just worked on this quarter's issue right now.

Belcher: It looks terrific!

Agunga: Each quarter the students work on this, and they come in with the same problems: 'What am I going to write about?' or 'I don't know what to do'. So we kind of go step by step until they get to the production stage.

Belcher: It sounds like a wonderful opportunity for the students.

Agunga: Yes, but to get back to your question, I grew up in Ghana.

Belcher: Were your parents eager to see you do well in school?

Agunga: Well, let me put it this way. Neither of my parents went to school. Actually, I was the first in my family to go to school. So, that in itself was unusual. My father used to work with the colonial structure. He was a chief and, you know, the chiefs, they are an indirect rule system in Ghana. My father, he would supervise the construction of roads to let the administrators go through, and so on. I always had the impression that he felt he could have been much, much higher if he was educated. He noticed what education did for the people who had it. He said to me, 'My son, I missed education, but my child, my son, shouldn't miss that opportunity'. And so that was the key behind him sending me to school. I am one of five brothers. But I was the youngest at the time when school came to our area. The others were fourteen or fifteen, so they couldn't go to school. But I was young enough.

Belcher: You were at the right age.

Agunga: Right, to make it. So, I was the beginning of education up there. Because of my father's interest that I make it, he didn't really spare the rod.

Belcher: Pretty strict?

Agunga: He was very strict. And there were days I didn't want to go to school but he said, 'You are going to school. It is not a choice.' So I'm grateful that he pushed me hard at that age; otherwise, it was easy to opt out because nobody else was going to school. I was the only one who would wake up early in the morning.

Belcher: That had to be hard.

Agunga: Right. So it was hard. And you have to walk. It was about six miles to school; return trip; we're talking about twelve to fourteen miles a day. At that tender age, it wasn't very easy. But there were a few other kids in the village going to school, so we would all team together and walk through the forest. So that was a very interesting beginning in the sense that it was instilled in me very early that you have to work hard to get what you want to get. I actually had no vision of what I wanted to get. I just wanted to go to school to please my dad. But that discipline was a good beginning for me.

As I got into school, I discovered that, generally, your roots dictate what you will do later in life. For me, agriculture was the mainstay of my people, and subsistence farming was the way of life. I felt that if I could help them improve their productivity and well being, that would be great. So that shaped my interest in agriculture right from the start. I never really gave too much attention to the arts, to literature, even though we had a rich, rich, rich literature. One of the little talents I have is art; you know, painting and so forth. I didn't develop that aspect, even though I had the opportunity to go to the University of Science and Technology to study art. I turned it down because at that time, in our society, they didn't think that was intellectual enough. *[Laughs]* You don't want to complain, you know. So that shaped my choice of a career very, very early.

Belcher: So was the school that you went to an English-medium school?

Agunga: Yes, it was. In the elementary years, we learned in the local language, which is Kusaal. But the Europeans call it Kusasi. Kusasi is the people and Kusaal is the language. But in many of the books they kind of mixed the two. Instead of learning the alphabet in our local language, we were taught English equivalents.

Belcher: So when did they introduce English? Or did you have to move to a different school?

Agunga: No, no, no. Actually, they gradually introduced English. From about primary three, they started introducing English. You used a slate to write the alphabet. So you could say that we just mixed the two languages together from the beginning and gradually tapered off the local language.

Belcher: Bilingual education?

Agunga: Yes, bilingual education. So that's how I got started. English became, more or less, the national language. You would go anywhere and English is spoken. As soon as you get past the elementary school, the rest is all English.

Belcher: Do you think people generally feel good about that – the fact that English is the national language?

Agunga: Well, because of the colonial heritage, we really are not too sensitive to the fact. I think that we should probably fight hard to preserve and protect our language. But we've been socialized at such an early age that we kind of accept it as a norm. But I know that in countries like South Africa, where the blacks really were not mixed and had the time to protect their language, they are very much sensitive to European influence. I know in Zaire, you couldn't wear a tie, and the girls couldn't wear mini-skirts. Mobutu wouldn't allow that. You wouldn't even have 'Robert' in your name; you wouldn't have any English names associated with you. You have two local names, period. So there were these areas where the resentment against the European influence was very, very strong. But in Ghana, I don't think it's that way.

Belcher: So you were able to go to the local school until you were thirteen or fourteen?

Agunga: Yes, I went to that school. It's a six-year school, from primary one to primary six. You could probably say age thirteen or something like that. Then we were moved to a different school. One of the things about my life is the fact that I was gradually moving away and away and away and away from home. I told you how I had to travel about six miles each way to the primary school. The middle school was even farther, located in Zebila, almost forty miles from my home. So I was at boarding school. In other words, we would stay there until school was over before we'd come back to our home. Thus from age fourteen, I began staying away from my family, and I would come home during the holiday period. But I was still doing my family responsibility. Any time I came home, I would weed, tend to the cattle, and so forth. School never excused me from doing my responsibilities or chores. So I would do that. And, you know, we had a horse; I would take the horse and water it, and so forth. I never got spoiled. I was still stuck to my roots. I went to middle school for three years.

Another thing that I need to point out along the way is the competitive nature of our education. Because, for example, even in primary four and primary five, at the end of each quarter we would take exams, and they would rank you first, second, third, all the way to the end. If you were among the top three, your name would be in red ink, and the rest would all be in blue. So it kind of makes you stand out. We were all striving to be at the top of the class. When you were up there, which was what I would have the opportunity to be, you never wanted to really drop back down. That kind of also influenced how much I committed myself to doing well. In middle school, it was still the same competition. You had to pass a test to go to secondary school, which was what I did. And that again took me more than a hundred miles away from home, because I went to Tamale secondary school, which is located in Tamale, another town of about, I would say, 150 miles away from where my family was. So there was secondary school for five years before I went to an agricultural college because of my interest in agriculture.

There was a difference in our country between an agricultural college and a university, and I believe the same holds here. The agricultural college was a three-year program and would qualify you to go out and work as an extension agent. So when I graduated, around 1971, 1972, I went back to work in my home region as a district extension assistant. I did that for a really very brief period because I had the opportunity to go back to the university to get – it wasn't quite a degree – but it was a diploma that would give you a senior status in the Ministry of Agriculture. But you have to continue for another four years to get the Bachelor's degree. So I got that and went back again to work with the Ministry of Agriculture, and I was working with the ministry until 1979, when I got a scholarship to get a Master's degree in communication at the University of Iowa.

Now one would say, why go from agriculture to communication? But that was a necessary major leap in my life because, working in agriculture, we discovered that we had the technical knowledge of agriculture. We knew what this crop could do and that crop could do, what animal breeds the best, and so forth. But we weren't the farmers; we were the technicians. The farmers were the ones who would take our ideas and put that to productivity, while they didn't have the information that we had. We weren't good communicators, unfortunately, to deliver that information to them. So we discovered such a wide gap that we, the technocrats with Ph.Ds and Master's degrees, were struggling with the concept that we were developing the people, but the people weren't getting anywhere. Fortunately, we had some people, foreigners, who came and said, 'Maybe you guys are not really giving attention to communication.' That professor actually became my mentor. He came to Ghana in 1976 as a consultant for the Food and Agriculture Organization. He had just done his Ph.D. at Michigan State in communication. So he was the person who said maybe we should look at what communication can do for development. He picked me up, literally picked me up, because he said, 'I'll take you to America and I'll train you and send you back.' That is how I came to study at the University of Iowa under him. This was around 1981. I studied with him until I graduated in

1989 with a Ph.D. He and I really shared a lot of philosophies. We have since written book chapters together.

Belcher: He was from Malawi?

Agunga: He was from Malawi. Yes, Joseph Ashgrove from Malawi. He's a very good scholar, a good writer, a storyteller, and I think the African oral culture comes through in his work. That was one of the things that he taught me. You wouldn't believe it, but he never read my dissertation beyond chapter one. He never did. This was his philosophy. He said, 'Look, if I don't understand the first part, there is no reason to think that I'll understand the last part.' 'First,' he says, 'you bring me five pages at a time.' So when I wrote the first five pages, I took them to him. He'd read to page three and say, 'There's no flow here; take it back'. And he says: What I'm looking for is continuity in everything that you say. In your introduction, you tell the reader what it is that you want him or her to get out of this passage. When the reader then finds out that there is no transition between this and that, then there is no continuity. So you go back and find the transition that would link the rest of it to that.' So I just kept doing that for almost a whole term. We were on the semester system. For the whole semester, I worked on chapter one. You can see how frustrated I was. When I got past chapter one, he said, 'Now you go write the rest.' As soon as I bring in chapter two, he would just put it there. Chapter three, he'd just put it there and say go and write chapter four and five and so on. When I'd bring the summary, he'd then look and say, 'OK, so if I go to chapter two, I'll find what you're saying over here?' I'd say, 'Yes, you'll find it if you skim through the chapters'.

To me, that was the moment I learned how to write. You have to really take the pains to organize. Because when I got to chapter two, I started to say, 'What is my goal in this chapter, and how am I going to convince people that I'm really meeting my goal?' People have to have fun when they're reading. They have to believe that you know what you say. They have to trust you that they can believe the facts that you are providing. All that I learned. I liken it to drying your clothes on a string outside in the summer. There is only one string, A to B. But between A and B you can hang your blankets, your underwear, anything, and you can see all that. That, to me, is how you weave an essay. You have to have humor in some places; you have to have facts in some places; you have to provide your own content to your own views of life; you have to assert yourself in certain places. All that together, to me, makes the story worth reading. But it doesn't come easy. It requires a lot of research, a lot of understanding of what it is that you are doing. That's one of the reasons why I worry about our students of today, because many of them don't want to take the time to visit the literature on their topic.

Belcher: What about your own reading? Did you love to read at an early age?

Agunga: Reading, yes, I loved to read. I read a lot of storybooks by African writers; I read Soyinka and many others. Reading was what we did, especially in the secondary school years. I also discovered that, the more you read, the wider the vocabulary you develop. The less you read, the more limited your vocabulary. Reading is really very helpful to writing; they complement each other very well. You see somebody's style and say, 'I like that! I like that arrangement of words!' Unfortunately, when you become a professor, your opportunities to read stories become limited. I switched from reading stories to reading professional texts, but that is also one of the reasons why I feel very comfortable in writing in my professional area, because to a large extent I have mastered what is out there. I stay on the cutting edge of the field because I am up to date with what people are doing. I can say with some degree of comfort that, especially in the development field, I think I've read so much that is out there that I can go to the World Bank and speak with ease even though they are supposed to be the experts out there. People know I have something to say.

Belcher: Of course, when you become an established faculty member, you have access to things even before they're published, as a reviewer of manuscripts.

Agunga: Exactly. Staying current in your field is so important. But it comes down to putting ink on paper; there's no substitute for writing. Initially, you might chew your pen and drink cups of coffee, and tear your paper several times. But that gradually begins to vanish, and you begin to enjoy your writing. The other thing about being a good writer is to be very critical of yourself. I remember my associate dean came in and I had just written a piece that I wanted him to look at. I had gone through and edited it like crazy. He asked, 'Whose paper is this? Your own paper?' I said, 'Yes, that's my own paper'. 'And you did that?' I said, 'Yes, I did that to my own paper'. That kind of commitment, to tear work apart and repackage it, is just essential.

Belcher: It's hard for a lot of people to do that.

Agunga: Yes, it is very hard for a lot of people.

Belcher: They can't distance themselves from their work.

Agunga: Exactly. But you have to do that. Otherwise your reader would be doing it for you.

Belcher: I was just going to say that – or the reviewers, the editors, and then you lose control.

Agunga: Right. And the other thing I found out is that, having published in my peer journals or refereed journals for quite a while, I have been able to at least judge what will get published and what will not get published. I know now that if I send out four papers, three of them will get published, or at least two of them. One or two may come back with a request for revisions. I know what they want, and I know how much work I have to put into it to get it published.

Belcher: Could you estimate how many articles you've published so far in your career?

Agunga: Oh, probably not a lot. But I have about probably 21 or 22 journal articles.

Belcher: Plus a 400-page book.

Agunga: Yes, this twelve-chapter book. And I have about four other book chapters.

Belcher: Do you have a goal? Every year, do you tell yourself, 'I'm going to try to publish *x* number of articles'? Or do you not think in those terms?

Agunga: Well, our department requires you to publish at least two a year. You could take that as the average expectation. But I feel that if I really commit myself and there are no distractions, such as faculty meetings and all these other things, I could publish easily three or four a year. That's not a problem at all. My problem is there are times I just don't feel like writing. You know those days.

Belcher: When the spirit doesn't move you?

Agunga: When the spirit doesn't move me, I don't try. But once I move myself, then I can put a lot into it. I just got one article published in the *Journal of Extension*, which arrived two days ago.

Belcher: When did you get your first article published? Were you still in graduate school?

Agunga: No, actually after. I never published whilst I was in graduate school. I could have, but it wasn't really what I wanted to do. I guess I am a delayed writer. I never felt that writing would be something I'd be spending a lot of time on. I never felt that I was going to be sitting in academia. I felt that after getting my Ph.D., I was going back to Ghana, back in the trenches, working in development, visiting with farmers, doing things day to day. Writing and being in academia was an afterthought. It was after I had gotten my Ph.D. that I began to evaluate my situation. I realized that the field of development wasn't where I had thought it was. When I read all the books, at least, all that I could read on 'what is development' and 'how do you get there', I felt so dissatisfied that people who I had thought knew all the answers really didn't know anything that much. So I said, 'I'd like to contribute to the literature on development'. If I could help people get my vision of what the work is and how we should do it, I would be multiplying my efforts many times.

Belcher: Reaching many more people?

Agunga: Exactly. Reaching many more people. Then I started asking myself where I could have the opportunity to do that. Knowing that back in my village there is no library, no electricity, and not a book to read. Worse yet, once I get back out there, I'm probably lost forever. So I weighed the circumstances, and when the opportunity came for me to teach at Ohio State, I said I would capitalize on that because maybe that would buy me time to contribute to the literature on development. That is how I made that decision to come here. I should also mention, though, that my job in Ghana had been lost because I was here for five or six years and the project I was working for had died down; there was no more project to get back to. But I could go back and find a job. That was not the excuse. I just felt that the people I wanted to talk to are the people at the World Bank and the people at the United Nations, and they are not in my village, but right here, in New York. If I stayed here, I would be closer to them and hopefully could be heard, and I have been talking with them ever since. So that is how I came late to academia, but it's never really too late to write.

Belcher: Not when you have ideas.

Agunga: Exactly. The key is having a message to convey.

Belcher: Were your first publications things that came out of your dissertation?

Agunga: Yes, my first publications came out of my dissertation. My dissertation actually was a conceptual dissertation. I got a lot of mileage out of it because conceptual dissertations are essentially a literature review. You really do an extensive review in the dissertation. That really opens your mind up. That was what I discovered. After I had written my dissertation, it opened so much of my mind that I could begin to see one thousand and one opportunities to write. For most writers, at least for new writers, the problem is what to write about. I didn't have that problem. Two things helped me: My field experience helped me a lot because I could see the problem from right up to the person, the farmer, the policy maker, and the field agent in between. I could see problems at each level, so there was so much to write about that you could write all day. And when I came to academia, then I got exposed also to the academic side of things, and I found a big gap between theory and practice. That has been what I've been trying to do, narrow the gap. How can we take theory and make it sound practice, and vice versa? How can what we learn in practice shape the theories that guide our thinking? This has been very challenging and interesting.

Belcher: You mentioned that you have collaborated with your advisor. Do you often collaborate these days? Do you like that approach to writing?

Agunga: I like collaboration when the opportunity arises, but I don't depend on it to write. Some students tend to rely very much on collaboration probably because they don't know what to write about. They lean on somebody for help.

Belcher: Like their advisor?

Agunga: Like their advisor. But in my case, it was more that I want to write an article with my advisor, and that kind of gratification: we have worked so many years together; let's write an article that will help us remember those years. I try to do that with my own students once in a while. I don't just want them to reference me as an advisor. I want them to be able to say that we did this together, that we presented a conference paper together. I think that brings the advisor much closer than just the formal setting. That's why my former advisor and I did the book chapter together. He has some strength in some areas in the collaboration process. He's a very good editor, and he really taught me a lot. I think I know a bit more of how to edit now, but there's always something more you can learn from your mentor. Your mentor will always be your mentor; that's what I've learned from him. Even when you are out in the wide world, you still need somebody to kind of confer with.

Belcher: What about when you're preparing a manuscript that you want to send out to a journal? Do you take advantage of your colleagues very much? Do you ask them to read what you've written?

Agunga: I do that too. I like that procedure very much. Not so much with my colleagues because some of the areas that I write about, not many of my colleagues are interested in or know about. But I try to draw on those who are interested in that. Sometimes I send my work to my friends in other towns, in other campuses, and say, 'This is an article I'm working on for this journal; can you take a look at it and give me feedback?' But the people I use most are my graduate students. I give it to two or three of my graduate students and say, 'Look at it and come back and tell me'. Because, believe it or not, many of the people who read what we write tend to be graduate students.

Belcher: That's a good point.

Agunga: Right. It's not so much our peers as graduate students. So, if you don't understand it or don't like it, I think there is room for me to improve on it.

Belcher: That's a nice approach. What about reviewers? Do you find that their comments are helpful? Or do you think sometimes they're too critical? I know I personally have found that, if I get several sets of reviewers' comments, sometimes they'll be conflicting and not very helpful.

Agunga: That happens. But I think even in that conflict, there is still some truth that you're not getting your message across, because if you hear dissonance in their minds, maybe they're not seeing the problem from the way you are seeing it, and obviously it's not easy always to see the problem from that way. But at least you get the view of one group of readers. Sometimes you are writing a paper that's critical of what they are doing for a living.

Belcher: And those are exactly the people the editors may send it to.

Agunga: So they would do everything they can to say you're not right. For people like that, there's nothing you can do except tell the editor sometimes. I'm supposed to provide references to support my thesis, and I believe I've given you sufficient references. I've never really had a big problem of arguing with editors. One instance I had was an article on sustainable agriculture. Sustainable agriculture is a new concept that is coming out, saying that farmers should be more mindful of the land.

Belcher: I've worked with one of your students who was writing about this.

Agunga: Right. So the mainstream agriculture people are still not very happy with that concept. When I wrote this, the people who had to review it were in mainstream agriculture, and they were very sensitive about what I had to say. But the editor was very supportive of me and said, 'There are some concerns expressed by the reviewers, but I don't share their concerns. I'm going to publish it'. So that was one instance.

Belcher: The last thing I really want to ask you about has to do with what kind of advice you would give to people who are just starting their graduate careers and maybe they're new to this country. It seems to me, from what you've been saying, that one of the most important things for you was having a mentor. You still have a good relationship with your own mentor.

Agunga: Yes, I still have a very good relationship with my mentor. I think that's very important. A mentor doesn't necessarily have to be, as in my case, somebody who comes from the same environment. I've had professors who were not African, but we had a very good relationship. It is the subject matter that really unites the student and the instructor. If you're doing a topic that is of interest to your mentor or any faculty member, I think they'll be happier to work with you.

Belcher: And you're more likely to find a mentor.

Agunga: Right. So that's very important.

Belcher: Don't look for the person; look for the subject first?

Agunga: I would look for the subject first because some people want nice guys. You know, 'He's a nice guy, but he doesn't know what I'm doing.' Nice guys tend to just help you through the program. I've known people who have had dissertations that they've never had an article out of because it didn't make any sense; it had nothing of value in it. They had a nice advisor who just said, 'OK, OK, OK'. You can get that degree and go, but your future as a writer is not really that bright.

Belcher: How successful will you be?

Agunga: Exactly. But you have to just develop an interest in writing and look at what is happening in society and say, 'How can I help make a difference?' I think that is where you begin a discovery of a niche. Good writers find niches. They find an area that has been less trod, and then they begin to take that as their calling, and begin to do something about it.

Belcher: You talked about having a message.

Agunga: Right. You have to have a message. Without that, I don't think you really have a story.

A Professional Academic Life in Two Languages: An Interview with María Juliá

María Juliá received her bachelor's degree in social science and her master's in social work from the University of Puerto Rico, and her doctorate in social work from The Ohio State University, where she is currently a professor of social work. Prior to joining academia, she served for more than a decade as social work consultant for both the Puerto Rico and Ohio Departments of Health, and as a social work practitioner and researcher for a number of human and health service organizations. She is actively involved in both the local and global community through participation in numerous task forces, committees and boards of state, national and international organizations, where she volunteers her time. Her research interests include maternal and child health, multicultural education and competence, international social work, and the role of women in international social development. Her research has appeared in such journals as *Social Development Issues, International Social Work, Sociology and Social Welfare* and *Global Awareness*.

Belcher: Would you like to start by talking about your background, childhood, growing up in Puerto Rico?

Juliá: Well, as I mentioned to you earlier, I come from a very verbal culture and a very verbal family. My parents always stressed the importance of education and of writing well or writing properly. They even had sort of a demeaning view of those lacking these abilities, and they stressed education as a way or the means to avoid degrading or demeaning kinds of jobs or occupations. My father would say, 'If you don't speak well, you're going to end up scrubbing somebody's floor'.

Belcher: And what did they do for a living?

Juliá: My mother was a professor and my father was a controller for NCR, the National Cash Register Company, in Puerto Rico.

Belcher: So they were both highly educated people.

Juliá: Yes, they were highly educated. Neither one of them achieved a Ph.D. degree, but they had a college education and they were self-educated too, especially my father.

Diane, you had a question regarding identity and the role that language played in identity. If language is an element of culture, my cultural identity and my self-image are very much based on the good command of the language. I believe that my self image became tied to a command of the language and to communication skills, probably based on my growing up in a family that valued and admired proficiency in languages. And that was the case with my peers, too. At school, I very much valued my peers and I admired the ones who were proficient in any language.

Belcher: Were your parents bilingual?

Juliá: Yes, both of them were. My mother was an English teacher and my father grew up, until he was about seventeen, in New York City. So they were proficient both in English and Spanish.

Belcher: Would they speak English at home?

Juliá: Not at all, no. I learned English as a second language and not by choice. Since Puerto Rico is a US territory, and Puerto Ricans are US citizens, English is mandated as a second language in the school system. Not happy enough with that, my parents enrolled me in a Catholic school staffed by North American nuns since becoming bilingual was so important and necessary to them. So I started learning the English language when I entered kindergarten. I was immediately exposed to literature in English and immediately resented it since I could not understand it. I never truly or really enjoyed the experience. The nuns were extremely demanding, and my parents, particularly my father, was very impatient with my mistakes. You're asking about my initial feelings or my first encounters with the English language. They were in an all-English school and they were painful. They were intimidating; they were humiliating at times, provoking feelings of inadequacy. Probably that's why I prepared all of these notes because I still don't feel confident with the language. Basically, English was a school activity for me, and once out of the classroom, there was no use for it – at home or with peers, anywhere. I never practiced it and, in fact, I avoided it. Outside of school I totally avoided it.

Belcher: Because you didn't enjoy it?

Juliá: Exactly. Your third set of your questions has to do with if I am enjoying reading and writing. Well, until recently, when I began discovering and enjoying the wonders of reading and writing off pressure, meaning post-tenure, I have basically seen reading and writing in a second language as a need or as a quality that one should possess, but not as a pleasurable activity. It was always a tool of survival for me.

Belcher: Do you do much pleasure reading?

Juliá: Well, I guess that's what I'm saying. Until recently, when I began discovering and enjoying the wonders of reading for the pleasure of it, I guess that the level of confidence and the realization of my capacity to express myself freely in my second language has been a rather recent discovery for me.

Belcher: But even now when you want to just read for enjoyment, do you prefer to read something in Spanish?

Juliá: No, either one. It doesn't make a difference.

Belcher: You're equally comfortable.

Juliá: Yes, I am. I'm comfortable in both. Not in speaking the language, but in reading or writing it. I think I feel equally comfortable in both languages now because in some ways my level of confidence in my Spanish writing has diminished.

Belcher: I was going to ask you about that.

Juliá: Yes, it has diminished due to the lack of daily contact with it. I have been here over twenty years now and have felt the lack of touch and lack of contact with Spanish-speaking people. We don't have that many Spanish-speaking people here. And my husband is from here. His first language is English. My husband, in fact, is one of the most, if not the most, severe critics of my writing – a very bright, compassionate, gentle, and supportive academic colleague and critic, but tough too at times. So, I don't have the opportunity or need to continue using Spanish.

Sometimes I feel like I'm losing command of my native language. My father is dead now, but I write to my mother a couple of times a month, and she takes my letters and she goes through them, how do you say that, with a toothpick? And she tells me about all of the mistakes that I'm making, and I am surprised that I am making those kind of mistakes because I was always very proud of how well I could write in my first language. So, I guess you lose it with time.

Belcher: Do you think that another problem is, beyond the lack of opportunity to use the language, the fact that working in Spanish is not valued by the academy here? For instance, I know you publish sometimes in Spanish; do you get the feeling that those publications are not as valued as English-language publications? Is there much more pressure to publish in English, and more rewards for publishing in English?

Juliá: In our field, it has to do with the quality of the journals and the quality of the publisher, the reputation of the publishing company. If I publish something in Spanish, but it is in a very highly regarded journal, then I think it's as valued. At least in our field it is. I certainly hope it is.

Belcher: I was just wondering to what extent people who are English speakers are even aware of what those journals would be.

Juliá: Oh, I make sure they do. *[Both laugh]* When the time comes, I bring information about the journal and about the editorial board and everything.

Belcher: I see. That would be important to do. So, we were talking about your early childhood experiences and how you started to learn English in school, and that wasn't a very pleasant experience. And you did your early college work in Puerto Rico?

Juliá: Yes, I completed both my bachelor's and my master's in Puerto Rico. And then I came to Ohio State for my Ph.D.

Belcher: So, your BA and MA, was that all done in Spanish?

Juliá: In Spanish. Again, with a lot of literature in English. But in Spanish, yes. And I don't even want to start talking about my experiences when I came here to go into a doctoral program, and working in a second language. It was very frustrating.

Belcher: You hadn't been living here at all, though, before?

Juliá: No.

Belcher: OK, so that was an abrupt and severe kind of transition.

Juliá: Yes, and I don't consider myself fluent now. But I think I was a lot less fluent at the time.

Belcher: You're certainly fluent.

Juliá: And I think that that really jeopardized my doctoral education. As I look back at the experience, I can identify the number of times in which I could have taken better advantage of a situation. Just as an example, you're in a classroom, and they are discussing a topic, and you start translating your contribution to the discussion. At the time, I was still translating before opening my mouth. By the time I finished my translation of what I wanted to say, they were talking about something else. Not only had I lost the opportunity of interacting, but I was then lost because in my spending my time translating, I lost track of what they were talking about. So I think in many ways that jeopardized my doctoral education. I think that there were times when I was sleeping four or five hours a night because I felt that I had to read things over and over to be able to be at the same place that the rest of the students were.

Belcher: And you were just saying earlier that you didn't really start to enjoy reading and writing until fairly recently.

Juliá: Basically, English is the only language that I use in my life now, although my first language enriches very much, I believe, my writing in English. I still think about the optimum way of expressing an idea in my first language and then I translate it into English. It's probably the result of my belief that my strength in terms of vocabulary is still in Language One. I think I have a better vocabulary in Language One. And neither language affects my preference in the kind of writing that I do. I love the story-telling type of writing. Perhaps, again, because of my verbal culture. It is easier for me to do that kind of writing.

Belcher: Do you use that very much in your academic writing?

Juliá: No.

Belcher: Because you're a quantitative researcher?

Juliá: Exactly. I like the emotional, the passionate, and the argumentative pieces. What happened is that I didn't have that much freedom of choice there for a while because I had to focus more on what was professionally publishable for purposes of tenure. And this kind of literature that I like to write about is not that publishable in our field.

Belcher: Or it's only just beginning to be.

Juliá: Yes, with the qualitative approach to writing it is. I enjoy academic writing now a lot more than before I was tenured. And I still lack, however, that level of confidence required for good writing. I still do.

Belcher: So when you were going through your doctoral program, basically a quantitative approach was the approach to use?

Juliá: Yes, oh, definitely.

Belcher: That was the scientific way.

Juliá: In fact, I remember a couple of people in our program who wanted to do some pieces that at the time were considered more ethnography. The qualitative concept was not that well known or used, and they had a hard time having that option accepted, if they ever did, as a piece for purposes of dissertation research.

Belcher: I think different departments tend to just have different styles.

Juliá: *[Nods in agreement]* You had some questions about the voice. I think that my voice in English is not completely free; I wouldn't call it free. It does not have to do with honesty, but with the level of emotions and feelings – the soul, if you will – that I am able to impart to the words and the writing that I do.

Belcher: You don't feel that it's really there?

Juliá: It doesn't come in the second language. It's still a struggle when I'm using Language Two to bring that out; I would even call it something personal. I think I mentioned to you, I still cannot pray in English.

Belcher: That's interesting.

Juliá: I still cannot pray in English. Some people say that you will really be a truly bilingual person when you can pray and make love in a second language. I still cannot pray in a second language.

Belcher: What about dreaming? Do you dream in English?

Juliá: Yes, I dream in both. I have paid attention to that because I have been surprised at dreaming in English.

You're also asking about ownership. If I define ownership as being in control of the format and control of the voice and the style, the freedom of content at times, I think that, up to recently, it's been essentially controlled by publishers and editors and reviewers. I think that's why I'm feeling so much better now. I think I am in better control of what I am writing because I'm writing at my own pace and what I want, and if publishers do not want it, then, so what? I do not need it to secure a job.

Belcher: So, in the past, before you had tenure, if you submitted a manuscript to a journal and the reviewers asked for a lot of changes, would you just make the changes?

Juliá: Yes.

Belcher: You wouldn't argue with the editor?

Juliá: I wouldn't argue, and, in fact, I would sometimes even bend my ideas.

Belcher: Compromise?

Juliá: Compromise just to be able to have the piece published. Especially as tenure approached. But now, I just say forget it. I am going to send it to somebody else who will understand what I am trying to say. As you know, what some people want is for you to eventually write what they wanted to write. It's not necessarily what you were trying to say. You might not be saying it clearly, but you can improve that message without having to change your ideas. But anyway, nowadays I don't compromise as readily as I used to. Maybe that's why I'm enjoying it now. Right now I'm working on a book on the cultural construction of gender.

Belcher: That sounds fascinating.

Juliá: And I still have difficulty. My main difficulty, I think, is finding the correct words in Language Two, and that slows me down.

Belcher: Is this an edited volume or a single-author work?

Juliá: It's an edited volume. Except for the first chapters. I'm writing the conceptual framework and the theoretical foundation. But it's hard to find the right words to express what you want to say in a second language.

Belcher: So do you have people from all around the world contributing?

Juliá: No, no, from the United States. I have twelve women, and each one of them belongs to the culture they are writing about. They are writing about the construction of gender in their own culture and, based on the understanding of that social construction, how you can work with women from those cultural groups. It's a very exciting project.

Belcher: Yes, that should be an important contribution.

Juliá: Oh, I am really thrilled with the comments from the reviewers. There is a woman – I am calling her a woman; I don't even know if it's a woman or a man, but I think you have to be a woman to be that sensitive. _[Both laugh]_ She says that she hasn't seen anything like this in the literature, and she is, according to the credentials that I've heard, an expert on culture and gender. So, that's great. I'm really thrilled with that. Um, can we move on to another topic?

Belcher: Oh, sure.

Juliá: After talking about ownership earlier, you had a question about collaboration. I really think that there are, of course, things that are better as solo projects. I don't have questions about that, but I'm very gregarious and I love collaboration. I'm fascinated by the interaction and the exchange of ideas that take place in collaboration, particularly with colleagues from other professions. And I believe that four eyes can see a lot more than two when you're writing. Collaboration also helps me stay focused on the task, and disciplined. It's very stimulating. I'm very much involved with the Interprofessional Commission of Ohio here, at Ohio State. I teach some of their courses too. So, I really enjoy that approach. The problem I find in collaborating is not the result of my writing in Language Two, but in the expectations brought in by the collaborators regarding my work capacity or my potential contribution. Yes, it has been very discouraging and disappointing to experience the lack of confidence of colleagues who, based on the sole fact that I am writing in a second language, dismiss, if not underestimate, my potential for contribution. In fact, I was talking with another person who writes in a second language here at the university and we came up with an analogy. We said, 'It's like when you are trying to cook a dish and you have a group of people cooking the dish. Everybody is supposed to do a part of it. And you were given the least important part because they don't have confidence that you're gonna do the right thing. Often your part is to just be there.'

Belcher: You can boil the water.

Juliá: No, even worse than that! It's 'Hey, you can clean the pot after this is finished'. It's a lack of confidence in the capacity of people. I don't know why, I guess. I suspect.

Belcher: The students talk about the same thing when they have to do collaborative projects with native-speaker students, domestic students. They're always given the numerical data analysis to do so they won't have any responsibility for the verbal part of the project.

Juliá: Yes. So anyway, that's what I think about collaboration.

Belcher: So, it's kind of a mixed blessing. You like to do it, but the reactions of the people you work with aren't always helpful.

Juliá: Yes. You were asking me also about how do I go about writing? I block time, I guess, like everybody else does, for writing-related activities every week. I try to block in my calendar, ideally, part of three days a week, on the average. And again, it depends on the rest of the demands. But at least an hour so that I can keep the discipline. If time permits, and I am rested and in the right frame of mind, I can write for three or four hours straight through. Again, it depends on the task and the topic I am writing about. I do a better job when I'm alone, when I have silence and no interruptions or distractions, like everybody else.

Belcher: Can you write here in your office?

Juliá: It's hard, but I do. I think I can write here better than at home. At home, I have too many distractions, things that I haven't done for six months. The dust is all over and I haven't looked at it for six months, but if I stay to work at home I will dust. And I will do a lot of other things and waste a lot of time. So, despite the interruptions, I tend to work better here. And here I have more resources I need on hand. I use the computer, but I grew up learning to write using pencil and pen and paper. And I still have a special relationship with pencil and paper that the computer hasn't been able to replace.

Belcher: So, when you're doing a first draft or just jotting down your ideas, do you do it with pencil and paper?

Juliá: Generally, yes. And people are telling me that I waste a lot of time by doing that, but I can be a lot more creative doing it that way. I go through rituals. My husband calls them rituals; he says he cannot understand. I go through rituals of writing and rewriting and rewriting and rewriting, and I'm never completely satisfied that I have it right, that I have done it correctly.

Reading plays a major role in my writing, both as a resource for documenting my ideas, but also in the development of the ideas. It improves my foundation knowledge, it informs my writing, it challenges my ideas, and it gives me, not only new ideas, or not necessarily new ideas, but it helps me to conceptualize abstractions that I have been playing with for a while, or with which I might have been struggling.

Belcher: Do you do a certain amount of reading each day?

Juliá: No, I tend to read in long blocks first. I tend to do all of these things in blocks. I tend to read first as much as I can before I start writing, and then I write for a while, maybe two or three weeks, and then I go back to reading again. And as I write, I identify the areas in which I need to read more. So, I go back and forth.

Belcher: Do you feel that your reading tends to be interdisciplinary? Are you reading mainly journals in social work, or are you reading in a lot of different areas?

Juliá: I'm reading in a lot of areas. I think a lot of the reading depends on what is the topic that I'm trying to work with. Like right now, I'm doing a lot of reading on gender and culture. But, I think it has to do more with what I am writing about at the time. I think that determines my reading. The Internet, by the way, serves as a source for me to identify information on materials to enrich my knowledge base, but not necessarily my skills in writing.

Belcher: So for gender and culture, you may be reading anthropology and psychology?

Juliá: All over campus, all over the twenty-some libraries, because I do the reading there a lot rather than staying here, because of the interruptions in the office. I also try as a writer to get a lot of feedback; feedback is extremely important to me. It reassures me. It gives me a little bit more confidence that

I have made good use of the language or that I use the language properly, that I'm saying what I intend to say, and that I am expressing myself appropriately.

Belcher: Are there people that you routinely give your work to?

Juliá: It depends on the topic again. Sometimes I give colleagues a piece I'm working on. There are a couple of people who are English majors that if I have serious questions about the language I tend to ask them to look at the piece and give me feedback. I do that all the time.

Belcher: And most of the reading you do, you probably don't do electronically.

Juliá: No, no no. In fact, if I have a couple of journal articles that I really like and want to use for my writing, even if I have already read them at the library, I have to copy them and bring them with me because I also need to underline and put exclamation marks and asterisks and questions all over the margins of the article. So, I still work in that paper/pencil/pen/highlighter relationship.

Belcher: You like the visual input.

Juliá: Yes, I guess that's it. And the ritual of underlining, maybe.

You were asking about success and other stories. I don't think that there are necessarily success stories, but disappointments, frequently discouraged, and doubting my ability, loads of questioning about my ability to make it. An instance I would consider a success: I always remember the first time that someone – it was a colleague here – told me that she thought that I was very articulate in the English language. We came out of a faculty meeting and she said, 'María, you're so articulate'. I almost died! 'Goodness sake', I said, 'let me go get a tape recorder! I want to put this down on a tape recorder! My father should be here to hear that, that I'm articulate in the English language. How can you say that?' I had never heard that in my life.

Belcher: So, what about your first publication? That must have made you feel more confident too. When did you publish your first article? Was that while you were in graduate school, or after you finished the dissertation, or later?

Juliá: When I was in graduate school and when I wrote my dissertation, there was not this kind of pressure for publishing that we have now in academia. Publishing wasn't really stressed in our doctoral program at that time. I think that, when I started thinking about joining academia, given my international interests and need for flexibility in my schedule, that's when I started thinking that I had to start writing. I was at the time a consultant with the state health department, and I was doing some research in black infant mortality in the state of Ohio. That's when I started developing my first papers.

Belcher: Well that must have given you confidence, when you started publishing.

Juliá: Well. not really. I think I still don't have it, you know.

Belcher: There are lots of native speakers who don't publish in English.

Juliá: But I still don't have it! And I can see, for example, if I give you a paper that I write, how little input you could give me now in terms of sentence construction and use of the language, and so forth. For comparison, I can take a recently written paper and place it by one of those first papers I wrote and had given to somebody for feedback, and the first paper looks like a beehive of written suggestions and corrections. Well, I guess that should increase my level of confidence in doing so much better. But still, it's as if you grow up with that insecurity, and I guess it's very hard to get rid of it.

Belcher: But you're also publishing in Spanish occasionally?

Juliá: Occasionally.

Belcher: Do you feel that it's important to do that to reach a different audience?

Juliá: Oh yes. I still feel very much responsible for making contributions to the Spanish-speaking audience. I do that more with presentations. For me, making a presentation in Spanish is so much better than doing it in English. My first presentations in English – you wouldn't believe it. I wouldn't sleep the night before. I would be sick; my stomach would be sick. I didn't know sometimes if I was going to be able to make the presentation without having to run to the bathroom before I was finished.

Belcher: No, I've been there.

Juliá: I'm going all over the map. But to answer your question, I do feel an obligation to make a contribution to a Spanish-speaking audience and I'm trying to do that.

Belcher: And when you do publish in Spanish, do the editors make a lot of comments on your text?

Juliá: Well, when I write something in Spanish the editors can say a lot about content but not about grammar because I shared it with my mother before I sent it in. [*Both laugh*] And she will give me feedback about grammar and so forth. Like I said, even the letters that I write to her she edits and then literally insults me over the phone telling me, 'How could you do that? How could you, at this ancient stage in your life, do that? What are you gonna do the day I die? You better learn before I'm gone'. So, I have in my mother a severe critic and teacher in Spanish, and the equivalent in English in my husband.

Something else that I would like to add – I had written this in response to one of your questions, and I'm not sure where it was supposed to fit. We were talking about academic life, I guess. I think there's a thin line between waiting for the ideas to develop and missing the boat along the way, versus rushing to get into the boat so quickly that the boat ride becomes meaningless, both for those who ride it and for others. There are no comparisons intended here with the type of work or the quality of work, or the quantity-versus-quality issue on which we embark every day in academia. But, this is a story that I recently heard and I thought illustrates it so well. And I think it was Botticelli, one of the great Italian artists, who went to see Michelangelo. Have you heard it?

Belcher: No, I haven't.

Juliá: He went to see Michelangelo while Michelangelo was painting the Sistine Chapel, and Botticelli was complaining. I think it was Botticelli; I'm not sure. He was complaining to Michelangelo about how long he, Michelangelo, was taking to paint the chapel. He, Botticelli, started mentioning all of the many sculptures and the many paintings that he had completed while Michelangelo was taking forever and ever in the same project. He went on and on, 'And I did this sculpture and I finished this painting, and you are still on this one'. And Michelangelo looked at him and simply replied, 'And it shows'. In other words, he was talking about the quality of the work. That's all he said, 'And it shows'. And I guess that's what we face here every day. And I think that I am moving now more towards spending a lot of time on projects that I really like and want to do as opposed to what I'm obliged to do in order to secure my job.

Belcher: And that's mainly because you now feel secure with tenure?

Juliá: I wonder. It would be interesting to find out how people who are writers, but are not in academia feel about this, because I'm sure that, without having the pressure of tenure, many of us would have developed in a different direction. Our writing here is so permeated by these pressures and these demands and, while I understand that a writer outside of academia still has the pressure of a publishing company and finishing something on time, I think it would be a pressure of a different nature.

Belcher: More self-imposed.

Juliá: *[Nods in agreement]* Yes, so, I don't know.

Belcher: Do you have many students that you work with who are working on big projects, or do you advise many doctoral students who are working on dissertations?

Juliá: Yes, I am on a number of dissertation committees and I teach one of the seminars in the doctoral program, the international social work and social development seminar.

Belcher: And are some of your students non-native speakers?

Juliá: Yes. And I understand their situation so much better, I think. I know where they are coming from. And some of them say they feel that the relationship with me in that regard is different because I know what they are going through, how much energy it takes for someone who is from a different country to adjust to the new environment. Now, to come from a different country *plus* talking in a different language... I remember when I first came to live in this state. I would go to bed and feel as if I had been working in a coal mine all day as opposed to being in school. One day, I think somebody mentioned to me that it would require twice the energy because I was working in a different language. It was a very exhausting period of time – at least the first couple of quarters were very exhausting.

Belcher: Well, I can understand that. I lived in China for a year and, as I was just a beginning-level learner of Chinese, had to struggle to communicate.

Juliá: So you know what I'm talking about. It takes so much energy; just to conceptualize takes energy, but then to conceptualize in a different language, especially when you're still translating in your mind before you open your mouth, is draining.

Belcher: So, do you think that international students maybe gravitate towards you because they feel that you will be more sympathetic?

Juliá: No, I don't think so. I think that our students, most of the time, reach out for people who share their area of interest and the topic of their research or the nature of their research design.

Belcher: I think one of the things I mentioned earlier that I'd ask you about was any advice that you would give to people, maybe people who are starting out as graduate students here.

Juliá: You had that kind of question. I guess I think that you have to ignore the references that are made, implicit or explicit, to your capacity to make it, because I think that directs your way then. You have to keep on trying. At the same time, the only way of focusing on doing it and keeping on track is also by ignoring all of these kinds of negative messages, implicit most of the time, that you get from other people.

I really appreciate the opportunity of doing this interview with you because it gave me the opportunity for some insights for which I haven't taken time before. There were things that I hadn't even thought or reflected about. Like while I'm trying to overcome my lack of confidence, I still get all of these implicit messages of inadequacy. It's interesting; sometimes it happens even in a faculty meeting, even in a committee meeting, when I am trying to make a contribution. And again, I am from a verbal culture – a culture that communicates very much verbally, but non-verbally too–and I sometimes see a little frown or a gesture in someone, and I can tell that that person isn't able to follow my thoughts, either because of my accent or because the person is doubting what I am saying. You have to really look in another direction, because otherwise you get paralyzed. And I'm not talking about paralyzed physically, but my ideas suddenly stop flowing when I feel that vibe. Sometimes I think, well, hell with it. But sometimes I don't. Am I getting paranoid? At the same time, sometimes other colleagues validate the observation or contribution of mine. So it's like a constant struggle. That's why my suggestion would be to try to stay away or totally ignore the negative and focus on the positive messages.

Belcher: Focus on what you will accomplish?

Juliá: Yes, focus on what you're gonna do.

Belcher: That seems like really good advice.

Juliá: Doing this interview with you has been an opportunity for me to grow. I have explored and realized more my levels of confidence in writing and in the ability to express myself. Thank you.

On Being a Citizen of the World: An Interview with Luis Proenza

A native of Mexico, **Luis M. Proenza** became President of The University of Akron in 1999. Prior to this, he was the vice president for research, dean of graduate education and professor of biological sciences at Purdue University. He holds a bachelor's degree in psychology from Emory University, a master's degree in psychology from The Ohio State University, and a doctorate in neurobiology from the University of Minnesota. He joined the faculty of the University of Georgia in 1971 and served as an assistant professor of psychology and as associate, then full, professor of zoology. In 1977, he became the study director for the National Academy of Science Committee on Vision. He was appointed assistant to the president of the University of Georgia in 1984. In 1987, he joined the University of Alaska Fairbanks as the vice chancellor of research, dean of the graduate school, and professor of biology, and from 1992-1994, was acting vice president for academic affairs and research for the University of Alaska system. The author of numerous journal publications and the editor and co-editor of two books, Luis Proenza has served as a member of the National Biotechnology Policy Board, chair of the Council on Research Policy and Graduate Education, founding president of the Arctic Research Consortium of the United States, and member of the Executive Committee of the Association of Graduate Schools in the Association of *American* Universities.

Proenza: My first language was Spanish, since I was born in Mexico. My family had relatively low levels of education. My mother probably only finished the sixth grade, and my father certainly had a high school education, but then he had some business training in New York. While they were both native Spanish speakers themselves – he from Cuba, she from Mexico – my father had lived in New York for many years. One of the influences he felt was a strong sense that English and the US were an important part of the future world, so he thought that I should learn English. Although there was no particular emphasis in those early years, primary education in Mexico included English lessons beginning in the first grade. And then I came to the US at age eleven and really immersed myself in English, and my formative education continued entirely in English. Of course, my family did keep a fair number of books at home, many of which were in English, and certainly in those years they were not a huge part of my life, but they were accessible. My family, also, had always subscribed to the *Reader's Digest* and this carried a lot of vignettes and things of the sort that I read regularly.

Mexico has a system of education perhaps more akin to that in European countries. I certainly felt that English was required right from grade one and we were expected to learn aspects of English as a second language from very early on. Secondly, there was a degree of compression, meaning that they had more to teach in a shorter period of time than I have found common in the US. When I first came to the US at age eleven and to the seventh grade, in terms of subject matter it was fully two years before I learned something new. Obviously, those first two years were exceedingly important in sharpening my knowledge of English, but not much else.

Right before I came to the US, and knowing that I would be going to school, my father arranged for me to have additional tutoring in English so that I would have a little more of a jump start. On arriving in the US in 1956, at a boarding military school in Northeast Georgia, I remember that the biggest difficulty I had was capturing the meaning of words from among the many nuances of accents and a lot of colloquialisms. But, with total immersion, that went very, very fast as I recall. By the end of the first year, I felt quite at ease, although I made some mistakes in the usage of terms and in relation to what was acceptable or not. I remember, for example, a story where someone put sulfur on the radiator in my room. As you know, sulfur doesn't smell very good when it is heated, and I suggested that it smelled like the 's' word. My teachers didn't quite understand that I wasn't trying to be the swearing type, I was just trying to be descriptive. But that early time went very quickly.

Along the same lines of your question, I was learning English as a second language very early and, I guess, voluntarily. It wasn't something I sought *per se*, but it was part and parcel of our culture, and part and parcel of what my father thought was important. That, in many respects, was the major reason that I came to the US, at least initially – to learn English. In fact, my father was concerned, as we looked at various schools, that if I were to go too far north in the US, I might be too cold, but if I were to go too far south, then there would be so much Spanish speaking influence that I might never learn English. But I really did not begin seriously reading or writing in any language until college.

I remember some writing in high school, but I just don't remember it being a major part of my life at that point. I wrote some copy for articles for the school yearbook, and I was drawing some editorial cartoons – all in English. As far as writing, I believe it really started seriously in college. Emory University provided a very fine background. Frankly, however, you asked about developing literacy, and I think that real literacy came to me in graduate school. It came when I really immersed myself, particularly in scientific writing, and it became very obvious how presentations needed to be made in order for them to have impact and to communicate a message and to do so with some degree of power. That's not the right word exactly; 'impact' might be the better word. In short, what I wanted to do was to communicate in a way that I would be listened to, I suppose.

Connor: For me, too, learning to write scientific reports in English was liberating because of the structure, the 'moves' in scientific research articles.

Proenza: The other thing that, to this day, I still do a great deal of, certainly in my teaching and in many of my presentations, is to use a series of visuals, as the, if you will, outline and then keying off for whatever I want to say. So, rather than having a written text, in many cases I simply have a series of slides and use them as the linkage for the thoughts that I want to express. That was, I think, very, very important in terms of developing my spoken voice in English. Today, I'm called upon to speak publicly quite frequently. However, with the groups that I speak to today, they want to just hear a five to fifteen-minute speech, and visuals aren't as important. I am not necessarily communicating highly detailed scientific content, but rather more of a point of view, opinion, message, typically of support for a program, and things of that sort.

I never thought that Spanish hindered my development of English. In fact, certainly by the time I was in college, Spanish became in a sense my second language, and English became my primary language. Today – obviously this is many, many years later; remember, I came to the US when I was eleven and I am now fifty-three; I've been here fundamentally continuously with the exception of one year – I even dream in English. The only thing that I still do in Spanish, occasionally, is my multiplication tables.

My mother and father are deceased, but my cousins, aunts, etc. are in Mexico. I'm an only child, no brothers or sisters. I can remember very clearly when I first went back to Mexico, after I got my Ph.D., and I was invited to make some presentations, not knowing the technical terms in Spanish prompted me to be inventive, and fortunately, of course, much of what I invented were the appropriate cognates and indeed were words that would be translated. However, as you undoubtedly know from throughout the world, you can get into trouble in different cultures, even in those that speak the same language, because often the same words will have separate meanings. Certainly in Latin American, a Spanish word that is perfectly neutral in Mexico may be an insult in Colombia, Chile, or Argentina. So, navigating those nuances, and also literal translations, was a challenge.

I remember another instance when I was asked to translate for a US scientist at a conference in psychology in Mexico. There is an area of experimental psychology that has worked with rodents, rats in particular, and colloquially has been known as 'rat psychology'. Well, trying to translate the term 'rat psychology', I used the literal translation, especially for a rat psychologist, a person working with rats, and used the Spanish term *psicologo ratero*. Well, technically that is correct, but *ratero* colloquially means thief. So I had just called everybody a thieving psychologist. But things of that nature have happened in various settings and one adapts and learns. I never thought of it as a hindrance.

While today I don't read Spanish regularly, if I'm confronted with a Spanish text, I find that there are a lot of words that I don't know. But in every case, if I have an opportunity to read the great writers of Spanish such as Pablo Neruda, I prefer to see them in the original rather than the translation.

Connor: Do you remember when you were in school if you kept on reading Spanish books also, or if all of your reading was in English?

Proenza: Once I came to the US, virtually all, I would say 99%, of my reading was in English. I have kept my speaking ability in Spanish only by virtue of trips back to visit family, and telephone calls, things of that nature. However, while my accent is still very much the standard of Mexico City Spanish, the range of my Spanish vocabulary is quite limited. I hold my own well in basic conversation, regardless of whether it is with scientists or business people, but clearly if I tried to read a news article in the paper or to try to write a serious message in Spanish, I would need help.

Connor: Did you write letters back home in Spanish when you were in high school?

Proenza: Yes, and when I was in high school I did write letters to send back home in Spanish, and I still do that. But again, spelling is limited, and vocabulary is more in keeping with what you would call an adult conversational Spanish, but certainly not literary Spanish. I don't think there is any text that I would prefer to write in Spanish. All of my writing today, and most of my speaking, is in English. I do find that my having retained a conversational ability in Spanish is very useful in what I do today. Clearly when I come across someone from anywhere in Latin America or Spain, it is wonderful to be able to relate to them in Spanish, and I'm quite comfortable in that domain.

For whatever it's worth, I had always considered myself more of a citizen of the world rather than of a particular country. So today, even when I speak Spanish, I'm not trying to promote my Hispanicity or anything of that nature. I just happen to know it, and it's nice to be able to relate to people who speak Spanish. It's very helpful.

Fundamentally, English is the language of my professional, academic life, and Spanish plays a role in my professional life only when I travel abroad. Yes, Spanish does enrich my English writing, largely because of the power of Romance languages. Certainly, the rhythm of Spanish has influenced how I try to use the English language because there is a certain beauty in language. Even though many people do not consider English as a beautiful language, I do.

Connor: You were speaking about your first language enriching second-language writing.

Proenza: That is more in terms of aesthetics than anything else. Occasionally, of course, I use Spanish to suggest a synonym, or to suggest another word, and that's very helpful. I love to write on more general topics these days, of course, as I have gotten more and more detached from the laboratory. The most difficult thing I have to do really is in assuring myself that what I want to say adequately represents the factual knowledge at hand. In other words, I try to be careful not too get too far into the realm of what a friend of mine calls the 'metaphorically extravagant'. I try not to get too much into hyperbole.

The audience is absolutely critical to me. For me, these days, that is more in terms of speaking than writing, but frequently when I make a presentation, I'm asked for the text. I guess I not only visualize the audience but, as I'm preparing a talk, I almost talk to myself and do so as close as possible to the rhythm that I expect that I will actually use. It is very helpful for me to do a rehearsal, even though I do it only in my head. Often, that will very clearly point out to me that something isn't working and that I need to change it. In a sense, it's a way of 'trying it out' for size, and as I 'hear' my text, I find out what works and what should be changed to create better impact.

Connor: Do you think communicating clearly is more difficult because you are a second-language learner?

Proenza: No. I came at an early enough age. Most of the Spanish speakers that I know who came to the US or who started speaking English after age fourteen or sixteen have had difficulty giving up their accent. Most people judge that I do not speak with a Spanish accent, so in most contexts I think I have kind of a neutral English accent. But no, somewhere probably at age eighteen or twenty, I found my English voice, and it has continued to develop. I don't think that I take particular pains to continue to develop it.

For me, if I go for weeks without a public presentation, then the next opportunity may not be as good a presentation as if I had been making presentations constantly. Obviously, making presentations too frequently, I don't have enough time to prepare and hence the degree of detail may suffer. I do think about my voice, again, mostly in terms of the message that I'm presenting, and Spanish does affect my voice in that context in that I'm probably somewhat more expressive in my body language when I speak than many native English speakers are. And obviously, I'm able to bring in some examples that come from other cultures.

Ownership of my text tends not to be an issue for me. I no longer write a great deal of technical literature. What I do today is really try to generate the broader ownership of ideas that I bring forward. I'm really delighted when people start picking up the ideas that concern me and that I have expressed.

Most of the projects that I'm working on are on themes relating to education, such as higher education as an infrastructure for the country, education as an investment instrument, higher education as a basis for economic development, and things of this sort.

I do collaborate with others. My wife helps me hone some ideas periodically and certainly, on a particular theme in what I do today, I will usually have input from three or four of my staff, and the ideas shape themselves as we develop them.

Connor: Do you think your training as a laboratory scientist and working in groups was helpful for you in learning to communicate?

Proenza: Very definitely. Without question, looking at the literature, reading about the literature, talking about the literature, and going to conferences made a huge difference to me in both writing and speaking.

How do I go about writing? *[Laughs]* Whenever it's needed, I guess. When I was writing scientifically, the structure of the scientific paper was very helpful because you knew what kinds of things needed to be where, and everything sort of followed that format. In what I do today, it's more of the borrowing of an idea. So what I do is, typically, borrow whatever phrases I have used in previous writings that may be helpful, and then begin simply to sketch out thoughts. Then, as they begin to be clearer in relation to the things I want to express, other things begin to suggest themselves as introductory to that thought, or as follow-ups to that thought. Things then take shape in many respects randomly, rather than within a particular structure.

Connor: Do you write by hand, or do you compose on the computer?

Proenza: Both. I typically find myself writing on an airplane or when I'm at a meeting waiting for something else. I then come back and put it on the computer and integrate other thoughts and shape them. I usually go through three to ten edits until I have something that I put in my briefcase to deliver, and I'm usually still editing even seconds before I give it or even in the midst of the delivery. Just this week I gave a talk to the Indianapolis Rotary Club and several things arose to add to my remarks – some, for example, from the previous speaker that was mentioned, and others from a person in the audience that made a particular reference possible. All of these things just kind of fall into place and hopefully don't get forgotten, which is the biggest difficulty.

Without question, reading plays a major role in my writing. I get a lot of ideas from the *Wall Street Journal, Forbes, Fortune, and Business Week.* Ironically, virtually none of my ideas come from the educational literature. It seems as if any of the ideas that I find valuable to communicate about education don't come from education itself; they come from the business literature.

Yes, reading has made me a better writer and, hopefully, communicator. Today the Internet does get me through to a lot of material, sometimes more in terms of networking in that I will find something on the Internet that suggests something else. Just the other day – as you know I'm going to be assuming the presidency at the University of Akron – I found out that there is an Inventors' Hall of Fame in Akron. It is independent of the University. Going to the Internet, I was immediately able to find out something about it and get the appropriate context in print and shape my thoughts about it. It is very useful for that.

I love to get feedback not only on my writing but on my speaking. My wife is my best help in that regard, and my best critic. Just recently, at a presentation I made, she said, 'You do a lot better when you don't look at your notes'. So yes, I can appreciate that and yet sometimes when you're trying to get a point across, you can't memorize every word, and notes help you do that. If I'm speaking more for, let's say, inspiration than for delivery of the message, notes may not be needed or even helpful, but if I'm trying to deliver a message, I will try to write it down more carefully.

Connor: So, for twenty years or so, you wrote for scientific publication. Now, you write as an administrator.

Proenza: This continues to be an evolution of a theme, so to speak. Clearly, I started out within a fairly narrow area in that my work was retinal neurophysiology. But as I moved into positions of organizational leadership, first in Washington, with a committee on vision research, I expanded the dimensions of vision research from ophthalmology to broader aspects of research and administrative responsibility. In Georgia, it had to do with biotechnology; in Alaska, it was Arctic research; here at Purdue, it is, of course, very, very broad – from agricultural economics and agribusiness to materials science and pharmacology and pharmaceutical practice, etc.

Connor: Writing for academic audiences versus popular audiences is very difficult for a lot of academics to do. Not all academics are good at it, and many of them don't want to do it.

Proenza: The other theme that has existed is that I tend today to want to instill change into various professional contexts, and by that I mean, at my level now, national administrative meetings of higher education, graduate education, research administration, you name it. And at these meetings, I'm prone to want to challenge the status quo and put out provocative ideas.

The greatest dilemma I have is that I seem to at times be a little bit ahead of where people want to be. For example, I am convinced that not necessarily the Internet, not necessarily television and electronic conferencing and all of these things, not necessarily any one of those elements is going to be *the* next wave in education. But that some major impact will be felt from these technologies and that, I believe, the private sector will be trying very hard to go into business for itself and compete with us is, I think, undeniable. I was speaking about that ten years ago. For some reason, I don't know why it is, I tend to be provocative about things that most people aren't ready to quite yet talk about. And I don't know where this comes from, whether it's part of the fact that I grew up in Mexico, very much looking to the future in other respects, or whether it is that I came forward and was fascinated by the rapidly developing technological world that we now live in.

Connor: Maybe, as a second-language speaker, you've always needed to take risks.

Proenza: I never thought about that; I don't know.

Connor: So would you have any particular horror or success stories about your publishing experiences?

Proenza: I don't think so, certainly not in my scientific writing, and I don't have any that I can share with gusto. Advice for others? I think practice, practice, practice is not a trivial statement, but practice with an audience, I guess, would be important. Even if you are not getting feedback from authors, comparing your writing to what you're seeing in the best articles and the best literature I think is very helpful. With regard to reading, be broad. A breadth of reading is useful. I find, as I was saying earlier, a lot of things of value in places outside of what would be considered the domain of my industry. I find often far too little in the literature about higher education itself and a lot more in other areas, how others see us. Without question, though, there's some splendid, splendid things being done in a scholarly sense and by others who are within the academy writing about the academy.

Connor: Thank you so much for your time and best wishes for your new position as President at the University of Akron.

The Advantages of Starting Out Multilingual: An Interview with Steven Beering

Born in Germany, **Steven C. Beering** has been President of Purdue University since 1983. He serves on a number of corporate boards, including the American Life Insurance Company, Arvin Industries, Eli Lilly and Company, and NIPSCO Industries. Before coming to Purdue, he served for decades as dean and director of the Indiana University Medical Center. He holds appointments as Professor of Medicine at Indiana University and Professor of Pharmacology at Purdue University. He has held numerous national offices, including the chairmanship of the Association of American Medical Colleges. He is a former regent of the National Library of

Medicine. He currently serves on the executive committees of the Association of American Universities and the National Association of State Universities and Land-Grant Colleges. He is a fellow of the American College of Physicians and the Royal Society of Medicine, and a member of Phi Beta Kappa, the Institute of Medicine of the National Academy of Sciences and the Indiana Academy.

Connor: You grew up in Germany and were multilingual before coming to the US.

Beering: I grew up speaking German and French. My mother was also fluent in English because of her background and education, and the family was international with Swiss and French, German, and English roots. At home, in order for their children not to understand what they were saying, the adults often spoke a foreign language. This, of course, doesn't achieve its intended purpose, but it's wonderful for improving the children's language skills. I also had a French lady as an au pair. So, I was comfortable with English, French and German as I grew up. My parents and grandparents encouraged me continually to develop language skills. The encouragement continued after we had grown up. We stayed in touch, and eventually my mother and grandmother – who lived to the age of 103 – lived together as widows. I would make the weekly phone call to the two ladies, always on Saturdays wherever I was in the world. I must have carried this on for the better part of three decades. It was terribly important to them, and after they died, I realized how important it had become to me. My grandmother would always begin our conversation by saying: 'Have you come across any new ideas this week?' Then, depending on what I would answer, she would say that she had read the most extraordinary book or seen a play or movie that she thought I would enjoy. She would encourage me to get involved with whatever was exciting her mind at the time.

Connor: Which language did your telephone calls take place in?

Beering: In the early years, it would be German, but since my grandmother was born in Paris, she frequently would revert to French in order to think of the right word or express an idea the way she wanted. But most of the time we spoke English.

Connor: What about writing, at what point did you learn English?

Beering: Well, we were in England before coming to America, so we decided early on that English was the language we needed to perfect. I tried to then get fluent in English writing, reading and speaking. This was a very good decision, of course, because now English has become the closest thing to an international language. It is the language of the European Union and of aviation.

Connor: Could you talk about your literacy experiences? Were your grandmother and mother big influences on you intellectually? What about reading, writing, and things like that? Do you remember having books read to you?

Beering: Yes, my mother not only read children's stories to me, but she authored and illustrated them. She was very, very talented – also played the piano. She and her mother were really more like twins than mother and daughter. They looked a lot alike, and they truly enjoyed each other's company. My father was so proud of escorting them around to various social functions. He was a very correct German whose parentage was really Austrian, and he was an international businessman. The three of them and, during his lifetime, my mother's father were a very, very close-knit family. A typical nuclear family in the best sense of the word: high values. Everyone read a lot; that was very important. I'm happy that my grandchildren are reading now. This is terrific.

Connor: What about writing experiences? Do you remember painful experiences when you were young, back in Germany? People usually enjoy reading more than they enjoy writing.

Beering: Of course, professionally I have had to write a great deal over the years. I give an average of 250 to 300 speeches a year. They are often extemporaneous, and I find that I do very well that way. I get a bit impatient if I have to write and edit and revise, because I think it makes me lose the spontaneity. Normally, I just have a note card with one or two ideas. This allows me to tailor the subject to my audience and its mood at a given moment. Most of my communication is really oral and verbal, but I have done a lot of writing, both scientific writing and letter writing.

Connor: I heard many of your speeches when I was working in graduate school at the commencement ceremony; they were always well received, very polished. Did you have a script for those speeches?

Beering: Yes. For commencement I do use a script because it is timed and there are so many people who have to speak. A lot of things are going on in a compressed moment there. We usually have two commencement ceremonies on the same day, so we cannot run over. So I use a script. I may depart from it slightly, but I'm disciplined to stay within that time frame, eight to ten minutes.

Connor: When you write those, do other people read them? React to them? Do you make revisions?

Beering: I do fifteen different commencement speeches a year at Purdue, as well as some on other university campuses. I go over the concept and ideas with Joe Bennett, the head of university relations at Purdue. Many years I have a theme. This year we are going to talk about family in America. This is motivated in part by the fact that last week was the 50th anniversary of my coming to America.

In developing the commencement speeches, Joe and I work as a team. We both explore resources for the theme, and then we sit down and rough out the ideas we are going to cover. Then I tailor it. For example, a School of Liberal Arts commencement ceremony presents a different set of challenges than the one for engineers. A medical audience, an agricultural group, and management students all are different and have special kinds of interests.

Last night in Chicago, I spoke to a couple of hundred alumni. The theme was raising money for athletic scholarships. In that kind of situation, I never just talk about athletics. I always talk about some general things that are important to the university and try to put athletics in the context of the overall mission and direction of the university. A few weeks from now, I will be talking to the retirees organization, which I do annually. The retirees are interested in everything because they represent all disciplines, and their backgrounds, in many cases, are quite extraordinary. In their case, I try to create a bridge between what they did when they were on our faculty or staff and what they are doing now, but also to show them how Purdue is moving forward. I might say something like: 'You started something important, and we are continuing it, but we have something new that was not available before you retired, and I think you would be proud of what we are doing. Even though you are not with us every day, you are still part of what we do in a variety of ways.'

Our retirees, by the way, are very busy and very important to us. The university's Visitor Information Center depends heavily on volunteers, many of whom are retirees. When I talk to a group like that, there are no scripts or outlines. I ask the leadership if there is something special that people want to hear. Well, they always want to hear about sports; they always want to hear about new buildings; and they always want to hear about new programs. They also want to know what happened to their special program. So there is lots to talk about each time.

Connor: When you look back on your first experiences in the States, or even now, are there ever times when you think that your other languages, German and French, either have interfered in your writing or have brought something special to your ability to express yourself in English?

Beering: Well I don't use phrases from other languages when I write or speak in English. There are people who like to do that. Germans are fond of inserting a lot of Latin or French phrases into their speeches.

Connor: Right, but I'm thinking of something different. In the field of study called contrastive rhetoric, in which I work, we have found that writers whose first language is something other than English will often write in English using their first-language speech and writing patterns. For example, Japanese writers I have studied tend to put their main points at the end of their paragraphs rather than at the beginning as the native English speakers would.

Beering: I'm very much aware of this. If you come from certain heritages, it's built in. One tends to be verbose and circular in one's reasoning, so I'm constantly striving to be direct and focused and brief. I'm having trouble as you and I talk now. I'm giving much too long answers to very short questions.

Connor: But German is associated with being direct and to the point. French, I guess, is associated with being more elaborate, but English is also associated with being direct. You say your main point first and then you give your examples. I was thinking, especially earlier on when you were doing academic writing in high school in the States, did you feel that you had to struggle? Was writing in English a problem? Did you have trouble getting used to what American teachers expected?

Beering: No, I guess I would have to say it wasn't, and I enjoyed English. I love poetry. By the way, I taught French and German at the University of Pittsburgh for a number of years, working my way through school. I did a comparative literature course doing Shakespeare in French, German, and English, and I came to the conclusion – which, of course, is not unique to me – that it is best to read poetry and to hear opera and to listen to drama in the original language. A literary work just loses a great deal when translated. It takes a major artist to capture the essence, and you really have to change the vocabulary. If you do a literal translation, you lose the power and the impact of the words. That's particularly true with music. An opera with new words put in that weren't part of the composition just doesn't sound right, to me at least.

Connor: So you have been very aware of differences between languages since you have done translation?

Beering: Let me add that I think my ability in English, which I wish were better, has been enhanced very much by my lengthy study of Latin – in a German *Gymnasium* Latin is required – and then by my early education in several languages. I think automatically about the proper positioning of words and syntax and grammar and spelling. I spell much better because I started with multiple languages. And I can edit material more quickly because of that background. I'll see the split infinitive, for example, almost every time. People are surprised by this facility because English is my second language, but I think it's a help rather than a hindrance.

Connor: How old were you when you came to America?

Beering: Fifteen. A little late actually for developing flawless English. My accent then was influenced by the fact that I had been in England for two years before that. Also, the German schools taught British rather than American English. I came here with a British vocabulary and inflections and intonation. I still can fall back to that in a hurry. We were in England two weeks ago and within two days I talked like they did. I didn't put it on. It was just automatic.

Connor: Well, you are a perfect orator and you sound like a native speaker.

Beering: I'm not a native speaker, although I might fool a lot of people. Let me tell you how this happened. When I taught at the University of Pittsburgh, I felt that I ought to speak flawless English if I expected my students to do a good job in German or French. So, I went to the drama department and I said, 'Give me elocution lists, the th's, the r's, the l's; give me exercises'. They said, 'Try to be like an actor. Put yourself in the position of someone who is playing a part, and mimic them. Listen to radio and try to imitate the announcers'. I did that. I also read the *Reader's Digest,* because a professor of English drama told me the *Reader's Digest* is written at the 6th-grade level. And that's the way the common people speak in America. Newspapers are written at the 6th-grade level, and there you will find the sentence structure and the vocabulary that you must master. I would work on these things, and then I'd come in to the English Department, and we'd have a seminar session. I almost switched my major to English drama and literature. I also hosted a very early educational program on the University's television station. We did literary criticisms and book reviews, and little enactments of pieces of good literature for high school audiences. They called it 'The Continental' because I talked like this [*in British accent*], you see. But the longer I went, the less I sounded like that, because I wanted to sound American. By the way, isn't it amazing that so much of our written communication in this country is written in the English equivalent of what the Romans would have called vulgate – the Latin of the streets? *USA Today* is read by more people than any other paper. It's not a literary masterpiece, but it communicates. The *Wall Street Journal* is an exception. The *Christian Science Monitor* is, too, and the *Los Angeles Times* used to be.

Connor: What about when you got into medical studies? Did you feel that learning to write for scientific audiences was a whole new language?

Beering: Yes. I think that is really true. In fact, I taught technical German at the University of Pittsburgh for Ph.D. candidates for a while. It's a whole different bag. At Purdue, we have an expert in Christiane Keck, who is now the head of our languages department. She is an expert on business German, which is yet another subset of what I would call technical German. It's a different vocabulary. I'm going to have to scratch my head tonight when I go to Washington. I'm going to meet with the Minister President of the State of Lower Saxony. Purdue is going to offer a master's degree in business in Lower Saxony, and the executive assistant to the Minister President said to me, 'It's going to be so exciting to hear you explain this program in German to Mr. Schroeder, who understands and reads and writes English fluently, but when he gets excited, he really likes to lapse into German'. I said, it would be easier for him to talk about technical things in German than it would for me, because I don't speak technical German on a day-to-day basis any longer.

When I have been in Germany in the last few years, it takes me two or three days to get comfortable, but I know my German is no longer very good. The President of the University of Hamburg said to me, 'I love to listen to you speak German'. I said, 'Come on, I'm no longer really up-to-date or fluent or current'. He said, 'That's just what I like. You sound like my father and you use expressions that I haven't heard in years'. And you know what has happened to German on the street now, and in their newspapers? It is laced throughout with American English. You hear all kinds of American expressions, and the people pronounce them properly. It's just amazing to me. On one of my early trips back to Germany – I guess in the 60s – I took a cab in Munich. I spoke to the driver in German, and he, of course, realized that I was from America. I had the clothing, the shoes, the aftershave; we really just give ourselves away all of the time. He was a college student, and he wanted to talk to me in English, which he spoke fluently. We ended up conversing alternately in both languages as he drove the cab, and I happened to say in German, 'You know, you have a marvelous *Flughafen* here'. This is the word I learned for airport; it means literally 'flying harbor.' He said, 'What was that word?' I said *'Flughafen'*. And he said, 'Oh, we call that an airport'. The road signs all said so many kilometers to the Munich airport in American English. I was shocked by that. Every time I was groping for a word, I taught myself, 'Say it in English; they all seem to understand'. Hamburger, French fries, McDonald's, Burger King, and so on. They learn English from age six up. They are very proud of it. Everywhere you go in the world English is understood. Two weeks ago, we were on a ship. Our cabin steward was Portuguese, and the maid was Polish. He didn't speak Polish and she didn't speak Portuguese, but they spoke fluent English with one another. English has become the glue.

Connor: There is a very nice book by David Crystal, *English As a Global Language* (1997). David Crystal is a linguist in England who writes encyclopedias of language. I don't know if you are familiar with his work.

Beering: No, I have not seen that book. I was active in the early days in trying to do Interlingua, which was the scientific version of Esperanto. It was clear to me that it was too difficult to translate into it because it was nobody's native language. No one would speak that. I welcomed the advent of a true international language; I didn't care which one it was, and English has become exactly that.

Connor: I'm still going back to the medical field. You have been a medical doctor, a faculty member, dean and so on. I guess looking from outside, I would think that writing in medicine or many scientific areas is a very narrow area of writing. So if you had these experiences, you loved poetry, you loved to experiment with language, you loved learning new things, did you have to shed the experimentation with language or the playfulness of the English language when you went into medicine?

Beering: No, I don't think so. In fact, poetry actually helped with that. I do some poetry writing. I enjoy it because it forces you to be disciplined and concise, and that's what medical writing is. It's not usually beautiful writing, but one must be concise and accurate. Also, there are some conventions about medical writing. What we call executive summaries in the business world are abstracts in science and medicine. These require a stylized approach that doesn't tend to produce writing that is particularly enjoyable to read. There are some exceptions, but you don't find many people in medicine who have written novels or poems or who have a beautiful command of the language. When you look at a strictly technical article, it's unusual to find it easy reading.

Connor: Then what about when you became a dean and began writing for more professional purposes, giving talks, writing articles for newsletters, and things like that? Was that an easy transition?

Beering: Yes, I didn't have any trouble with that. But I worked at it. It didn't just come automatically. I had to practice and do it and redo it initially, and after a while it became second nature.

Connor: There is a question about voice in your professional writing. Do you consciously think about your voice in your professional writing? Along those lines, what advice would you have for language learners who come to this country – how to make it; what is the key to success?

Beering: I think the key to success, to quote Dr Ralph Ware, my wonderful former English professor, is that you have to put yourself into the other person's shoes and be like an actor and try to act out what it means to be an American, thinking, acting, feeling and speaking like that. And then want to do it well. The problem with the current debate about bilingual education in our schools is that if you teach people in some other language, you take away their opportunity to succeed as Americans. Unless you are planning to go somewhere else to do your work, you are going to be obliged to communicate in the language of the majority. Therefore, you must be very good at that. I say it's wonderful to worship in your own language and maintain the family ties and celebrate the history and practices of wherever you came from and to talk with grandma in her own language. But, if you want to be a success economically, if you are the head of a family, a business person, it is imperative to be very, very good at the language of the culture in which you live.

References

Crystal, D. (1997) *English As a Global Language.* Cambridge, UK: Cambridge University Press.

Appendix

The following list of guiding questions and accompanying instructions was given to all contributors to this volume.

Guiding Questions[1]

Please note that the following questions are only intended as suggestions. Feel free to address as many or as few of the questions as you like. The goal is to compose an L1/L2 literacy autobiography that would help both L2 learners and teacher-researchers better understand how highly advanced L2 literacy can be achieved.

L1 literacy development

(1)   How would you describe the education and literate activities (reading and/or writing) of current and preceding generations of your family?
(2)   What are your most vivid memories of the role that written language (i.e. your L1) played in your home and family's social, cultural, occupational, or religious practices as you were growing up?
(3)   What role(s) do you remember written language (again, your L1) playing in your relationships with peers as you were growing up?
(4)   What kinds of L1 reading and writing did you do in and out of school?
(5)   Were libraries, bookstores, television, radio, computers, or even toys important influences on your L1 literacy?
(6)   Who (specific teachers, family, friends?) most influenced your L1 reading and writing?
(7)   Do you have vivid memories of specific successes or failures with L1 literacy?
(8)   Do you feel that L1 literacy has played a major role in shaping your identity?

L2 literacy and professional success

(1)   Did you voluntarily choose to learn your L2 (or L3, L4, etc., whichever language other than your L1 that you use extensively as a literate professional)? Or was your L2 somehow imposed on you? If you chose

it, why were you attracted to it? If it was 'imposed' on you to some extent, what were your initial feelings about being a learner of this particular language?

(2)   When did you begin reading and writing in L2? What types of texts did you like to read and write?

(3)   How did you feel initially about your L2 writing? Did these feelings differ significantly from your feelings about yourself as an L2 reader?

(4)   Do you associate your developing L2 literacy mostly with classroom or extra-curricular activities? Were teachers or non-teachers (friends and family) the most significant influences on you?

(5)   Did you feel (or do you still feel) that your L1 literacy helped/helps or hindered/hinders your developing L2 reading and writing competencies?

(6)   When did you begin to see L2 reading and writing as pleasurable activities? Or, do you see L2 reading and writing in very different lights, the latter perhaps never truly pleasurable?

(7)   Do you remember your progress as an L2 reader/writer in terms of definable stages, or has your progress been steady and continual, with no memorably different phases?

(8)   Are there certain types of texts that you prefer to read in your L1 rather than your L2?

(9)   Are there certain types of texts that you prefer to write in your L1 rather than your L2?

(10) How would you describe your self-confidence levels as an L2 reader and writer and as an L1 reader and writer?

(11) Is L2 the sole language of your professional academic life, or does your L1 play a role too?

(12) Do you feel that your L1 generally enriches the L2 writing you currently do? If so, how?

(13) Is academic writing something that you enjoy doing, or do you see it more as a necessary evil? Does your L2 or L1 literacy have an impact on your attitude toward academic writing?

(14) What kinds of academic writing do you typically do? Which do you most prefer (e.g. research articles, book reviews, proposals, manuscript reviews)? Does your L1 or L2 affect your preferences?

(15) What type (or stage) of writing do you find the most difficult?

(16) Is audience important to you as you do your professional writing? For instance, do you try to visualize a specific audience as you compose? Do you feel you can anticipate the reactions of native-speakers of your L2? Do you try to write for an international audience, or does this vary, depending on purpose and the type of text?

(17) Do you consciously think about your 'voice' in your professional writing, i.e. the way you come across or the persona you present? Do you feel that being an L2 writer affects your 'voice'?

(18) Is ownership of your own texts ever an issue? Do you feel that you own or control your L2 writing or that others own and control it (e.g. publishers, editors, and manuscript reviewers)?

(19) What academic writing projects are you currently working on? Are you pleased with the ways your current L2 literacy affects your progress on these projects?

(20) Do you frequently collaborate with others when working on writing projects? Do you see collaboration as posing any particular problems for you or those you collaborate with? Do you prefer collaboration to single authorhood, and if so, why? Do you recommend collaboration to other L2 writers?

(21) How would you describe your L2 writing habits? How do you go about writing? How often do you write? For what length of time do you write? In what environments do you like to write? Do you use your L1 at all when writing in your L2?

(22) Does reading play a major role in your L2 writing? Do you see your reading as an important resource for your writing, both in terms of ideas and your sense of style as a writer? Do you feel that you have improved as an L2 writer because of your reading (either professional or strictly pleasure reading)?

(23) What role does the Internet play in your use of L2 as a reader, writer, or more specifically, as a professional?

(24) What kind of feedback do you get or would you like to get on your L2 writing? Are there people that you routinely show your work-in-progress and finished texts to? How important is this feedback to you?

(25) Do you have any particularly memorable 'horror' or success stories about your publishing experiences that you'd like to share? What might other L2 writers learn from your experiences?

(26) What advice would you give to other L2 speakers who would like to achieve your advanced level of proficiency as an L2 reader and writer?

(27) What specific advice about academic reading and writing in an L2 would you give to those who wish to enter your profession?

Notes

1. Adapted by Diane Belcher and Ulla Connor from Gesa Kirsch (1993) *Women Writing the Academy: Audience, Authority and Transformation.* Carbondale: Southern Illinois University Press; and Steve Fox, Unpublished manuscript.